STRAWBERRY
LEAVES

POUR Y PARVENER

The Most Noble John Duke of Rutland

STRAWBERRY LEAVES

An Account of some
Ducal Families and their
Bookplates

Colin R. Lattimore

THE BOOKPLATE SOCIETY

2016

Acknowledgements

I wish to express my grateful thanks and appreciation to the following members of the Bookplate Society for their considerable help and support without which this book may never have been accomplished. Peter Youatt who acted as my editor and also scanned numerous illustrations from the Franks collection in the British Museum and elsewhere. Jim Shurmer who designed and prepared the text and illustrations for publication. Anthony Pincott who provided me with many scans of ducal plates from his own collection and other sources. In addition I received a number of illustrations from the following: the late Dr John Blatchly M.B.E., Peter Dakin, Peter McGowan, John Titford and Dr Geoffrey Vevers.

All the references for the quotations in the text may be found in the books listed in the bibliography, the majority of them in the footnotes to *The Complete Peerage*, revised ed. 1910.

Images have been obtained from various sources. The majority have been scanned and are at actual size. It has not been possible to verify the size of all and some may be reduced or enlarged.

The illustrations on pages 25, 43, 153 and 169 are reproduced by kind permission of the Syndics of Cambridge University Library, references LA.8.69- and Oo.41.8.

This is the members' book of The Bookplate Society for the year 2016

Text © Colin R. Lattimore

Published by The Bookplate Society, 2016

ISBN 978-0-9555428-3-1

Copy-editing by Peter Youatt

Design and formatting by James Shurmer FCSD

Printed by Henry Ling Limited at the Dorset Press, Dorchester DT1 1HD

The Bookplate Society is an international society of collectors, bibliophiles, artists and others dedicated to promoting bookplate use and study.

For details of publications and membership benefits visit
The Bookplate Society's website: www.bookplatesociety.org

(*Frontispiece*) A large and very impressive early armorial bookplate for John Manners, 9th Earl of Rutland, who in 1703 was created Duke of Rutland (*see page 154*)

(*Front cover*) A fine example of a panel armorial bookplate for John Douglas, 9th Duke of Argyll (*see page 18*)

(*Back cover*) Bookplates for: His Grace John Duke of Atholl (*see page 26*); Henry George Percy, 7th Duke of Northumberland (*see page 132*); Mary Duchess of Bedford (*see page 60*)

Contents

To the memory of
His Grace John, 13th Duke of Bedford,
1917–2002
who showed the way for ducal estates
to survive in modern times

'Since the first was created in 1337 approximately
500 individuals have been granted the right to
call themselves Duke, although barely two dozen of
the exalted survive today.'

English Country House Eccentrics
David Long, 2012

Introduction

A duke's coronet of rank consists of a gold circlet of eight strawberry leaves (see title page) hence the main title of this book. Not all dukedoms are included in detail, only some of those which were extant at the beginning of the eighteenth century and remained so throughout the whole or part of the next two hundred years or were created during that period.

The reason for this timescale is that bookplates did not exist, in England, in any great quantity prior to 1700 but there was a sudden outburst in the reign of Queen Anne 1701–14 and their usage continued to expand throughout the next two centuries. Furthermore not all the dukedoms in this period are included only some of those where bookplates were used by one or more holders of the title and, to a lesser extent, by their near relations.

Dukedoms held by Princes of the Royal Blood, such as York, Gloucester or Cambridge, are excluded but ducal titles held by illegitimate offspring of the Sovereign are included. Charles II was the great provider in this respect, so far as dukes are concerned. He ruled England for twenty-five years from 1660–85 and died leaving no legitimate male heir. He left plenty of illegitimate children by various mistresses. Six of these, sons, were created dukes and four of the titles are extant to this day. William IV also had a large number of illegitimate children but none were created dukes.

Although a number of the early ducal bookplates are very impressive others of them are not brilliant and look as though little thought has been given to their design, production or usage. This was typical of armorial bookplates at that time; they were not always the minor works of art they later became. They were printed in sheets often using up odd scraps of paper. Their owners were sometimes quite careless in the way they allowed the plates to be cut out. Frequently they were trimmed very close to, or even encroaching onto, the design itself. This is a general observation not limited to any particular family. The impression given is that bookplate design did not feature very largely in ducal lives. The quality, in some cases, is poor throughout the period. The placing of the order with the printer was probably left to an upper servant such as the steward or librarian. The designs are often standard. There is, sometimes, not much evidence of individuality until we get to the later period when it is the designers themselves who raise the quality.

A similar situation arose in the mid-nineteenth century with the introduction of postage stamps. These were originally in un-gummed unperforated sheets which had to be cut up for use. As they were only being stuck on disposable envelopes users, generally, did not take much care in cutting them out. As a result carefully cut out stamps, with clear margins, of the period are today worth a considerable amount of money. One would have thought that more care would have been taken with plates to be placed in books for posterity but this does not seem to have been the case.

Armorial bookplates were the fashion of the day originally and remained so, on the whole, with dukes, if not their families even after pictorial and other designs were introduced. The styles of bookplates followed very much the prevailing decorative fashions of each period. In the early part of the eighteenth century the simple armorial, sometimes described as early armorial was used often with a profusion of mantling and with an often detailed inscription below. After about 1715 the Baroque style (previously called Jacobean) was prevalent with scallop shell motifs, fish scale patterning and symmetrical architectural structuring. Across the middle of the century the Rococo style (previously called Chippendale) occurred with its asymmetrical designs, S and C scrolls and floral decoration. This was followed in the 1770s and 80s by the neo-classical Adam style with its spade shaped shields, swags, drops and paterae. Across the turn of the century and well into the nineteenth century the familiar 'dog eared' shield (the two little wings at the top corners of the shield) made its appearance and designs were more simplistic and, on the whole, rather boring. In the third quarter of the nineteenth century the round seal type armorial was popular

By the late nineteenth century artists such as C.W. Sherborn, George Eve and Miss C. Helard in England, and Graham Johnson and his colleagues in Scotland, were giving much more careful thought to the design of armorial bookplates which probably reached a peak of perfection with the panel armorials of the period. These were universally popular and continue to be so down to the present day.

The last two decades of the nineteenth century saw a widening interest in the use of bookplates and the collecting of them resulting in the formation of the Ex Libris Society in 1893.

Unless the plate is signed and dated the style used is not an absolute indication of age but the type of paper used can be a help. Up until about 1755 laid paper with its distinctive chain lines was the only type used. Thereafter wove paper was introduced although laid paper was used on occasions. As each succeeding style emerged the older styles remained popular with some owners. In the case of ducal plates if the inscription simply states 'The Duke of X', or as frequently happened the heir bore the same forename as his predecessor, then the plate could be used by successive holders of the title without the need to commission a new plate. On the whole however as can be seen dukes were individualists and tended to have their forenames on their bookplates sometimes replacing the name of their predecessor with their own and reusing the plate.

Every ducal seat would have had a library and therefore the need for bookplates but some ducal families were far more prolific in this respect than others. The dukes of Bedford being a good example; almost every generation, since 1700, commissioned a new bookplate and some more than one, providing individual ones for each of their various residences so the book could be returned to its rightful place. There is no doubt that the use of bookplates by successive generations of dukes adds considerably to the interest of their libraries in the present day.

Strawberry Beds

An historical survey

The title 'duke' comes from the French 'duc' and the Latin 'dux'. It goes back to Roman times when it originally referred to a military commander. Over the centuries the title has been used throughout Europe and in all the countries where it is used it is the highest order of nobility below the Sovereign.

In the British Isles dukedoms were created in the Peerage of England from 1337–1707 and in the Peerage of Scotland from 1398–1707. From 1707 to 1801 English and Scottish peerages have been created in the Peerage of Great Britain and from 1801 to the present day in the Peerage of the United Kingdom. Dukedoms in the Peerage of Ireland were created between 1661 and 1868.

In mainland Europe dukes ruled over small states known as duchies, usually under a higher authority such as a king or emperor. In England there are only two duchies, Cornwall and Lancaster, both created by Edward III and belonging to the Crown. At the present time the Sovereign of the day holds the title Duke of Lancaster and the eldest son and heir the title of Duke of Cornwall. Both receive revenues from their respective duchies. Dukes in Great Britain did not rule over duchies as such but usually owned large areas of land and, in the past, exerted considerable powers. Such powers are greatly reduced today. All British subjects are subject to, and protected by, the law of the land and owe allegiance to the Sovereign.

The first duke to enter England was William of Normandy also known as 'William the Bastard'. He inherited his father's title as Duke of Normandy and invaded England in 1066 to defeat Harold and become William I of England.

The first three native dukedoms in England were created by Edward III (1327–77) mainly to provide titles for his sons. In 1337 he created his eldest son, Edward the Black Prince, Duke of Cornwall. On the duke's death the title passed to his nine year old son, Richard, who eventually succeeded his grandfather as Richard III.

Edward's closest and trusted friend was Henry of Grosmont (1310–61). He was the son and heir of Henry, 3rd Earl of Lancaster, a well known diplomat, politician and soldier. He was a founder member of the Order of the Garter and also one of the founders of Corpus Christi College, Cambridge. In 1351 Edward made him the first commoner duke by creating him Duke of Lancaster. The title became extinct on the duke's death in 1361. However, the following year the title was re-created for Edward's fourth son, John of Gaunt, who had married the first duke's daughter. At the same time Edward also created his second son, Lionel of Antwerp, Duke of Clarence.

In 1385, eight years after Edward's death, his grandson and heir, then Richard III, created dukedoms for his two remaining uncles. Thomas of Woodstock became Duke of Gloucester and Edward of Langley became Duke of York. With the exception of the dukedom of Clarence, which is in abeyance following the death of Queen Victoria's grandson, Prince Albert Victor, Duke of Clarence and Avondale, in 1892, all these titles, having been recreated a number of times, are in use by members of the Royal Family today.

Following this spate of royal dukedoms a number of commoner dukedoms were created and by 1483 the total number of distinct creations had risen to sixteen. However the survival rates were not high, due to early death, natural or otherwise, and failure of the male line. By 1485, following the Battle of Bosworth Field in which the 1st Duke of Norfolk lost his life, only two royal dukedoms remained extant, Cornwall and Lancaster. Because Norfolk was on the losing side, having fought for Richard III, the victor, Henry VII, denied Norfolk's son, Thomas, Earl of Surrey, the right to his father's dukedom. The dukedom was eventually restored to Thomas by Henry VIII in 1513 following the Earl's victory over the Scots at the Battle of Flodden (see Norfolk).

The first half of the sixteenth century was, again, a dangerous and turbulent time for English dukes. For various reasons, although they were being created they were also being beheaded, often on the flimsiest of excuses, or becoming extinct in other ways. Consequently by the time Elizabeth I came to the throne in 1558, Thomas, 4th Duke of Norfolk, was the only surviving duke. Elizabeth did not create any dukedoms of her own. The only one she had she abolished by having Thomas beheaded in 1572 for plotting to marry her cousin Mary, Queen of Scots, and seize the throne for Mary. For the remainder of Elizabeth's reign there were no English dukedoms other than Lancaster, held by the Sovereign.

The seventeenth century began with the emergence of the Stuart dynasty. James VI of Scotland succeeded Elizabeth as James I of England in 1603. Although he was married to Anne of Denmark and had children he was, almost certainly, bisexual and attracted to various young men both in Scotland and England.

One such was George Villiers who was appointed his cup bearer in 1614. Thereafter he rose rapidly through the ranks of the peerage to become the most powerful man in the kingdom after the King. Having been knighted in 1615 he became Earl of Buckingham in 1617, Marquess in 1619 and Duke of Buckingham in 1623. Following the death of James I in 1625, although he remained in favour with his son, Charles I, he was not popular in the country at large due to his various intrigues. He was assassinated on the 23rd August 1628 by an army officer, John Felton, who was later executed for his crime.

With the outbreak of civil war matters became even more chaotic. After the Battle of Worcester, in 1651, the heir to the throne, the future Charles II, was smuggled abroad and George Villiers' heir, the 2nd Duke of Buckingham, also fled the country. Needless to say no dukedoms were created during the Commonwealth.

With the restoration of the monarchy in 1660 the new King, Charles II, set about establishing his position and rewarding those who had supported him and his late father during the period of the Civil War and Commonwealth. One of the best and most sought after marks of royal favour, was for an individual to be raised to the peerage, of which there are, in ascending order, five ranks – baron, viscount, earl, marquess and duke. The higher up the ranks the greater is the honour. In any case the highest rank of the peerage, that of duke, was in urgent need of replenishment being virtually denuded of members.

Within the first year of his reign Charles created or recreated five new dukedoms including Norfolk, Hamilton and Albermarle.

Following the execution of the 4th Duke of Norfolk by Elizabeth, the Howard family had been petitioning successive monarchs for the restoration of the dukedom. Finally, with the support of a large number of peers, they were able to persuade the new King to restore the title. It was, to say the least of it, unfortunate that their candidate for the honour Thomas Howard, a direct descendent of the fourth duke, was living abroad in Italy having suffered a severe illness which had left him mentally deranged. Nevertheless he was raised to the peerage as 5th Duke of Norfolk and held the title for seventeen years whilst still living abroad in Padua. On his death he was succeeded by his brother, Henry, as sixth duke.

James, Marquess of Hamilton, had been created 1st Duke of Hamilton in the peerage of Scotland by Charles I in 1643 with remainder, failing male heirs, to his brother William and his sister Anne. Following his defeat at Preston fighting for the King the first duke was beheaded and was succeeded by his brother William as second duke. He in turn was killed at the Battle of Worcester in 1651 and, having no male heirs, was succeeded by his sister Anne as 3rd Duchess of Hamilton in her own right. She had married William, 1st Earl of Selkirk, and in 1660, for no other apparent reason than that he had married a duchess whose relatives had given their lives in defence of the crown, Charles II created him Duke of Hamilton for life. On Anne's death the title went to their eldest son.

General George Monck, a professional soldier, led an interesting life. He originally fought for Charles I and was captured and imprisoned for three years in the Tower of London. Under the Commonwealth he agreed to fight for Cromwell against the French, Irish and Scots and became General-in-Chief of Land Forces. In 1660, with the Commonwealth falling into disarray, Monck was quick to seize the opportunity and lead negotiations for the restoration of the monarchy. In this he was successful and was rewarded by Charles who created him 1st Duke of Albermarle. He played a significant role in restoring order after the Great Fire of London in 1666. Unfortunately his son Christopher, the 2nd duke, died childless in 1688 and the dukedom became extinct.

Amongst others raised to the first rank of the peerage by Charles II was William Cavendish, Marquess of Newcastle who was a great equestrian and the King's former tutor. He became Duke of Newcastle in 1665. In 1672 John Maitland was created Duke of Lauderdale in return for controlling the Scots north of the border and in 1682 Henry Somerset, Marquess of Worcester became the 1st Duke of Beaufort. The reason given for his elevation was that he was descended from Edward III and had served the King well.

As well as creating dukedoms for commoners Charles provided a quantity from his own loins. He had a large number of illegitimate children from various mistresses.

Six of these, sons, were given dukedoms. When he ascended the throne he already had one illegitimate son James, by Lucy Walters, born in Rotterdam in 1649. He became Duke of Monmouth and, later, Buccleuch. The Monmouth title expired with the Duke's execution in 1685 but the Buccleuch title survived through his marriage to Anne Scott Countess of Buccleuch in her own right. She remained Duchess of Buccleuch in her own right after her husband's death and on her death her grandson inherited the dukedom.

Charles spent his first night in England with Barbara Villiers, Countess of Castlemaine, who went on to provide him with six children, the three sons becoming the Dukes of Cleveland, Grafton and Northumberland. In 1670 the famous Nell Gwyn produced a son who became Duke of St Albans. Lastly, in 1672 Charles's French mistress, Louise de Keroualle, obliged him with a son whom he created Duke of Richmond. The titles and descendants of four of these lines – Buccleuch, Grafton, St Albans and Richmond – are extant and their royal arms, suitably differenced, can be seen displayed to this day.

In earlier times illegitimacy did not carry quite the stigma it acquired in the nineteenth and early twentieth centuries. Thomas Farington noted in his diary in 1796 'Nollekens showed me his bust of Miss Le Clerc, a natural daughter of the Duke of Richmond. She is about twenty years old, tall and handsome. She lives at the Duke's and the Duchess is very fond of her. She has been introduced at Court. The Duke comes with her sometimes to Nollekens and seems very fond of her.' This was the 3rd Duke of Richmond who, apparently, had three natural daughters, all by his housekeeper, and settled money on each of them and on the housekeeper. Similarly at Devonshire House and at Chatsworth the natural children of William, 5th Duke of Devonshire, lived under the same roof and enjoyed the same privileges as his legitimate family. Although gossip worthy this would not have been regarded as unusual, simply a question of 'noblesse oblige'.

Among the aristocracy and gentry who used arms an illegitimate child's future did not depend on his or her lineage but on how far the father was prepared to recognise and accept the child into his household. If a natural son was accepted and allowed to use his father's arms they had to be differenced by a mark of distinction. Here the term is not used in the sense of 'honour' but in the sense of distinguishing the arms from the legitimate family arms. No particular mark was identified for this purpose but the bend and bordure were sometimes used. Illegitimate children had no right of inheritance of titles and no absolute right of inheritance of goods and property but could receive bequests from their father.

Many people will be familiar with the term 'bar sinister' which they believe sounds evil and is an heraldic mark of bastardy. This is a misconception. It is a corruption of the French term 'barre sinestre' which in English translates as 'baton sinister', sinister, from Latin, meaning left. The bend or bendlet (narrow bend) sinestre comes from the top left of the shield. If the bendlet does not reach the edges of the shield but falls short at each end it is referred to as a 'barre' in French or a 'baton' in English. In practice the baton or barre sinister across the arms was reserved for royal illegitimate children and carried charges to distinguish one child from another. Whilst royal illegitimate children and those of the aristocracy were usually proud of their lineage, birth out of wedlock for the remainder was not usually a matter for rejoicing.

These illegitimate royal creations cost the country dear in taxation to provide for their support. The King also put himself out to find suitable marriage partners to further enhance their financial security.

Charles II died in 1685 and, leaving no legitimate male issue, he was succeeded by his brother James, Duke of York, who was a staunch catholic. As James II he promoted many catholics into influential positions and, encouraged by the catholic monarchies in France and Spain, was keen to see Britain become a catholic country once again. Most of the population generally, and the aristocracy in particular, were not in favour of such change. Many aristocratic families had benefited considerably under Henry VIII, and the Dissolution of the Monasteries, with the redistribution of monastic lands. They were anxious to retain their holdings and feared retribution if the Catholic Church became powerful again. The result was the so called 'Glorious Revolution' of 1688 which saw James deposed and his daughter Mary and her protestant cousin and husband, William of Orange installed as joint monarchs.

The result of this upheaval, in ducal terms, was interesting. James was deemed by Parliament to have abdicated, so far as England and Scotland were concerned, in December 1687 although he remained King of Ireland until the Battle of the Boyne in 1690. He fled to France in 1688 where Louis XIV allowed him to establish himself in the Chateau de St Germain, a royal residence some twelve miles west of Paris. Here he continued to create peerages in all three countries including a number of dukedoms. This practice was continued after his death in 1701 by his son James Edward, the Old Pretender, as *de jure* James III until his death in 1766 and by his son Charles Edward, the Young Pretender, until his death in 1788. His last ducal creation was in 1783 when he created his illegitimate daughter, Charlotte, Duchess of Albany. She died in 1789.

These creations became known as the Jacobite Peerages (see Appendix III) but were not recognised in Britain by William and Mary or their successors. They included seven dukedoms in England, eight in Scotland and one in Ireland. Most of these did not survive beyond the eighteenth century either from failure in the male line, being subsumed into legitimate titles or simply being abandoned through lack of official recognition.

Following their accession William and Mary continued the practice of their predecessors in dealing out honours and rewards to those who had supported them. First of these, in ducal terms, was to William's main army commander Marshal Schomberg.

Frederick Schomberg was a naturalised Frenchman of German birth. He had fought for a number of different monarchs and following his support for William he was stripped of his French nationality and lost his French estates so he promptly became an English national. As a reward for his support he was created Duke of Schomberg in 1698, and, on the request of the King, Parliament awarded him £100,000 to compensate for the loss of his French estates. He was appointed to command the troops in Ireland but lost his life at the Battle of the Boyne. He was succeeded by his two sons as second and third dukes but the dukedom died out in 1719 through lack of an heir.

A fellow countryman and close confidant of the King was William Bentinck whom he created Earl of Portland. He also gave him various estates but an attempt to rent him a large part of Denbighshire at an annual rent of 6s.8d. was defeated by Parliament. There was no further rise in the family fortunes until the next century when George I bestowed a dukedom on William's son, Henry, the second earl (see Portland).

Another of William's army commanders was John Churchill whom he rewarded by making him Earl of Marlborough. Churchill married Sarah Jennings a great friend of the then Princess Anne soon to become the last of the Stuart monarchs.

William's last ducal creation was in 1701 when he created Archibald, 10th Earl of Argyll, Duke of Argyll. Archibald had served under Marlborough but relations between the two were less than cordial due to intense jealousy (see Argyll).

On her accession in 1702 Queen Anne created John Churchill Duke of Marlborough in recognition of his many and great military achievements. Oddly enough his wife Sarah was against the promotion fearing they did not have adequate resources to support a dukedom and, anyway, they already had a peerage (see Marlborough). Anne also honoured John Earl of Rutland, who had sheltered her during the 1688 Revolution, by creating him Marquess of Granby and Duke of Rutland, and James, Marquess of Atholl, who became Duke of Atholl (see Rutland and Atholl).

The death of Queen Anne in 1714 brought to an end the Stuart dynasty and the throne passed to the Hanoverians. The new Sovereign, George I, as usual, was besieged by requests for honours and privileges and he rewarded those who supported him against the Jacobites. One such was a young man Thomas Pelham. He was the son of Baron Pelham and at the age of eighteen, in 1711, he inherited large estates from his uncle John Holles, 1st Duke of Newcastle of the second creation, but unfortunately the title did not pass with the estates. However, the death of his father brought him further estates and the title Lord Pelham. He strongly supported the Hanoverian cause and as a result he rose in the peerage finally being created 1st Duke of Newcastle, of the third creation, in 1715. He became one of the great intriguers and politicians of the eighteenth century becoming Prime Minister for the first time in 1756. He had no heir to his many titles so, in 1756, George II raised him to a second dukedom that of Newcastle under Lyme with special remainder to his favourite nephew Henry Clinton (see Newcastle). This was the only dukedom that George II created although he had offered dukedoms to some who had refused (see page 180). Nevertheless by the time George III succeeded to the throne in 1760, outside the royal family, there were some forty dukedoms, the highest number ever.

In the early years of his reign George III was also besieged by requests for preferment particularly by those seeking the highest rank of the peerage. However he was, initially, reluctant to respond to these pressures.

Sir Hugh Smithson, a Yorkshire baronet, had married Lady Elizabeth Seymour, grand-daughter of the Duke of Somerset. She was also related to the earls of Northumberland. She had married Sir Hugh much against her grandfather's wishes who regarded Sir Hugh as an upstart,

Johnny-come-lately. On the death of her brother, shortly after her marriage, she inherited the vast Percy estates in Northumberland. Her grandfather had tried unsuccessfully to disinherit her. In 1748 he died and Lady Elizabeth's father became Earl of Northumberland. Two years later he died and Smithson, having changed his name to Percy was created Earl of Northumberland. However he was not satisfied with that and felt that his vast estates justified him in being made a duke. By way of response the King wrote to his Prime Minister, William Pitt, Earl of Chatham, *'Undoubtedly few peers have so great an estate in point of income and scarce any in point of extent: therefore if you will co-operate with me in declaring I don't mean to open a door for the creating of many dukes I will consent to it.'*

Another aspirant to a dukedom was George Brudenell, 4th Earl of Cardigan, who had married the co-heiress of the 2nd Duke of Montagu. He had assumed the name and arms of Montagu on marriage and by his persistence was rewarded with the dukedom which had been in abeyance due to lack of male heirs.

Finally, in the first ten years of his reign, George III created a third dukedom when James Fitzgerald, the Irish politician and grandee, became Duke of Leinster, there being no Irish dukes at that time.

The nineteenth century saw the final days of ducal creations, with a further eight being created. The first of these was Wellington, in 1814, in recognition of his great military service to the King and state before, finally, defeating the French at Waterloo in 1815. The remainder were largely political appointments or in recognition of great wealth. George IV created Richard Temple Nugent Brydges Chandos Greville 1st Duke of Buckingham and Chandos. It was said to be as a mark of personal friendship but in fact it was a political move whereby the Grevilles lent support to a Tory government and took the side of the King against his Queen, Caroline. The dukes of Buckingham and Chandos led troublesome lives overburdened by debt and although the third duke made attempts to restore the family fortunes the dukedom became extinct on his death in 1889 due to lack of a male heir.

William IV added to the sum total of dukes by creating two more, Cleveland and Sutherland and Queen Victoria finished the century by creating another four. Her first was an Irish dukedom, Abercorn, conferred on James Hamilton, Marquess of Abercorn in 1868. He had previously been a Groom of the Stole to Prince Albert. He had seven daughters whom he successfully married off into the peerage,

two to dukes, one to a marquess and the remaining four to earls.

In 1874 Victoria conferred a dukedom on the very wealthy Hugh Grosvenor, Marquess of Westminster. Wealth, friendship and high standing were the driver rather than any outstanding service to Queen and country (see Westminster). The following year her choice fell on the 6th Duke of Richmond. He had inherited a large property in Scotland and was descended on the female side from the last Duke of Gordon. Rather oddly, since she was the fount of all honours, the Queen enquired of him why he had never been made Duke of Gordon and decided that it was right, because of his great wealth, estates and lineage, that the old Scottish title, extinct since 1836, should be restored and so he became Duke of Richmond and Gordon in 1875.

Her final creation was in the nature of a semi-royal appointment when she created William George Duff, 6th Earl of Fife, Duke of Fife on his marriage to her granddaughter, the eldest daughter of the Prince and Princes of Wales. This was mainly done at the instigation of the Prince who wanted a duke for a son-in-law. This was the last nonroyal dukedom to be created.

The following are some of the reasons which have been used over the centuries for creating dukedoms:

1 To provide a title for an illegitimate son of the Sovereign e.g. Grafton and St Albans.
2 For love and friendship, e.g. Buckingham.
3 In compensation for the execution of an ancestor by a previous monarch e.g. Bedford.
4 Serving the country by winning great battles e.g. Marlborough and Wellington.
5 By virtue of being a great landowner and of long distinguished lineage e.g. Norfolk and Westminster.
6 Marrying the right person – someone who has or will inherit land, wealth and or titles e.g. Hamilton and Northumberland.
7 For supporting, or not supporting, a particular political cause or Sovereign e.g. Beaufort.

As will become clear from the ducal histories that follow successive Sovereigns bestowed dukedoms as a reward for past services or in order to buy loyalty and favour from some of their more powerful and wealthy subjects or simply on a whim or in response to pressure from the family concerned. Often political pressure from the governing party of the day played a hand in order to obtain powerful political support. Titles could be created, recreated or granted with special remainder, this would allow the title to slip sideways if the main line failed (see Newcastle).

Some families had to work their way through the lower ranks of the peerage over generations before emerging triumphant at the top whilst others could make the ascent in one generation. It has to be said, once the process had started, the reasons for advancement to the higher ranks of the peerage seem in some cases very flimsy indeed. Multiple titles were the order of the day so a duke rarely had less than four titles.

Those families who had worked their way up through the ranks retained their subsidiary titles one of which, usually the second highest, was used, as a courtesy title, by the eldest son and heir, in the lifetime of his father. A lower title might be used by the eldest son of the eldest son, in the lifetime of his grandfather. For example the eldest son of the Duke of Argyll uses the title Marquess of Lorne; the eldest son of the Duke of Bedford is the Marquess of Tavistock and his eldest son uses the title Baron Howland in the lifetime of his grandfather. When the duke dies the son and grandson move up one. It must be stressed that these subsidiary titles are courtesy titles only and did not normally entitle the user to a seat in The House of Lords. The exceptions to this rule occurred sometimes with eldest sons of earls and above who may have been summonsed to Parliament under one of their father's lesser titles in the lifetime of their father (see Leeds).

When a dukedom was created, as a first honour, subsidiary titles would be bestowed at the same time so that the son and heir would have the use of a courtesy title. Land and income could also be provided by the crown. Arthur Wellesley, 1st Duke of Wellington, was given the estate of Stratfield Saye and an income to go with it and John Churchill, 1st Duke of Marlborough, was given the necessary funds to build Blenheim Palace.

Ducal armorial bearings, often with many quarterings, are of considerable interest and a word of explanation might be helpful. Armorial bearings are a means of identification, originally in battle and later on possessions such as houses, silverware, glassware, porcelain, tombs and, of course, books. A duke would normally marry into an armigerous family and for the duration of his marriage would display his father-in-law's arms together with his own on a shield. The shield is always described as though held in front of you so the left side is the one on the right when facing you. The shield is divided by a vertical line down the centre with the owner's arms on the right side and his wife's family on the left. Any offspring of the marriage use only their father's arms.

However if the wife is an heraldic heiress (i.e. she has no brothers to carry on her father's arms) then her family arms pass to her offspring on her death. During the marriage the husband displays his wife's arms on a shield of pretence in the centre of his own shield. In due course, after the death of the wife her offspring quarter their maternal arms with those of their father. The shield is divided into four quarters, the top two being 1 and 2 and the bottom two 3 and 4. The father's arms, the pronomal arms, are placed in 1 and 4 and the maternal arms in 2 and 3. The sons pass these quartered arms to their sons and, if no sons were produced, any daughter could transmit her arms, via her armigerous husband, to her offspring. As dukes would always try to arrange the best marriages for their children, particularly the son and heir, often in the case of sons to rich heraldic heiresses, over time a very large number of quarterings could be accrued as will be seen from some of the ducal book-plates. It is often impossible to show all the quarterings because of the number but a select few may be chosen from the more prestigious of the marriages providing the pronomal arms are always displayed in the first quarter. Many dukes choose to display only their pronomal arms.

The armorial blazons which follow under each dukedom have many armorial terms some of which will be familiar and some not. There are many good reference books available. One of the best is Stephen Friar, *A New Dictionary of Heraldry*, A.C. Black, London, 1987.

One point worth mentioning is the difference between a duke's coronet of rank and a ducal coronet. A duke's coronet of rank is a circlet of strawberry leaves always depicted in gold. In a two dimensional presentation it is shown as three strawberry leaves full face and two sideways, one at each side. It is usually shown above the shield and below the helmet and crest. A ducal coronet on the other hand is shown as three strawberry leaves one full face and two sideways. This may form part of a crest or be a charge on the shield or supporters. It can be used by any armiger, be of any tincture and does not indicate ducal rank or connection. It is however found in some ducal arms. Book-plate artists do not always appreciate the point and depict a duke's coronet of rank when they intend a ducal coronet. The point is well illustrated in the Leonard Wooddeson (sic) plate shown here. The crest of Woodeson of Middlesex is blazoned 'out of a ducal coronet or, flames issuant proper'. What is shown is clearly a duke's coronet of rank.

Dukes were expected to live as befitted their status and to play their part in society. They should be very wealthy, own great estates and make advantageous marriages to improve

Leonard Wooddeson

Appointments as a Knight of the Garter were distributed freely amongst dukes as vacancies became available. This is the senior and oldest Order of Chivalry under the crown instituted in 1348 by Edward III. The Order is restricted to twenty-four members and members of the Royal Family and other reigning royals. Appointments were originally in the gift of the Sovereign but from the eighteenth century until 1946 were made by the Sovereign on advice from the Government of the day. Since 1946 they have reverted to being in the gift of the Sovereign for those who have served well in high office in public life or have served the Sovereign personally. Originally appointments were restricted to the aristocracy particularly the upper end of the peerage but today appointments come from a much wider sphere. The only non-royal duke holding the Garter at the present time is The Duke of Abercorn (1999). A similar history and pattern applies to the Order of the Thistle which was resurrected by James II in 1687 and was given to succeeding generations of Scottish dukes amongst others.

The principal residencies of dukes also had many features in common. Many of these stately homes were built in the eighteenth century often based on earlier buildings. They were sited in large deer parks surrounded by miles and miles of brick wall to keep the deer in and the peasantry out. Within the park would be a water feature, river or lake, well stocked with fish. If not present then one could be created by diverting a nearby water course. Deep inside a convenient hill near the house, again one could be manufactured if not available, would be an ice-house with bricked interior protected by at least two stout wooden doors for insulation. In the winter large sheets of ice were taken from the lake and stored there ready for chilling the wine, making ice-cream etc. A large stable block and carriage house would be situated close to the house. There would be a church on the estate with a resident chaplain and usually a mausoleum to give the dukes a final resting place.

The parks would be landscaped in the latest fashion by designers such as Lancelot 'Capability' Brown and Humphrey Repton. Getting away from the structured formal gardens of the previous century many featured follies built specifically as ruins to enhance the scenery. For best effect they were meant to be viewed at a distance, on closer inspection some were found to conceal a dwelling inside for a gamekeeper or other estate worker.

The mansions would be staffed by enormous numbers of servants, a self sustaining community, and filled with works of art and other treasures collected on The Grand Tour and

their situation. They should participate actively in public life at national and local level in both political and ceremonial capacities, from serving as Prime Minister to handing out prizes at the local show. They were expected to entertain their Sovereign with great pomp and ceremony when required and to spend a considerable amount of money in the process.

In spite of all this high living and status dukes and duchesses were as prone to the ills of the time as anyone else. One has only to note the number of premature deaths, in infancy, middle life and childbed to realise this.

Dukes often had a number of features in common. They tended to give their forenames to their eldest son thus sometimes making identification difficult historically. They usually married into the peerage, often a fellow duke's daughter, although in the late nineteenth and early twentieth centuries there was a move to marry rich American heiresses to restore the family fortunes. As well as doing that these marriages also improved the gene pool which had become somewhat inbred over the centuries.

They were frequently members of the Royal Society and the Society of Antiquaries. They regularly served as Lord Lieutenants and, before succeeding to their dukedom, sat as members of Parliament. They were regularly appointed as Privy Counsellors, the Sovereign's trusted advisors.

elsewhere. Family portraits would adorn the walls. Visitors, of an appropriate class, would be shown round the house and grounds, by the housekeeper or butler, on certain days, in return for a small monetary contribution payable to them. In addition to their principal residence a duke would have a town house, usually in the Mayfair district of London, and often other country residences.

The sons of dukes, on the whole, were well educated, attending Eton, Harrow or other public schools of note and then going on to Oxford or Cambridge. In the process they became familiar with books and often accrued large, well selected libraries, many with rare incunabula. In the nineteenth century a number of these ducal libraries came on the market, in an attempt to restore family fortunes. The sales caused a considerable stir amongst the bibliophile world because of the large sums of money which were raised at a time when a labourer's wage was less than £1 a week.

The first of these sales was in 1812 when the library of John Ker, 3rd Duke of Roxburghe, came on the market. In a sale lasting forty-six days ten thousand one hundred and twenty lots went under the hammer raising £23,397.

The next in line came in 1849 when Richard, 2nd Duke of Buckingham and Chandos, put the Stowe library up for sale. Sotheby's sold the library over twenty-four days, this time six thousand two hundred and eleven lots of books and prints produced £14,155. The Stowe manuscripts were sold by private treaty to the Earl of Ashburnham for a further £8,000. One enterprising bookseller, Mr. Lincoln of Westminster Road, London had a book label printed to insert into his purchases, no doubt to tempt buyers.

In the 1880s two more ducal libraries were sold. The first was the Sunderland library which had been formed by Charles, 3rd Earl of Sunderland, who died in 1722. The library came into the possession of the Dukes of Marlborough in 1733 when Charles, 5th Earl of Sunderland, became the 3rd Duke of Marlborough. Unfortunately the library was not well cared for whilst at Blenheim and many

of the leather bindings suffered from sun damage. Nevertheless when John, the seventh duke, put them on the market, thirteen thousand eight hundred and fifty-eight lots were sold in four sales between December 1881 and November 1882, each sale lasting ten days and the total amount realised was £56,581.6s.0d.

At about the same time William Beckford's library from Fonthill Abbey in Wiltshire was also sold. After Beckford's death in May 1844 his daughter Susana Euphemia, who had married the 10th Duke of Hamilton, inherited the library. The duke wished to sell the library and was offered £130,000 for the whole library *'the money to be paid within a week'*. The duke was keen to accept the offer but his duchess would not agree as she did not wish to see her father's library sold. So the library remained unsold until 1889 when her grandson, the twelfth duke, decided to sell. Like the Sunderland library it was sold in four parts the first three taking twelve days each and the fourth four days. In all there were nine thousand eight hundred and thirty-seven lots raising £173,551.

The 12th Duke of Hamilton's own library which he had collected as Marquess of Douglas before succeeding to the dukedom had been sold five years earlier in May 1884 when an eight day sale disposed of two thousand one hundred and thirty lots for £12,892

Finally, also in 1889, a part of the library of the Duke of Buccleuch was sold, one thousand and twelve lots in total selling for £3,705.

Some dukes managed their estates efficiently and were able to support the family and their many dependants, whilst other survived by dint of selling off artworks and other valuables and marrying rich, often American, heiresses. Many ducal families were able to live in grand style well into the twentieth century. Life in ducal households could be hectic particularly at festive times as illustrated by the Earl of Stockton, Harold Macmillan, whose wife, Lady Dorothy Cavendish, was the daughter of the 9th Duke of Devonshire. In *Winds of Change*, published in 1966, Macmillan described Christmas at Chatsworth in the 1920s:

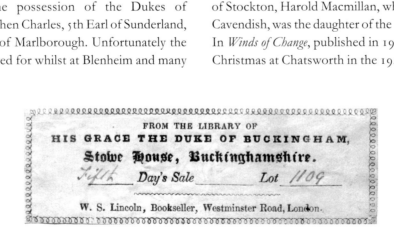

FROM THE LIBRARY OF
HIS GRACE THE DUKE OF BUCKINGHAM,
Stowe House, Buckinghamshire.
Fifth Day's Sale   Lot *1109*

W. S. Lincoln, Bookseller, Westminster Road, London.

'Christmas at Chatsworth was conducted on traditional lines. Every year was the same except for the increasing number of children. The Devonshire's own family in addition to the Duke and Duchess consisted of two sons and five daughters all married. The average number of children in each family was about four. These with their attendant nurses and nursery maids amounted therefore to something like fifty souls. Then there were the lady's-maids and valets bringing the total to at least sixty. In addition there were other guests including generally two or three cousins of the Duke or Duchess's

With all these Christmas visitors and their attendants together with the permanent and temporary servants in the household the number gathered under that vast roof must have been something like one hundred and fifty people. The children, of course, delighted in this strange and exciting world. They were spoilt and pampered by the servants and made many long friendships with them. It was always a new pleasure to be conducted through the great kitchens, the huge pantries, the larders with their stone floors and vaulted roofs; above all, the great building, larger then many butchers' shops, where hung rows of carcasses of oxen and sheep and game of every kind. Many of the families arrived with their ponies with their attendant grooms.

One special treat was to be taken through the plate rooms. Here was kept, in the care of an old retired under butler, a great collection, much of it dating from the seventeenth and eighteenth centuries. The beautiful William and Mary dressing sets were there; and, in addition the gold plate. On certain occasions, at Christmas, or at other great parties, the best of the plate was shown in the dining room. But for the most part, except for the pieces in daily use, these treasures were kept in the vigilant care of their devoted guardian. The ritual did not differ from year to year.'

Dukes, so far as their dependants were concerned seemed to come in three varieties, benevolent, despotic and nondescript. Benevolent dukes were highly to be desired by those who worked in their households and on their estates or were tenants. They were likely to be treated with consideration, have good working conditions according to the values of the time and be provided for in their old age. Whereas despotic tyrannical dukes were much to be feared because of the considerable powers they exercised over their domains and their dependants. Life could be very hard on such estates. The nondescript dukes were neutral, neither one thing nor the other and tended to pass unnoticed leaving little impression behind.

What of the dukes themselves, how did they see life? In 1919 the 8th Duke of Northumberland was being cross questioned by the Coal Commissioners at a time when His Grace's revenues from coal mined on his estates was of the order of £84,000 per annum. The following exchange took place:

Sir Leo Money, Chairman of the Commissioners – *As a Coal Owner what service do you perform to the community?*

The Duke – *As the owner of the coal I do not think I perform any service to the community, not as the owner of the coal.*

Sir Leo – *Do you not think it is a bad thing to own as much as you do?*

The Duke – *No! I think it is an excellent thing in every way.*

What other answer could any sensible duke give? However, great wealth, in itself, did not make great men. It is how it was used that counted. Used in the right way it could allow a duke to support his many estates, provide life long employment, security and support for large numbers of people, support for charitable institutions such as schools, hospitals and orphanages to say nothing of dowries for daughters, luxury yachts and, in their time motor cars and aeroplanes all of which provided work and livelihood for many other people.

This is borne out beautifully by a passage in an article by Robert Hardman in the Daily Mail as recently as the 3rd October 2014 reporting on the attendance of a very large number of uniformed estate workers at the funeral service of Deborah, Dowager Duchess of Devonshire, widow of the 11th duke and known to her friends as 'Debo', who had died at the age of ninety-three:

'She may have spent her last years in a semi on the estate (Chatsworth) but Debo and her late husband once had the run of seven ancestral seats and 72,000 acres.

Old lefties might growl at such a sight but every one of those respectful, uniformed mourners represented a job that might not have existed had Debo and her husband not turned this place around when they inherited an empty crumbling wreck (and 80 per cent death duties) in 1950. With 700 on today's payroll, Chatsworth is the biggest employer in the entire area after the State.'

It must be remembered that in the eighteenth and nineteenth centuries and earlier dukes were held in considerable awe, esteem and reverence even by other ranks of the peerage. This is something that modern generations might find hard to understand.

In the nineteenth century the College of Arms gave the following advice relating to orders of precedence:

'The Aga Khan is held by his followers to be a direct descendant of God. English Dukes take precedence.'

I think that sets the scene rather nicely.

ARG I **Duke of Argyll** NIF

A fine example of a panel armorial bookplate for John Douglas, 9th Duke of Argyll.

His ducal arms are shown accollee with those of his wife, the Princess Louise, daughter of Queen Victoria, as it is not permitted to impale the royal arms with those of a commoner. It is signed faintly in the bottom right hand corner 'A. Downey.'

ARMS: Quarterly 1 and 4, gyronny of eight or and sable (Campbell); 2 and 3, argent, a lymphad her sails furled and oars in action, flags and pennons flying gules (Lorne). Behind, in saltire, a baton topped by an imperial crown thereon the Crest of Scotland and a sword proper hilt and pommel or designating the Hereditary Master of the Royal Household in Scotland and Justice General of the Shrievalty of Argyll (*not shown on this plate but see, e.g. ARG 4*).

CREST: On a wreath of the colours a boar's head erased or.

SUPPORTERS: Two lions rampant guardant gules.

MOTTOES: Ne obliviscaris – Do not forget.
Vix ea nostra voco – I scarce call these deeds of our ancestors ours.

The royal arms are shown with those of Saxe-Coburg in pretence and a label of three points denoting a child of the Sovereign.

Dukes of Argyll

FAMILY NAME: Campbell

CREATION OF DUKEDOM: 23rd June 1701

COURTESY TITLE OF ELDEST SON: Marquess of Lorne

COURTESY TITLE OF GRANDSON AND HEIR: Earl of Campbell

PRINCIPAL RESIDENCE: Inverary Castle, Argyllshire

The fortunes of the Clan Campbell of Argyll began to rise in the fifteenth century when Sir Duncan Campbell was created the 1st Lord Campbell in 1445. When he died, in 1453, his son Archibald Campbell of Luckow had predeceased him so he was succeeded by his grandson, Colin, who was a minor at the time. Nevertheless four years later in 1457 he was created Earl of Argyll by King James II of Scotland.

After having worked in various embassies in England and France he rose to high office as Master of the Household and Chancellor. He joined a conspiracy of nobles against James III in 1487. After the rebellion which ended with the death of James III he was deprived of the chancellorship but was reinstated by James IV the following year. He died on 10th May 1493.

He was succeeded by his son, Archibald, who, as well as the title, inherited many of his father's offices including Master of the Household. Archibald married Elizabeth, daughter of John, 1st Earl of Lennox, and had issue but unfortunately was slain in September 1513 at the Battle of Flodden against the English.

Successive generations continued to hold high office with more or less success as we come to Archibald Campbell, Lord Lorne who succeeded his father as 8th Earl of Argyll in 1638. He was a protestant and a strong supporter of the Covenanters but when Charles I came to Scotland in 1641 he made peace with him and was then created Marquess of Argyll with a pension of £1,000 a year. Shortly afterwards he rejoined the Covenanters and thereafter continued to switch sides as seemed expedient. In 1648 he brought Cromwell to Edinburgh but two years later he was crowning Charles II in Scotland following his father's

execution (having first obtained a promise to be made a duke and to be given the Garter). Then he was present at the Proclamation of Oliver Cromwell as Lord Protector and signed a promise to live peaceably under the new government.

In 1660 he was in London to wait on the arrival of the new King, Charles II. However, for all his machinations Charles ordered him to be confined in the Tower and later taken to Edinburgh Castle where he was tried for high treason. He was convicted, attainted and executed – all his honours were forfeited.

He was described by Lord Clarendon as *'a person of extraordinary cunning who carried himself so, that they who hated him most were willing to compound with him'* and having *'neither material qualifications nor the reputation of more courage than violent and imperious persons, whilst they meet with no opposition, are used to have,'*

His son and heir, Archibald Campbell, Lord Lorne, born on 26th February 1628, had a stormy passage throughout his whole life. Having fought on the royalist side at the Battle of Dunbar in 1650 he was excluded from Cromwell's Act of Grace in 1654. He later submitted but had to find £5,000 as security. At the Restoration he was imprisoned and sentenced to death but was later released. Under Letters Patent dated 16th October 1663 some of his father's titles were restored to him. He became Earl of Argyll and Barons Campbell, Lorne and Kintyre. In December 1681 he was again sentenced to death for high treason for refusing to subscribe to the Test Act.

Lord Halifax said of the sentence at the time – *'I know nothing of Scotch law, but this I do know, that we would not hang a dog here, on the grounds on which my Lord Argyle has been sentenced.'*

However, he escaped from Edinburgh Castle and fled to Holland. Having been attainted all his honours had been forfeited. In 1685 he returned to Scotland as General of a force in support of the Duke of Monmouth's rebellion but was captured and executed on his former sentence on 30th June 1685.

His son and heir, by his first marriage to Mary, daughter of James, Earl of Moray, Archibald, Lord Lorne, on hearing of his father leading the rebellious invasion had offered to fight against him on the side of James II but, receiving little encouragement, went on to support William of Orange. As a result, following William and Mary's accession he was, in 1689, admitted to his father's earldom as 10th Earl of Argyll and his father's attainder was rescinded. As well as being Colonel of the 4th Regiment of Horse Guards he also commanded a regiment of foot comprised almost entirely of his own clansmen.

On 23rd June 1701 he was created Duke of Argyll, Marquess of Kintyre and Lorne, Earl of Campbell and Cowall, Viscount of Lochow and Glenyla and Lord of Inverary, Mull, Morven and Tirie with remainder to his heirs male. After enjoying this vast range of honours for only two years he died at Chenton House near Newcastle on 25th September 1703.

He was succeeded by his son John as second duke, born on 10th October 1680. As an adult he was greatly in favour of the Protestant succession and the Union of England and Scotland. In 1705 he was created Baron of Chatham and Earl of Greenwich in the peerage of England and had a long and successful military career. He fought under Marlborough with distinction against the French. In 1715 he defeated the Jacobites at the Battle of Sheriffmuir and in 1719 was created Duke of Greenwich in the peerage of Great Britain. He married twice and had five daughters by his second wife but no sons. He died in October 1743 when his titles of Duke of Greenwich, Earl of Greenwich and Baron Chatham became extinct.

He was succeeded by his brother Archibald, aged sixty-two at the time of his succession. Archibald was very akin to his brother, a soldier he fought alongside him at the Battle of Sheriffmuir. He was a great promoter of the House of Hanover. He held the offices of Lord Privy Seal (Scotland) and Keeper of the Great Seal (Scotland), Under the Jurisdiction Act of 1747, four years after his succession, he was allowed £21,000 for the hereditary offices of Justiciary of Argyllshire and the Isles and the Sheriffship of Argyll.

The third duke (ARG 2) collected a large library and also built the present Inverary Castle on the shores of Loch Fyne on the site of the old fifteenth century castle. He married, on 19th January 1712, Anne, daughter of Major Walter Whitfield MP. She died early, in 1723, leaving no children. He remained a widower for thirty-eight years and died suddenly in London, in April 1761, aged seventy-eight.

He seems to have attracted the attention of various people who were not slow to express their views of him. He was described by Lady Louisa Stuart as of *'strong clear sense, sound judgement and thorough knowledge of mankind, ... cool, shrewd, penetrating, argumentative, an able man of business and a wary if not crafty politician, ... interested in philosophical experiments, mechanics and natural history'*. Hugh Walpole's view of him was *'He was slovenly in his person, mysterious, not to say with an air of guilt in his deportment, ... he loved power too well to hazard it by ostentation.'* Lord John Hervey's comment was *'a man of parts, quickness, knowledge, temper, dexterity and judgement, a man of little truth, little honour, little principle and no attachment but to his interest.'*

With the failure of the main line the dukedom now passed to a cousin, John, son and heir of the Honourable John Campbell of Mamore. Another elderly inheritor, being born in 1693 he was sixty-eight when he became the 4th Duke of Argyll. In 1720 he had married Mary, daughter of John 2nd Lord Bellenden. He, also, was a career soldier having held a colonelcy in various Scottish regiments. He rose to be Major General and finally General in 1765. He fought in the wars in Flanders and at the Battle of Dettingen.

At the same time as being a soldier he managed to serve as Member of Parliament for various burghs until assuming the dukedom. After his succession he became the first President of the Highland Agricultural Society of Scotland.

He died in 1770 and was succeeded by his son, another John and another career soldier, as fifth duke. He had married, in 1759, a calculated beauty of her day, one of the Gunning sisters, Elizabeth, Dowager Duchess of Hamilton. Through her two marriages she became the mother of four dukes. She died in 1790 aged fifty-seven and he died in 1805 aged eighty-two.

His first son having predeceased him he was succeeded as sixth duke by his second son George William who, in 1799, on the death of his half brother, the Duke of Hamilton, had succeeded, in right of his mother, to the Barony of Hamilton. He followed his father as second President of the Highland Agricultural Society and later became Lord Steward of the Household to William IV and then Queen Victoria. Although married, in 1810, to Caroline Elizabeth, daughter of George, 4th Earl of Jersey, he left no male heir when he died in 1839 and, as a consequence, he was succeeded by his brother.

John Douglas Edward Henry, 7th Duke of Argyll, born in 1777, had a short career in the army before becoming Member of Parliament for Argyll 1799–1822. He was Keeper of the Great Seal of Scotland and became a Fellow of the

Royal Society in 1819. He held the dukedom for a relatively short period dying in 1847 at the age of sixty-nine.

He was followed as eighth duke (Arg 4) by George Douglas Campbell his second, but first surviving, son by his second marriage. Born on 30th April 1823 he succeeded to the title aged twenty-four. He had a distinguished career, being Lord Privy Seal, Chancellor of the University of St Andrews, Secretary of State for India 1868–74 and a Fellow of the Royal Society. He was a Knight of the Thistle and also a Knight of the Garter and had the rare distinction of being allowed to hold both Orders at the same time. He was one of only four holders allowed to do so. Normally one was required to relinquish the Thistle on being offered the Garter.

The Gentleman's Magazine said of him in 1857 when he was thirty-four *'Remarkable for an extreme juvenility of appearance and hair which his enemies might call red. A slim person, features intelligent and regular, a good voice and excellent delivery, great confidence and self possession of manner and considerable industry constitute some of his characteristics.'*

In later life he proved himself a very able man both in politics and other fields but was said to be somewhat arrogant and cocksure. He married three times and died at his home, Inverary Castle in Argyllshire on 24th April 1900. Lord Colin Campbell (Arg 5) was his fifth son by his first wife.

He was succeeded by his eldest son, by his first marriage, John Douglas Campbell (Arg 1 and 6), styled Marquess of Lorne during his father's lifetime a title he held for fifty-five years, who inherited a long string of accumulated titles: 9th Duke of Argyll (Scotland), 2nd Duke of Argyll (United Kingdom), Marquess of Kintyre and Lorne, Earl of Argyll, Earl of Campbell and Cowall, Viscount Lochow, Lord of Kintyre and Lord of Inverary, Mull, Morven and Tirie all in the Peerage of Scotland and also Lord Sandridge and Lord Hamilton in the Peerage of Great Britain.

Hereditary Master of the Royal Household (Scotland) he was born on 6th August 1845 and educated at Eton and Trinity College, Cambridge. On 21st March 1871 he married HRH Princess Louise (Arg 7) fourth daughter of Queen Victoria and, on the same day, he was created a Knight of the Thistle. He became a Privy Counsellor in 1875 and then became, a very successful, Governor General of Canada 1878–83. He was described as a man of *'pleasant and picturesque appearance, thoroughly courteous and kindly, of reflective habits, studious tastes and no mean intellectual endorsements.'* He died on 2nd May 1914.

He was succeeded as tenth duke by his nephew, Niall Dermot Campbell, son of Lord Archibald Campbell and grandson of the eighth duke. Born in 1872 he was educated at Charterhouse and Christ Church, Oxford. He was of somewhat eccentric behaviour throughout his life and spent his latter years in what was described as *'monastic seclusion'*. Fearing that his eccentricities might be inherited he never married and died, childless, in 1949 and was succeeded by a cousin, Ian Campbell, a grandson of the third son of the eighth duke.

The eleventh duke, born in 1903, married four times; the first three marriages ended in divorce. He had two sons by his second marriage to Louise Clews. His third marriage was the most famous being to Margaret Sweeny, nee Whigham, whose daughter Frances, from her marriage to Charles Sweeny, became Duchess of Rutland. Margaret, Duchess of Argyll, was a notorious socialite in the 1950s who had numerous affairs with various men which ended with the duke divorcing her in 1963. His fourth marriage, in the same year, was to Matilda Mortimer (Arg 8), daughter of Stanley Mortimer an American landowner from Lichfield, Connecticut. She was raised in France by her grandparents and later studied philosophy at Harvard. She died in Paris on 5th June 1997.

The duke died in 1973 when he was succeeded, as twelfth duke, by his elder son, Ian, (Arg 9). In 1980, in a letter to the then President of the Bookplate Society, Jim Wilson, the duke describes the plate as follows: *'my bookplate was given to me by my wife on my fortieth birthday (1977). The shield at the bottom is that of the Colquhouns as my wife is the daughter of the Chief of that clan. Needless to say the house is ours and has played a particularly important role in my life. The plate was designed here in Scotland and executed by an engraver retained by Smithsons in London.'*

Ian, 12th Duke of Argyll was born in 1937. He spent his early life abroad in France and Portugal before going on to study engineering at McGill University in Canada. In 1964 he married Iona Mary, daughter of Sir Ivar Colquhoun, the eighth baronet, and they had a son and a daughter. He died, suddenly, in 2001.

ARG **2**

ARG 3

ARG 4

ARG 2 **The Honourable Archibald Campbell Esqr.** **1708** F4975

An early, full armorial bookplate. The arms are Campbell quartered with Lorne with a crescent in the centre for difference (second son). Archibald Campbell was the second son of the first duke. When his elder brother John died without a male heir he succeeded him as 3rd Duke of Argyll in 1743.

ARG 3 **Frederick Campbell** F4990

A late eighteenth or early nineteenth century simple armorial with name below. The arms bear a crescent in the centre point for difference (second son). The fact that the cadency mark is in centre point rather than centre chief indicates that the plate was made after his father's death in 1770.

Lord Frederick Campbell was born in 1729 the second son of John, 4th Duke of Argyll, and his wife Mary, daughter of John, Lord Bellenden. Educated at Westminster and Christ Church, Oxford he was called to the bar in 1754 and later elected to Parliament in 1762. He died in 1816.

ARG 4 **GEORGE DOUGLAS DUKE OF ARGYLL KC KT** NIF

A seal type full armorial bookplate commissioned by John Douglas, Marquess of Lorne, for his father the eighth duke. The design, by G.W. Eve, was produced in 1893 but, reputedly, not used in the ducal books.

ARG 5 **Lord Colin Campbell** NIF

A simple armorial bookplate for the younger son of a duke. It is for Colin Campbell, the fifth son of George Douglas, 8th Duke of Argyll, by his first wife, Elizabeth Georgiana daughter of George, 2nd Duke of Sutherland. She bore him twelve children in all, five sons and seven daughters. Lord Colin was born on 8th March 1853 and went on to become Member of Parliament for Argyllshire in 1878. In 1881 he married Gertrude, youngest daughter of Edmond Blood of Brickhill, County Clare. He divorced her in 1884 and died, without issue, on 19th June 1895.

ARG 6 **Anonymous** F4945

A simple armorial bookplate for John Douglas, 9th Duke of Argyll, showing the arms, with supporters beneath a duke's coronet, the shield surrounded by the motto of the Order of the Thistle. The duke, then Marquess of Lorne, was made a Knight of the Order on the occasion of his marriage to Princess Louise in 1871.

ARG 5

ARG 6

ARG 7

ARG 9

ARG 8

ARG 7 **LL** (interlaced) NIF

A monogram plate for Louise, Marchioness of Lorne, in a diamond showing interlaced 'L's' encircled by a marchioness's coronet with a royal coronet denoting a princess of the royal blood above. Princess Louise, daughter of Queen Victoria, married John Douglas, Marquess of Lorne, in 1871. He succeeded to the dukedom as ninth duke in 1900. [*Royal Collection Trust ©H.M. Queen Elizabeth II 2016.*]

ARG 8 **Mathilda Mortimer Duchess of Argyll** NIF

A modern bookplate for Mathilda Mortimer who married the eleventh duke in 1963 as his fourth wife. It probably dates after the duke's death in 1973. It depicts a stylised crested bird, possibly an egret, on top of a stylised tree with motto and inscription below. The plate was produced by William Day Ltd. London.

ATH 9 **IAN XII DUKE OF ARGYLL** NIF

A good modern armorial plate for the twelfth duke showing his arms and, on a separate shield, those of his wife, with a view of Inverary Castle.

Archibald Campbell First Duke of Argyll.

From the original of Sir Peter Lely, in the Collection of

His Grace The Duke of Argyll

Archibald Campbell, 1st Duke of Argyll, 1658–1703, from an original painting by Peter Lely. Both his grandfather and father were executed for high treason and their honours forfeited. However Archibald was a supporter of William of Orange and on his accession, as William III in 1689, in recognition of that support, William restored the earldom of Argyll to him as tenth earl. On her accession in 1701, Queen Anne created him 1st Duke of Argyll.

ATH 1 His Grace John Duke of Atholl 1711 NIF

A large early armorial bookplate for John, 1st Duke of Atholl, with the arms surrounded by the chain and insignia of the Order of the Thistle beneath a duke's coronet, with supporters and the motto on a ribbon below. The badge of the Order of the Thistle is shown top left and the family crest surrounded by the motto and insignia of the Order of the Thistle top right.

ARMS: Grand quarters: I and IV, quarterly, 1 and 4 paly of six or and sable (Atholl); 2 and 3, or, a fess chequey azure and argent (Stewart); II and III, azure, three mullets argent within a double tressure flory counter flory (Murray).

CREST: A demi savage proper wreathed about the head and waist vert, in the dexter hand a dagger pommel and hilt or, in the sinister a key of the last.

SUPPORTERS: Dexter, a savage wreathed about the head and loins vert, feet in fetters chained to dexter hand. Sinister, a lion gules gorged with a collar azure charged with three mullets argent.

MOTTO: Furth fortune and fill the fetters

Dukes of Atholl

FAMILY NAME: Murray, Stewart-Murray

CREATION OF DUKEDOM: 30th June 1703

COURTESY TITLE OF ELDEST SON: Marquess of Tullibardine

COURTESY TITLE OF GRANDSON AND HEIR: Earl of Strathtay

PRINCIPAL RESIDENCE: Blair Castle, Perthshire

In the fourteenth and fifteenth centuries the earldom of Atholl was created and recreated many times for various sons of the Scottish Kings. It became extinct in 1625 for lack of a male heir. It was recreated again, in 1629, for John Murray, son of William Murray whose wife, Dorothea, was the eldest daughter and co-heir of John Stewart, Earl of Atholl (1563–95), and therefore heir of that line.

John Murray was born c.1605 and he married, in 1630, Jean, daughter of Sir Duncan Campbell of Glenorchy. They had a son, John, born on 2nd May 1631 who, on the death of his father in 1642, inherited the earldom aged eleven. He joined the King's army against Cromwell in 1653 and, at the Restoration of the monarchy in 1660, was made a Privy Counsellor. In January 1670 he succeeded his cousin as Earl of Tullibardine and became Captain General of the Royal Company of Archers. He was obviously in favour with Charles II who created him Marquess of Atholl in 1676. On the 29th May 1687 James II revived the old Scottish Order of the Thistle and John Murray was one of eight knights created on that occasion. He married, on 5th May 1659 Amelia, daughter and sole heir of James Stanley, 7th Earl of Derby. He died at Dunkeld, Perthshire in 1703 aged seventy-two and was succeeded by his son, John, born on 24th February 1659/60.

John was a strong supporter of William III and one of his Principal Secretaries of State. He was appointed a Privy Counsellor by the King and reappointed by Queen Anne on her accession. He was Chancellor of the University of St Andrews. On the 30th June 1703, a month after succeeding to his father's titles, he was created Duke of Atholl (ATH 1 and 2), Marquess of Tullibardine, Earl of Strathtay and Strathardle and Viscount Balquidder, Glenalmond and Glenlyon with special remainder, failing heirs male of his own body, to those of his father. He was made a Knight of the Thistle in February 1703/4.

In 1705 he resigned his Office of Privy Seal and strongly opposed the Union of England and Scotland. He was reappointed to that office in 1713.

He married firstly, in 1683, Katherine, daughter of William, Duke of Hamilton. She bore him three sons and died in 1707. He married secondly, in 1710, Mary, daughter of William, Lord Ross. He died in 1724 at Dunkeld.

His eldest son, John, studied at the University of Leyden and later was Colonel of a regiment in the service of the Dutch. He fought at the Battle of Malplaquet in September 1709 where he was killed.

The second son, William, matriculated at the University of St Andrews and entered the navy in 1707. He joined the Rising of 1715 to restore the House of Stuart and was attainted for high treason. However, he managed to escape to Brittany. The following year he was created, by the titular James III, whose exiled Court was at St Germain, Duke of Rannoch, Marquess of Blair and Earl of Glentilt (Jacobite Peerage). He returned to Scotland and was defeated at the Battle of Glenshiel in 1719. He again escaped, this time with a price of £2,000 on his head. He was back in 1745 to help raise the Jacobite Standard at Glenfinnan but after the defeat at Culloden in 1746 he surrendered and was committed to the Tower of London where he died, unmarried, later that year.

In 1715, following William's attainder for high treason, the first duke had obtained an Act of Parliament under George I vesting his honours and estates in his third son, James, after his death. Consequently James succeeded his father in 1724 (ATH 3 and 4).

James, who was born in 1690, had a career in the army and in 1717 was Lieutenant Colonel of a Grenadier Company. He was Member of Parliament for Perth 1715–24. In 1733 he obtained an Act of Parliament to say that the attainder on his elder brother William should apply only to William and his heirs and not to any other heirs male of their father.

James was Lord Privy Seal 1733–63, a Privy Counsellor from 1737 and created a Knight of the Thistle in 1733. In 1736 in accordance with the Act of Parliament of 1715, despite his elder brother, William, still being alive he succeeded his cousin James, 10th Earl of Derby, to the Sovereignty of the Isle of Man and also to the Barony of Strange in the Peerage of England (created 1627). In which barony he was summoned to Parliament sitting both as an English baron and a representative Scottish peer for four years.

He married first, in 1726, Jane, widow of James Lannoy of Hammersmith, a London merchant. She died in London in 1748. He married secondly, in Edinburgh in 1749, Jean, daughter of John Drummond. He died in 1764 at Dunkeld without leaving a male heir. His two sons, by his first wife, had both died as infants.

He was succeeded, as third duke, by his nephew John Murray, son of Lord George Murray his younger brother. Born in 1729 John was a captain in the 54th Highland Regiment of Foot. He served as Member of Parliament for Perth 1761–4. As a result of the attainder of his father, who was a Lieutenant General in the force of Charles Edward in the 1745 Jacobite Rising, his right to the dukedom was in some doubt. He presented a petition to the King who referred it to the House of Lords. Their Lordships resolved that the petitioner had a right to his uncle's titles.

He married, in October 1753, his cousin Charlotte (ATH 5) only surviving daughter and heir of his uncle James, the second duke. On her father's death she had inherited the Sovereignty of the Isle of Man. She and her husband sold the Sovereignty to the Government in 1765 for £70,000 and an annuity of £2,000 for their joint lives. The third duke died at Dunkeld on 5th November 1774 having drowned himself in the river Tay in *'a fit of delirium'*.

He was succeeded by his son John who, in 1777, three years after his succession, raised a regiment known as the 77th Regiment of Foot or the Atholl Highlanders. He was a representative Scottish peer and in 1793 was made Captain General and Governor in Chief of the Isle of Man. He was made a Privy Counsellor in 1797 and a Knight of the Thistle in 1800.

He married first, in 1774, Jane, daughter of Charles, 9th Lord Cathcart. She died in 1790 and he married secondly, in 1794, Margery, widow of John Mackenzie and eldest daughter of James, 16th Lord Forbes. He died in 1830 at Dunkeld.

The fifth duke was his son John. Born in 1778 and educated at Eton he became an Ensign in the 61st Regiment in 1797. In 1798 he was said to be *'of unsound mind'*. What exactly that involved is not clear. However he was sufficiently lucid in 1845 to entertain Queen Victoria at Blair Castle. This involved moving to a smaller house on the estate while Queen Victoria, Prince Albert and their seventy-

ATH 2

five servants inhabited the castle. This was their first visit to Scotland, they both fell in love with the country and, as a result, went on to buy the nearby Balmoral estate which remains the Royal Family's Scottish home to this day. The Queen was impressed by all things Scottish and was so entertained by the Atholl Highlanders that she gave the Dukes of Atholl the right in perpetuity to keep them as a private army; the only such army in the United Kingdom. Recruits come from local landowners and estate workers and their function, today, is purely ceremonial. The fifth duke died died, unmarried, in 1846.

He was succeeded by his nephew George Augustus Murray, son of Lord James Murray, Lord Glenlyon (created 1821). Born in 1814 he was an officer in the 2nd Dragoon Guards. He succeeded his father as 2nd Lord Glenlyon in 1837 and went on to hold various offices; Grand Master of Freemasons (Scotland), Hereditary Sheriff of Perthshire and President of the Highland and Agricultural Society. He became a Knight of the Thistle in 1853.

In 1829 he married Anne, only daughter of Henry Home-Drummond, who bore him a son and heir. He died on 16th June 1864 of *'a cancer in the neck'*.

The seventh duke was his son John James, Marquess of Tullibardine (ATH 8 and 9), born in 1840 at Blair Castle. He followed a military career in the Scots Fusilier Guards. In 1865 he succeeded his maternal uncle, Algernon Percy, 4th Duke of Northumberland, in the barony of Percy (created by Writ 1722). In the same year he assumed the name of Stewart before that of Murray. He was installed a Knight of the Thistle in 1868 and became Lord Lieutenant of Perthshire ten years later. He was President of the Highland Agricultural Society.

He married, in 1863, Louisa, daughter of Sir Thomas Moncreiffe of Moncreiffe, the seventh baronet. Their first son John Stewart-Murray, Marquess of Tullibardine, died the day after his birth so he was succeeded, as eighth duke (ATH 10), by his second son John George Stewart-Murray, Marquess of Tullibardine when he died in 1917. At that time the duke owned two hundred and two thousand acres of land in Perthshire.

The 8th Duke of Atholl had claim to the greatest number of titles within the Peerage of the three kingdoms of England, Scotland and Northern Ireland. As well as the dukedom he held two marquisates, five earldoms, three viscountcies and eight baronies as well as being a Knight of the Thistle. That is twenty distinct titles which takes no account of the Jacobite peerages (ATH 10).

ATH 2 His Grace John Duke of Atholl 1711 F21379

This is a similar plate to ATH 1 but a smaller plate and a different engraving, for the first duke, it is also dated 1711.

ATH 3 His Grace James Duke of Atholl Lord of Man & the Isles. Lord Strange &c. 1737 F21381

A large early armorial bookplate for James, the second duke who was the third son of John, the first duke and who succeeded his father in 1724. It mimics the style of his father's bookplate (ATH 1).

ARMS: Grand quarters: I, azure, three mullets argent within a double tressure flory, counter flory or (Murray); II, gules, three legs in armour proper and spurred or conjoined in triangle at upper thigh (Lordship of Man); III, quarterly 1 and 4 argent, on a bend azure three buck's heads caboshed or (Stanley); 2 and 3 gules, two lions passant in pale (Strange); IV, quarterly, 1 and 4 paly of six or and sable (Atholl); 2 and 3 or, a fess chequey azure and argent (Stewart).

The Duke had been made a Knight of the Thistle in 1733 and had succeeded to the Lordship of Man and the English barony of Strange in 1736 which are recorded in the arms and inscription which is dated 1737.

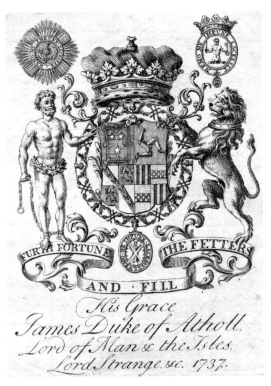

ATH 3

ATH 4 **Anonymous** F21380

A full armorial for James, 2nd Duke of Atholl, in the baroque style from the second quarter of the eighteenth century with the arms displayed as in ATH 1. James (1690–1764) was the third son of the first duke and succeeded him in 1724. Although married twice he left no male heir and on is death was succeeded by his nephew John.

ATH 5 **Charlotte Duchess Dowager of Atholl Baroness Strange** F21384

An Adam style plate showing the arms in a lozenge which in this case denotes a widow. Note the supporters are reversed. It dates after 1774 the year of her widowhood.

Charlotte was the second daughter of James, 2nd Duke of Atholl. On 23rd October 1753 she married her cousin John who, later in 1764 succeeded his uncle as third duke. At her father's death she succeeded to the sovereignty of the Isle Man and the barony of Strange. She had five sons and four daughters and died in 1805.

ATH 6 **Lord Henry Murray** F21414

A very late eighteenth century plate showing an early example of a 'dog eared' shield.

ARMS: Quarterly of eight, 1 and 8, Murray; 2, Stewart; 3, Atholl; 4, Stanley; 5, Lathom; 6, Isle of Man; 7, Strange; 8, Murray. There should be a cadency mark, a martlet, for difference.

Henry Murray was the fourth son of the 3rd Duke of Atholl. Born in 1767 he had a military career, albeit a short one, then in 1804 he was appointed Lieutenant Governor of the Isle of Man. He died in office a year later at the early age of thirty-eight.

ATH 7 **Lord Charles Murray** F21401

A simple crest plate within a wreath showing the crest of Murray, a demi savage proper wreathed about the head and waist vert, in the dexter hand a dagger pommel and hilt or, in the sinister a key of the last.

ATH 4

*Charlotte Duchess Dowager of Atholl
Baroness Strange*

ATH 5

Lord Henry Murray

ATH 6

Lord Charles Murray

ATH 7

Charles Murray was the fifth son and last child of John, 3rd Duke of Atholl. Born in 1771 he entered the church becoming Dean of Bocking in Essex and Archdeacon of Sodor and Man in 1803. He married, 18th June 1793, Alicia Mitford daughter of George Mitford and heiress of her great uncle, Gawen Aynsley. Upon marriage Charles assumed the surname of Aynsley after that of Murray. He died in 1808 aged thirty-seven.

ATH 8 John James Hugh Henry, 7th Duke of Athole
F21382

A typical nineteenth century plate dating from the 1860s between 1864 when he inherited the title and 1868 when he was installed as a Knight of the Thistle. The quartered arms show Murray in the first quarter, the Lordship of Man in the second, Stanley quartering Lathom and Strange in the third and Atholl quartering Stewart in the fourth. He had assumed the surname of Stewart before that of Murray in 1865. The supporters are reversed as in ATH 6.

ATH 9 Anonymous F21383

Although unnamed this plate is nineteenth century in design and almost certainly for the seventh duke after he was awarded the Thistle in 1868. The helm, crest and mantling are identical with the previous plate but this time the supporters are the right way round.

ATH 8

ATH 9

Ath 10 **JOHN GEORGE 8ᵗʰ DUKE OF ATHOLL** NIF

A nice panel armorial bookplate signed and dated 1921 by A.J. Downey.

ARMS: Grand quarters: I, quarterly, 1 and 4, paly of six or and sable (Atholl); 2 and 3 or, a fess chequey azure and argent (Stewart); II, azure, three mullets argent within a double tressure flory counter flory or (Murray); III, quarterly, 1 argent, on a bend azure, three buck's heads caboshed or (Stanley); 2, gules, three legs in armour proper and spurred or conjoined in triangle at upper thigh (Isle of Man); 3, or, on a chief indented azure three plates (Latham); 4, gules, two lions passant in pale argent (Strange); IV, quarterly, 1 and 4, or, a lion rampant azure (Percy); 2 and 3, azure, five fusils in fess or (Percy).

CREST: A demi savage proper wreathed about head and waist vert, in the dexter hand a dagger also proper pommel and hilt or, in the sinister a key of the last.

The shield is surrounded by the collar and badge of the Order of the Thistle.

The duke succeeded to the title in 1917.

ATH 10

Bᴇᴀ 1 **The Most Noble Henry Duke of Beaufort 1706** ꜰ27573

An early, full armorial for Henry, 2nd Duke of Beaufort. It is typical of its period and dated 1706 the year of Henry's second marriage to Rachel, daughter and co-heiress of Wriothesley Noel, 2nd Earl of Gainsborough whose arms are shown in pretence.

Aʀᴍs: Quarterly, 1 and 4, azure, three fleur-de-lys or (France); 2 and 3, gules, three lions passant guardant in pale (England); all within a bordure compony argent and azure. On a shield of pretence, or, a fretty gules, in dexter chief a canton ermine (Noel, Earls of Gainsborough).

Cʀᴇsᴛ: On a wreath of the colours a portcullis or nailed azure with pendant chains or.

Sᴜᴘᴘᴏʀᴛᴇʀs: Dexter, a panther argent with flames issuant from mouth and ears, gorged with a collar and chain or. Sinister, a wyvern wings addorsed vert, holding in the mouth a sinister hand couped at the wrist.

Mᴏᴛᴛᴏ: Multare vel timare sperno – I scorn to change or fear.

Dukes of Beaufort

FAMILY NAME: Somerset

CREATION OF DUKEDOM: 2nd December 1682

COURTESY TITLE OF ELDEST SON: Marquess of Worcester

COURTESY TITLE OF GRANDSON AND HEIR: Earl of Glamorgan

PRINCIPAL RESIDENCE: Badminton, Gloucestershire

Henry Somerset, born 1629, was the son and heir of Edward, 2nd Marquess of Worcester. He became Member of Parliament for Monmouth and was one of the twelve commoners deputed, on 7th May 1660, to invite the return of Charles II. He succeeded his father as 3rd Marquess of Worcester in 1667 and was elected Lord Provost of Wales 1672–89. He became a Privy Counsellor in 1672 and in the same year was given the Garter.

On 2nd December 1682 he was created, by Charles II, Duke of Beaufort in consideration, it was said in the patent, *'of his noble descent from King Edward III by John de Beaufort eldest son of John of Gaunt, Duke of Lancaster'*. However this *'noble descent'* was via two generations of illegitimate offspring, hence the bordure around the royal arms in his armorial bearings.

He carried the crown of the Queen Consort at the coronation of James II and was a firm supporter of James against the rebellion of the Duke of Monmouth in 1685 and against William of Orange in 1688. Being a staunch Tory he refused the Oath of Allegiance when William became king.

He married, in 1657, Mary, widow of Henry Seymour and sister of Arthur, Earl of Essex. He died of a fever, on 2nd January 1699/1700, aged seventy.

His first son and heir apparent died as an infant. His second son Charles Somerset, styled Marquess of Worcester, lived to adulthood, married and had a family but died, following a coaching accident in Wales, in 1698 in his thirty-eighth year and eighteen months before his father. (The bookplate of his second son, also Charles Somerset, is BEA 2)

Thus Henry was succeeded, as second duke (BEA 1 and 3), by his grandson Henry, eldest son of Charles, Marquess of

Worcester. Born in 1684, he inherited the dukedom when only fifteen and two years later, in August 1702, he entertained Queen Anne, and her consort Prince George at his family home, Badminton. However, being a staunch Tory, like his father and grandfather before him, he absented himself from court until the Tories came to power in 1710, in which year he was also appointed a Privy Counsellor.

He became Lord Lieutenant of Hampshire, and later of Gloucestershire, in 1712 and remained so until his death. He was installed as a Knight of the Garter in 1712

He married firstly, in 1702, Mary, daughter of Charles, Earl of Dorset. She died, three years later, in childbed. He married secondly, in February 1705/6, Rachel, daughter and co-heiress of Wriothesley, 2nd Earl of Gainsborough. She brought to the marriage a dowry of *'upwards of £60,000'*. She also died, after four years of marriage, again in childbed in September 1709. He married thirdly, in 1711, Mary daughter of Peregrine, 2nd Duke of Leeds.

Lady Henrietta (BEA 4) was his sister.

He died in May 1714 *'of inflammation caused by drinking small beer on a long journey which he rid in one day'*. He was aged only thirty-one.

He was succeeded, as third duke, by Henry (BEA 5) his son by his second wife Rachel. Henry was born in 1707 and educated at Westminster School and University College, Oxford. Like his father before him he was a Tory and became High Steward of Hereford in 1729.

He married in June 1729 Frances, only daughter of James, 2nd Viscount Scudamore. She was born in 1711 and, aged five, succeeded her father, in 1716. Following his marriage the duke took the name of Scudamore by Act of Parliament in 1730 on succeeding, in right of his wife, to Holme Lacey, Hereford and other estates of that family.

He divorced his wife, by Act of Parliament, in March 1743/4 because of her infidelity. She had eloped with William, Lord Talbot, himself a married man.

Henry died in February 1744/5 without leaving any children. He was only thirty-eight and was said to have been *'worn out by a complication of disorders'*. Mrs Delany said of him *'His death is not to be lamented, he was unhealthy in his constitution and unhappy in his circumstances, though possessed of great honour and riches; his brother is qualified to make a better figure and his wife, I hope, will prove an honourable and virtuous Duchess of Beaufort'.*

Henry was succeeded by his brother Charles Noel Somerset as fourth duke (BEA 6). Born in September 1709, like his brother he was educated at Westminster School and University College, Oxford. In the 1730s he was Tory Member of Parliament. for Monmouth.

He married, in 1740, Elizabeth (BEA 7), daughter of John Berkeley and sister and sole heir of Norborne Berkeley, Lord Botetourt. He died aged forty-eight in 1756, his widow survived him for the rest of the century dying in 1799 at the age of eighty.

He was succeeded by his twelve year old son Henry as fifth duke who later matriculated from Oriel College, Oxford in 1760. He went on to hold various offices, Grand Master of Freemasons 1767–72, Master of the Horse to Queen Charlotte 1768–70, Lord Lieutenant of Monmouthshire (1771) and of Brecknock (1787) until his death. He was given the Garter in 1786.

He married, in 1766, Elizabeth (BEA 8), daughter of Admiral the Honourable Edward Boscawen and sister of George Evelyn Boscawen, 3rd Viscount Falmouth.

In 1803 he obtained, by Writ, a declaration in his favour, of the termination of the abeyance of the Barony of Botetourt, to which, by right of his mother, he was one of the co-heirs. Unfortunately he died later that year of '*gout in the stomach*'. His widow died in 1828 aged eighty-one, having lived to see nearly eighty of her descendants of the name of Somerset.

The sixth duke was the fifth duke's son, another Henry, born in 1766 and educated at Westminster School and Trinity College, Oxford. He was Tory Member of Parliament for Monmouth and later Bristol. He married, in 1791, Charlotte, daughter of Granville, 1st Marquess of Stafford. He became Lord Lieutenant of Monmouthshire and Brecknock (1803) and of Gloucestershire (1810) and served until his death. He was made a Knight of the Garter in 1805 two years after his succession.

He died at Badminton in November 1835. He seems to have been one of the benevolent dukes. It was reported of him that '*he was a man of generous disposition, plain and straightforward in his speech, punctual in his dealings and of strict integrity. He was kind and open in his manner, very benevolent in his conduct and always willing to oblige*'.

The seventh duke was his son, yet another Henry. Born in 1792 he joined the 10th Hussars aged eighteen and was Aide-de-Camp to the Duke of Wellington in Spain and Portugal 1812–14 and Lord of the Admiralty 1815–19. He was later Member of Parliament for Monmouthshire and West Gloucestershire and High Steward of Bristol.

He married firstly, in 1814, Georgiana, daughter of the Honourable Henry Fitzroy. Her mother was Anne, sister of the Duke of Wellington. She died in 1821. He married secondly, in 1822, her half sister Emily (BEA 9), the daughter of Charles Culling and his wife Anne, widow of the Honourable Henry Fitzroy. He was installed as a Knight of the Garter in 1842 and died at Badminton in 1853. The Gentleman's magazine said of him '*He was an excellent landlord and a great patron of the sports of the field... his inherent courtliness was enhanced by a fine port and commanding figure and a countenance whose features were cast in a truly noble mould. He was a consistent supporter of conservative politics*'.

The eighth duke was the fourth Henry in a row. Son of the seventh duke by his second wife he was born in 1826 in Paris. After Eton he went into the Life Guards and, like his father, he too became Aide-de-Campe to the Duke of Wellington in 1842. He followed the general trend of his predecessors, being Member of Parliament for East Gloucestershire, High Steward of Bristol, Master of the Horse and Lord Lieutenant of Monmouthshire (1867) till his death. He was given the Garter in 1867.

He married, in July 1845, Georgiana, daughter of Richard 1st Earl Howe. A year before his death from gout in April

MUTARE VEL TIMERE SPERNO

The R.t Hon.ble Lord Charles Somerset Second son to y.e Late Marquefs of Worcefter 1703

BEA 2

1899 he made over all his estates to his eldest surviving son thus avoiding the heavy succession duties.

Henry Adelbert Wellington Fitzroy Somerset, the eighth duke's second, but eldest surviving, son and heir inherited a string of titles. 9th Duke of Beaufort, Marquess of Worcester, Earl of Worcester, Lord Botetourt and Lord Herbert. Born in 1847 and styled Marquess of Worcester he had a career in the Horse Guards retiring in 1877. Before succeeding he held many of the offices previously held by his predecessors and in 1899 he was Aide-de Campe to Queen Victoria. He also commissioned a very fine bookplate (BEA 15).

He married rather late in life in October 1895, Louise, daughter of William Harford and widow of Carlo, Baron De Tuyll.

BEA 2 The Right Honble Lord Charles Somerset Second son to ye Late Marquess of Worcester 1703
F27579

A very fine full early armorial with profuse mantling and an inscription below. The arms are Beaufort with a crescent for difference in the centre point.

Lord Charles Somerset was the second son of Charles, Beaufort. However in 1698 he predeceased his father who was therefore succeeded by his grandson Henry.

BEA 3 The Most Noble Henry Duke of Beaufort 1705
F27572

A similar but smaller plate than BEA 1 and without the arms in pretence. It is dated '1705' and predates his second marriage.

BEA 4 The Right Honble Lady Heniretta [sic] Somerset 1712 F27582

An early eighteenth century plate in the baroque style for a maiden lady with the arms of Beaufort shown in a lozenge. There is an inscription below.

Lady Henrietta Somerset was born in 1690 the daughter of Charles, Marquess of Worcester and the sister of Lord Charles Somerset and Henry, 2nd Duke of Beaufort. In 1713 she married Charles, 2nd Duke of Grafton but later died in childbed in 1726 aged only thirty-six.

BEA 3

BEA 4

BEA 5

BEA 6

BEA 7

BEA 5 **BEAUFORT** NIF

A simple armorial bookplate from the first half of the eighteenth century for Henry the third duke who succeeded his father in 1714 at the age of only seven. Educated at Westminster School and University College, Oxford he went on to have a disastrous marriage, divorcing his wife for infidelity and, suffering ill health, he died in 1745 aged thirty-eight

BEA 6 **The R^t Honble The Lord Charles Noel Somerset 1725** F25780

An early style armorial bookplate for Lord Charles Somerset second son of Henry, the second duke. The plate is signed 'Hulett Sculp.' and depicts the arms within a lined border. Rather strangely there is a mullet on the fess point, this is the cadency mark for a third son but he was the second son so should bear a crescent which should be in centre chief anyway. It must be due to artistic error which was not spotted nor appreciated by the owner who was only fifteen at the time.

Born on 12th September 1709 Charles was educated at Westminster School and University College, Oxford graduating in 1725. He was elected Member of Parliament for Monmouth 1734–45. In 1740 he married Elizabeth, the daughter of John Symes Berkeley. He succeeded his elder brother Henry as 4th Duke of Beaufort in 1745 and died in 1756.

BEA 7 **Anonymous** F27575

A mid eighteenth century armorial plate for Elizabeth, 4th Duchess of Beaufort, in the rococo style, close cut following the outline of the design. the arms, in a lozenge, are Beaufort impaling – gules, a chevron ermine between teen crosses patty argent, six in chief and four in base (Berkeley).

Elizabeth, born in 1719, was the daughter of John Berkeley. She married Lord Charles Noel Somerset in 1740 and he succeeded his brother as 4th Duke of Beaufort in February 1744/5. He died in 1756. As the arms are in a lozenge they denote, in this case, a widow and must date after 1756. She lived on to the end of the century dying, aged eighty, in 1799.

BEA 8 **ELIZABETH DUCHESS of BEAUFORT** F27576

A simple armorial bookplate for a peeress in the early nineteenth century style with the typical 'dog eared' shield. It shows the arms of Somerset impaling Boscawen, ermine, a rose gules barbed and seeded proper.

Elizabeth Boscawen was the daughter of Admiral the Honourable Edward Boscawen, brother of the 2nd Viscount Falmouth. In 1766 she married Henry Somerset, 5th Duke of Beaufort. He died in 1803 and she died in 1828 aged eighty-one. She had lived to see nearly eighty of her descendants of the name of Somerset.

BEA 9 **EFB** F27577

A small monogram plate showing the initials EFB under a duchess's coronet before a draped cloak.

Emily Francis was the daughter of John and Anne Culling. In 1822 she married, as his second wife, Henry Somerset, Marquess of Worcester. He succeeded his father as 7th Duke of Beaufort in 1835. This plate post dates that event.

BEA 8

BEA 9

BEA 10

BEA 10 **Anonymous** NIF

A plain simple nineteenth century armorial bookplate depicting shield surrounded by the Garter bearing the garter motto, supporters and coronet all above a ribbon containing the family motto. The plate bears a manuscript shelf reference number – '*M 2–3*'. It is difficult to ascribe this plate to a particular duke as the sixth, seventh and eighth dukes were all called Henry and all given the Garter in 1805, 1842 and 1867 respectively.

BEA 11 **Anonymous** NIF

A small simple armorial bookplate showing the shield in outline without tinctures surrounded by the Garter with the garter motto and surmounted by a duke's coronet. This plate also bears a manuscript shelf reference number – '*C = 2 = 12*'. The same comment applies as for BEA 10.

BEA 11

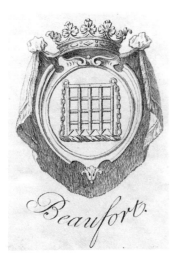

BEA 12

BEA 14 **ISABEL SOMERSET – REIGATE PRIORY** F27583

A simple late nineteenth century plate showing the inscription within a wreath suspended from a true lover's knot.

Isabella Caroline Somers-Cocks (1851–1921) was the eldest daughter of Charles Somers-Cocks, 3rd Earl Somers. She married, on 6th February 1872, Lord Henry Charles Somerset, second son of the 8th Duke of Beaufort. Although he provided her with a son he was homosexual and the marriage ended in legal separation. He retired to Italy; she became active in temperance work and women's rights.

BEA 12 **Beaufort** F27574

A small anonymous Beaufort plate showing the portcullis crest surrounded by a mantle and surmounted by a duke's coronet. It is on wove paper and probably dates from the nineteenth century.

BEA 13 **Lord Granville Somerset** F27581

A simple armorial from the first half of the nineteenth century showing the arms of Beaufort impaling Carrington, with supporters, crest and motto.

Lord Granville Charles Henry Somerset, born in 1792, was the second son of Henry, 6th Duke of Beaufort. Educated at Christ Church, Oxford he married, in 1822, the Honourable Emily Smith, daughter of Robert Smith, 1st Lord Carrington. He held various Government posts; Lord of the Treasury 1819–27 and 1828–30, Privy Counsellor 1834, Chancellor of the Duchy of Lancaster 1841–6. He died in 1848.

BEA 13

BEA 14

BEA 15 Henry Somerset 9th Duke of Beaufort
MDCCCC NIF

A fine full panel armorial bookplate showing the achievement against a gothic background with an inscription in the base.

Henry Adelbert Wellington Fitzroy Somerset was the second son of the eighth duke and succeeded his father in 1899, his elder brother having predeceased his father.

BEA 16 Arthur William FitzRoy Somerset of Castle Goring in the County of Sussex, Esq. 1920 NIF

A modern bookplate by Harry Soane, dated 1920 and in an early eighteenth century style. The quartered arms are those of a branch of the Somerset family with another quartered coat in pretence. The pronomal arms in each case are Somerset as the owner married his second cousin.

Arthur William Fitzroy Somerset was the great grandson of the 5th Duke of Beaufort and the son of Colonel Fitzroy Molyneux Henry Somerset. He was born in 1855 in Chatham, Kent and in adult life moved to Castle Goring a country house near Worthing, Sussex. He was a Deputy Lord Lieutenant and Justice of the Peace for Sussex and a first class cricketer playing for Sussex and London Counties Cricket Club. In 1887 he married Gwendoline Adelaide Kathleen Matilda Somerset daughter of Sir Alfred Plantagenet Frederick Charles Somerset, his second cousin. He died in 1937 at the age of eighty-one.

BEA 15

BEA 16

Edward Somerset, Second Marquis of Worcester.

From the original of Vandyke, in the Collection of

His Grace The Duke of Beaufort.

Edward Somerset, 2nd Marquess of Worcester, 1602–67, from an original painting by Anthony Van Dyke. A catholic aristocrat who had a mixed career of military service and scientific study and inventions. His son, the third marquess, became 1st Duke of Beaufort.

by assassinating King Charles II and his brother, the Duke of York on their journey from the Newmarket races to London. He was put on trial and, somewhat dubiously, was found guilty of high treason, condemned to death and attainted. He was executed in Lincolns Inn Fields on 21st July 1683.

Following the accession of William and Mary in 1688 the attainder was declared void and in 1694 King William created his father, the fifth earl, Marquess of Tavistock and Duke of Bedford. Basically this was as a recompense for having lost his son. The preamble to the Letters Patent creating the dukedom specifically state that he is receiving the honour by virtue of the fact that he was *'the father to the Lord Russell, the ornament of his age, whose great merit it was not enough to transmit by history to posterity.'*

The following year the new duke's grandson, Wriothesley aged only fourteen, was married to a rich heiress Elizabeth Howland, aged thirteen, only daughter and heiress of a wealthy merchant John Howland of Streatham. Her dowry was £100,000. A month later his grandfather, in addition to all his other honours, was created Baron Howland of Streatham to commemorate the marriage and preserve the name. The title, Baron Howland, is used as a courtesy title by the eldest son of the eldest son in the lifetime of his grandfather down to the present day. The first duke only enjoyed his new honours for six years before dying in 1700 at the ripe old age of eighty-seven. No bookplate is known for him. He was perhaps too old and died just too soon to indulge in the new fashion for bookplates.

He was succeeded, as second duke, by his grandson Wriothesley (1680–1711) (BED 1), son of the executed Lord William Russell. Wriothesley and his wife Elizabeth had lived apart for some time following their early marriage; she with her mother and he on the Grand Tour where he developed a taste for collecting works of art. Later they were to have six children including four sons. The first two died in infancy but the second two survived to become 3rd and 4th Dukes of Bedford and between them served the Honour for sixty years. Although it has to be said, the third duke did not serve it very well or very long.

Shortly after the birth of their youngest son, John, in 1710, the family went to live for a while at the wife's family home in Streatham despite the advice of their doctor, the famous Dr Hans Sloane, who considered it an unhealthy area. Unfortunately the duke caught smallpox there and died in 1711. He left two daughters, a three year old son, now the third duke, also called Wriothesley (1708–32) (BED 2) and the infant John to be brought up by their mother and grandmother, the dowager duchess.

In adult life the third duke was a wastrel and a gambler; he was a bad duke. Although during his eleven year tenure the second duke had managed to double the rent roll from his vast estates the third duke spent enormous sums whilst doing little to maintain or enhance his inheritance. Fortunately for the future of the family his health failed and he died on a voyage to Lisbon, in 1732, aged only twenty-four which was an effective form of damage limitation. He left no heir and no bookplates and was succeeded by his younger brother, John, as fourth duke (BED 3).

John was to be a good duke. He had inherited the skills of his merchant ancestors and managed by hard work to recover the estates and make them profitable again. He was also a member of the Whig party and very active politically. He held a number of high offices including First Lord of the Admiralty and Lord Lieutenant of Ireland. At the time the family seat was still at Chenies in Buckinghamshire but this was about to change to Woburn Abbey in Bedfordshire.

It is to John that we owe the Woburn we see today. He inherited the building in a very poor run down state and, having got his affairs in order, in 1747 he instructed the architect Henry Flitcroft to undertake a major rebuild. At about the same time the Duke of Devonshire was rebuilding Chatsworth and the Duke of Portland was rebuilding Welbeck Abbey.

As a young man he did what many scions of aristocratic families did; he undertook the Grand Tour. During his wanderings he arrived at the city of Venice where he met the resident artist Antonio Canale (Canaletto). He was much taken with his work and commissioned a number of paintings purchasing twenty-four in all. He set aside a room at Woburn for their display where they remain to this day. In his appreciation of the artist he was in good company, George III and Catherine Empress of Russia were both patrons of Canaletto.

The duke served as Lord Lieutenant of Bedfordshire from 1745 and concurrently as Lord Lieutenant of Devon from 1751 holding both posts until his death. He also served periods as Master of Trinity House, President of the Foundling Hospital and Chancellor of the University of Dublin.

He married firstly, in 1731, Diana youngest daughter of Charles Spencer, 3rd Earl of Sunderland, son-in-law of the 1st Duke of Marlborough. She brought him £30,000 on marriage and, after the death of her maternal grandmother Sarah, Duchess of Marlborough, a further £100,000. She died of consumption, aged only twenty-five in 1735 after which the duke married secondly, in 1737, Gertrude, eldest daughter of John, 1st Earl Gower.

He died on 14th January 1771 and was buried in the family mausoleum at Chenies in Buckinghamshire. Horace Walpole said of him:

He was a man of inflexible honesty and goodwill to his country; his great economy was sometimes called avarice; if it was so, it was blended with more generosity and goodness than that passion will commonly unite with. His parts were certainly far from shining and yet he spoke readily, and, upon trade well; his foible was speaking upon every subject and imagining he understood it, as he must have done, by inspiration. He was always governed; generally by the Duchess, [his second wife] though immeasurably obstinate when once he had formed or had an opinion instilled in him. ..... If he could have thought less well of himself, the world would probably have thought better of him.

There is a story that a certain Mr Heston Humphrey, a country solicitor, following a quarrel horsewhipped the duke with *'severity and perseverance'* on the race course at Lichfield. Subsequently the King, George II, having heard that Sir Edward Hawke had given the French a 'drubbing' asked Lord Chesterfield the meaning of the word, to which Chesterfield replied *'Sir, here comes the Duke of Bedford who is better able to explain it to your Majesty than I am.'*

His first wife had given birth to a son, John, who died on the day of his birth, 6th November 1732. His second son Francis, his only son by his second wife, also predeceased him in 1767, following a fall from a horse, but not before he had married and produced two sons. The elder, Francis, succeeded his grandfather as fifth duke at the age of six.

Francis was born in 1765 and educated at Westminster School before entering the field of politics as a Whig taking his seat in the House of Lords in 1787. He died, unmarried, on 2nd March 1802 after a fortnight's illness and a too long delayed operation for a hernia.

He was succeeded by his younger brother, John, who was born on 6th July 1766. In his early years the sixth duke (BED 4) served a short period in the army before becoming Member of Parliament for Tavistock and Recorder of Bedford. He was appointed a Privy Counsellor in 1806 and was Lord Lieutenant of Ireland 1806–07. He was installed as a Knight of the Garter in 1830.

He married firstly, in 1786, Georgiana Elizabeth (BED 5), second daughter of George Viscount Torrington. She died at Bath in 1801. Two years later he married another

Georgiana, this time the younger daughter of Alexander, 4th Duke of Gordon. He died on 20th October 1839.

The sixth duke had a younger brother, Lord William Russell, whose descendent inherited the barony of De Clifford from the maternal side. The barony of De Clifford was first created in 1299 for Robert de Clifford. It was a barony by writ and therefore could descend to the heirs general, i.e. through the female line. It fell into abeyance and was recreated a number of times. In 1852 Edward Southwell, 21st Lord De Clifford died without issue and the barony again fell into abeyance.

Edward's sister, Catherine, eldest daughter of the 20th Lord De Clifford, married George Coussmaker and they had two children, George who died in 1821 and Sophia who was, in right of her maternal grandfather, one of the co-heirs to the barony of De Clifford. The barony was called out of abeyance in her favour in 1833 and she went on to marry John Russell R.N. son of Lord William Russell above. They had a son, Edward Southwell Russell (1824–77) (BED 6) who, on the death of his mother in 1874 succeeded to the barony of De Clifford (BED 7). He had married, in 1853, Harriet daughter of Admiral Sir Charles Elliot K.C.B. and they had a son Edward Southwell Russell who succeeded his father in 1877. He married Hilda daughter of Charles Balfour in 1879 and died in 1894 at the age of thirty-nine being succeeded by his son Jack Southwell Russell.

The 6th Duke of Bedford's successor was his son by his first marriage, Francis, born on 13th May 1788. Educated at Westminster School and Trinity College, Cambridge he went on to become Member of Parliament for Peterborough 1809–12 and for Bedfordshire 1812–32. He was summoned to Parliament, as a peer, in his father's lifetime in his father's subsidiary title as Baron Howland before succeeding to the dukedom in 1839 (BED 8, 9, 10, 11 and 12). He was appointed a Privy Counsellor in 1846, given the Garter in 1847 and served as Lord Lieutenant of Bedfordshire from 1759 until his death. He was the most prolific of the dukes, in bookplate terms, providing a quantity of examples for his various establishments.

He married on 8th August 1808, Anna Marie (BED 13), daughter of Charles, 3rd Earl of Harrington. The country owes a great debt of gratitude to Anna for it was she who introduced the idea of afternoon tea into England in the mid-1840s. Up to that time the aristocracy had two meals a day, breakfast and dinner, both substantial meals. Tea, if taken, in the afternoon was just a cup of tea and possibly a ratafia biscuit. Anna decided she required something more filling and so the afternoon tea with sandwiches, cakes, biscuits etc. was born. It was at this time that, the previously unknown, tea plates became standard issue in tea services. The seventh duke died at Woburn in 1861 and is buried in the family mausoleum at Chenies in Buckinghamshire.

His successor was his only son, William (BED 14 and 15), who was born on 1st July 1809 and educated at Eton and Christ Church, Oxford. He sat as Member of Parliament for Tavistock from 1832–41. He suffered from depression for most of his life and became a recluse. He rarely visited Woburn preferring to live in his London residence. It is perhaps surprising, therefore, that he managed to commission a bookplate for the Woburn Library and another for his property at Endsleigh in Devon – albeit not very inspiring ones. He never married and died suddenly on 27th May 1872.

His heir was his first cousin, Francis Hastings Russell. Born in 1819, he was the eldest son of Major General Lord George Russell G.C.B. who was the younger brother of Francis the seventh duke. Lord George had two other sons the younger being Odo William Russell born in 1829 and educated at Westminster School. He worked for the Foreign Office and was attaché at various embassies. He married, in 1868, Emily daughter of George Villiers, 4th Earl of Clarendon. He was Under-Secretary of State for Foreign Affairs 1870–1, Ambassador to Berlin 1871–81. In 1881 he was created Baron Ampthill. He died in harness at Potsdam near Berlin in 1884 and was succeeded as second baron by his son Arthur Oliver Villiers Russell (BED 16). Born in 1869 and educated at Eton and New College, Oxford he was Governor of Madras from 1900–05. He married, 6th October 1894, Margaret daughter of Fredrick, 6th Earl Beauchamp (BED 17) and died 7th July 1935.

Francis Hastings, the 9th Duke of Bedford (BED 18, 19, 20 and 21), had served in the army from 1838–44 before becoming Member of Parliament for Bedfordshire 1847–72. He was installed as a Knight of the Garter in 1880 and was Lord Lieutenant of Huntingdonshire from 1884–91. He married, on 18th January 1844, Elizabeth, daughter of George, 5th Earl Delaware. He died on 14th January 1891 at his London home in Eaton Square having shot himself, whilst suffering from a deep depression, following a bout of influenza and pneumonia.

The tenth duke was his son George, born on 16th April 1852. Educated at Balliol College, Oxford he went on to become Member of Parliament for Bedfordshire for ten years 1875–85. He married, in 1876, Adeline Mary daughter and co-heir of Charles, 3rd Lord Somers. He held the dukedom for less than three years dying suddenly on 23rd November 1893, from diabetes. He had no children. His contribution to the family collection of bookplates was to adapt a small plate of his father's by simply changing the date from '1873' to '1893' (BED 22). His wife, Adeline, had a small monogram bookplate (BED 23) and his unmarried sister, Lady Ela Russell, a plate (BED 24) showing the family arms on a lozenge within a stylised frame work.

His successor was his brother Herbrand (BED 25, 26 and 27). He, too, was a scholar at Balliol after which he entered the Grenadier Guards. He served in Egypt in 1882 and was Aide-de-Campe to the Viceroy of India 1885–6. It was whilst in India that he met his wife, Mary, daughter of the Venerable Henry Tribe, Archdeacon of Lahore. She was a redoubtable lady who led a full and interesting life. She established a cottage hospital at Woburn, was a competent needlewoman and a first class shot. Although suffering from severe deafness, late in life she discovered a fascination with flying and obtained a flying licence thus becoming known as 'The Flying Duchess'. Sadly she lost her life in 1937 on a flight to Cambridge. She never arrived and days later the wreckage of her Gypsy Moth was washed up on the Norfolk coast. Her two bookplates (BED 28 – designed by J.A.C. Harrison – and BED 29), show the interest in wildlife which she shared with her husband.

Herbrand served as Lord Lieutenant of Middlesex, was President of the Zoological Society of London, a Trustee of the British Museum and, in 1908 was Aide-de-Campe to Edward VII. In his domestic life he was something of a cold fish, finding it difficult to give affection to his wife or children, a trait he shared with other members of his family. He found it difficulty in interacting with people generally. If his servants saw him approaching they were to stand aside perfectly still and he would pass by totally ignoring them.

When, at the outbreak of the Second World War, in 1939, he was approached to see if part of his vast estate could be used by the Foreign Office he is reputed to have replied *'Can't you see that there is someone living here already?'*. However, he did agree to the Riding School and Tennis Court being used as offices and the Foreign Office staff were allowed limited use of the grounds for recreation on condition that if the eighty-one year old duke should appear they were to hide behind trees and shrubs until he had passed. He died in 1940 and was succeeded by his only son Hastings as 12th Duke of Bedford.

Hastings (1888–1953) took after his father, being largely deprived of parental affection. In adult life he was somewhat eccentric and suffered from depression. Throughout the 1939–45 War he favoured trying to reach an agreement with Nazi Germany to the point were his actions were described as 'verging on the subversive' by a government spokesman.

His contribution to Woburn Abbey was a destructive one. After the war the Riding School and Tennis Court together with the east wing of the Abbey were found to be riddled with dry rot so he had them demolished.

He died in October 1953, being found dead from gunshot wounds on his estate at Endsleigh near Tavistock. Third party involvement was not suspected and the coroner returned a verdict of accidental death.

The story of the Russell family would not be complete without mention of his successor, John, 13th Duke of Bedford. Born in 1917, he inherited the title and vast estates at the age of thirty-six. He also inherited a huge debt in the form of death duties amounting to many millions of pounds. By successfully turning the Woburn estate into a safari and theme park and opening the Abbey to the public he not only paid off the debts and saved the family home but also blazed the trail for many other members of the peerage to follow.

BED 2 The right Noble Wriothesley Russell Duke of Bedford &c. NIF

An early full armorial the shield being quarterly of fifteen with the pronomal arms in the 1st and 15th quarters to give balance. This is, almost certainly, the bookplate of Wriothesley the 3rd Duke of Bedford rather than Wriothesley, the second duke.

BED 3 The most Noble John Duke of Bedford 1736 F25700

A dated bookplate in the baroque style; a full armorial for the fourth duke. This was produced whilst he was between marriages, his first wife having died in 1735 he remarried in 1737.

BED 4

BED 4 **John, Duke of Bedford** F25702

A bookplate in the continental style with shield and supporters surrounded by a mantle dependant from a duke's coronet. The shield shows the arms of Russell impaling those of Gordon which are: quarterly, 1, azure, three boars heads or (Gordon); 2, or, three lions' heads erased gules (Badenoch); 3, or, three crescents within the royal tressure of Scotland gules (Seton); 4, azure, three cinquefoils argent (Fraser). John, the sixth duke, married in 1803, as his second wife, Georgiana daughter of Alexander, 4th Duke of Gordon.

BED 5 **Georgiana Bedford** F25721

A bookplate in the continental style for Georgiana, second wife of John the sixth duke showing the arms of Russell impaling those of Gordon.

BED 6 **Arma eduardi southwell russell** NIF

A seal armorial bookplate for Edward Southwell Russell and his wife Harriet daughter of Admiral Sir Charles Elliot K.C.B.

ARMS: Quarterly 1 and 4, argent, a lion rampant gules, on a chief sable three escallops argent (Russell); 2 and 3, chequey, or and azure, a fess gules (De Clifford); impaling, gules, on a bend engrailed or a baton azure, a bordure vair (Elliot).

CREST: A goat statant guardant horned and unguled or.

BED 5

BED 6

Edward Russell was the son of John Russell R.N. and the grandson of Lord William Russell, younger brother of the sixth duke. His mother, Sophia, had inherited the barony of De Clifford on the death of her uncle without issue and on her death in 1877 Edward inherited the barony. This plate, therefore, dates before 1877.

BED 7 **LORD DE CLIFFORD** NIF

This seal type armorial bookplate dates after 1877 and either belongs to the Edward Southwell Russell owner of BED 6 or to his son of the same name. It shows the un-differenced arms of the Duke of Bedford but the arms should be shown as in BED 6.

BED 8 **Arma ducis de bedford** F25708

A mid-nineteenth century seal early type armorial bookplate showing the arms of Russell impaling those of Stanhope. The bookplate of Francis, 7th Duke of Bedford who, in 1808, married Anna, the daughter of Charles Stanhope, 3rd Earl of Harrington.

BED 7

BED 8

BED 9 **Anonymous** NIF

A simple armorial bookplate for Francis, the seventh duke, without title, with the impaled shield under a duke's coronet surrounded by the Garter motto. The duke was installed as a Knight of the Garter in 1847.

BED 10 **Francis Duke of Bedford, OAKLEY HOUSE** F25704

A full armorial bookplate with title made for one of the duke's smaller properties, Oakley House in Bedfordshire. An identical plate is known with the inscription 'COPLE' instead of OAKLEY HOUSE.

BED 11 **FRANCIS, DUKE OF BEDFORD** NIF

A small, post 1847, armorial bookplate with the garter motto and title below for Francis, the seventh duke.

BED 12 **Four small monogrammed plates** F25714/5/6/9

A series of four small monogram plates with a 'B' under a duke's coronet for Francis, the seventh duke.

12a. B

12b. Woburn Abbey

12c. Hundreds Farm

12d. Woburn Abbey. This plate dates after 1847 the year the duke received the Order of the Garter.

BED 12A

BED 12B

BED 12C

BED 12D

BED 13

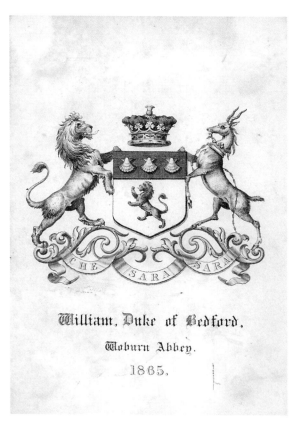

William, Duke of Bedford.

Woburn Abbey.

1865.

BED 14

William, Duke of Bedford.

Endsleigh.

BED 15

BED 13 **Anna Maria Duchess of Bedford** F25720

A simple armorial bookplate with the arms of Russell impaling Stanhope beneath a duchess's coronet for the wife of the seventh duke.

BED 14 **William, Duke of Bedford, Woburn Abbey 1865** F25709

A simple armorial for the eighth duke showing the pronomal arms with supporters. A similar plate is known with the date '1867'.

BED 15 **William, Duke of Bedford, Endsleigh** NIF

A similar plate for the duke's property Endsleigh House in Devon.

BED 16 **Arthur Oliver Villiers Russell. Baron Ampthill** NIF

A full panel armorial designed by C.W. Sherborn and dated 1896 for Arthur Oliver Villiers Russell, 2nd Baron Ampthill. The shield depicts the arms of Russell impaling Lygon: argent, two lions passant double queued gules. The shield and supporters are marked with a mullet or and the crest with a mullet sable for difference. The mullet is the cadency mark for a third son. Arthur's father, the 1st Baron was the third son of Major General Lord George Russell G.C.B. who was the younger brother of Francis, 7th Duke of Bedford. Arthur married, in 1894, Margaret, daughter of Frederick Lygon, 6th Earl Beauchamp.

BED 17 **Margaret Ampthill** NIF

This features the initials 'MA' beneath a baron's coronet within a cartouche which is surrounded by a swag and ribbon design within a decorative panel border. Margaret Ampthill was Lady Ampthill, wife of Arthur, 2nd Baron Ampthill.

BED 16

BED 17

BED 18 **Francis Charles Hastings Duke of Bedford Woburn Abbey 1873** F25711

A seal type armorial bookplate for the ninth duke, the shield showing Russell impaling the arms of Earl Delaware: quarterly, 1 and 4, argent, a fess dancetty sable (West); 2 and 3, quarterly, or and gules, a bend vair (Sackville). The duke married Elizabeth, daughter of George Sackville, 5th Earl Delaware in 1844.

BED 19 **HASTINGS DUKE OF BEDFORD WOBURN ABBEY** F25723

A square panel armorial for the ninth duke by Harry Soane showing two shields accollee, Russell and Delaware: quarterly, 1 and 4, argent, a fess dancettee sable (West); 2 and 3, quarterly, or and gules, a bend vair (Sackville).

BED 20 **WOBURN ABBEY 1873** F25712

A small crest armorial for Hastings the ninth duke with the Russell crest surrounded by the family motto 'Che sara sara' under a duke's coronet.

BED 21 **Anonymous** F25718

A rather elegant small crest label under a duke's coronet and displaying the Garter chain, George and motto. For the ninth duke who was installed as a Knight of the Garter in 1880.

BED 19

BED 20

BED 21

BED 22

BED 23

BED 26

BED 24

BED 25

BED 22 **WOBURN ABBEY 1893** NIF

A small crest armorial bookplate for George the tenth duke adapted from a bookplate of his father's by simply changing the date from '1873' to '1893'. As he died on 23rd November 1893 this is almost certainly his plate rather than his brother's who succeeded him.

BED 23 **AMB** NIF

A small bookplate showing the initials 'AMB' under a duchess's coronet within a decorative cartouche. Adeline Mary was the daughter of Charles, 5th Lord Somers, she married George Marquess of Tavistock in 1876. He succeeded as 10th Duke of Bedford in 1891 but held the dukedom for less than two years, 1891–3.

BED 24 **ELA MONICA RUSSELL** F25735

A late nineteenthth century plate for a maiden lady showing the arms in a lozenge within a stylised framework.

Lady Ela Russell was the second child and first daughter of Francis Charles Hastings Russell, 9th Duke of Bedford. She was born in 1854 and died, unmarried, in 1936. She lived,

with a staff of servants, at Chorleywood House about a mile from Chenies, the family estate and mausoleum in Buckinghamshire.

BED 25 **Herbrand, xi**th **Duke of Bedford** NIF

A fine panel full armorial bookplate within a decorative border. The plate is signed along the bottom 'Ortner & Houle Sc. 3 St James's Street S.W.'

BED 26 **Herbrand eleventh duke of bedford woburn abbey** NIF

A large panel type full armorial bookplate. The lion supporter is holding a very large lance in its forepaw. The plate designed by Sebastian Evens is signed with a monogram in the bottom right hand corner.

BUC I **Duke of Buccleugh** [*sic*] F26257

The dukes of Buccleuch were not prolific
users of bookplates and this anonymous
example was probably produced for the
third duke (1746–1817), judging by the
style, and could easily have been used
subsequently.

ARMS: Grand Quarters: I and IV, quarterly,
1 and 4, azure, three fleur-de-lys or
(France); 2 and 3, gules, three lions
passant guardant in pale or (England);
II and III, or, on a bend azure an estoile
between two crescents of the field (Scott).

CREST: A stag trippant proper, attired and
unguled or (not shown).

SUPPORTERS: Two female figures wearing
three ostrich plumes in their hair.

MOTTO: Amo – I love

Dukes of Buccleuch and Queensberry

FAMILY NAMES: Montagu-Douglas-Scott

CREATION OF DUKEDOM OF BUCCLEUCH:
30th April 1663

COURTESY TITLE OF ELDEST SON: Earl of Dalkeith

COURTESY TITLE OF GRANDSON: Lord Eskdaill

CREATION OF DUKEDOM OF QUEENSBERRY:
3rd November 1684. Henry 3rd Duke of Buccleuch
succeeded to this dukedom in 1810

PRINCIPAL RESIDENCE: Drumlanrig Castle,
Dumfriesshire

The dukedom of Buccleuch was created for James the illegitimate son of Charles II by Lucy Walters. He was born on 9th April 1649 in Rotterdam. As a child he was placed in the care of William, Lord Crofts and thereafter was known as James Crofts. He was educated in Paris and brought to London in 1662. Although Charles II officially recognised him as his natural son there was at the time, and subsequently, doubt over his actual parentage. At the age of fourteen, on 20th April 1663 Charles created him Duke of Monmouth, Earl of Doncaster and Baron Scott of Tindall in the Peerage of England. Having changed his surname to Scott in anticipation of his forthcoming marriage to Anne Scott, suo jure Countess of Buccleuch, he was, on the day of his marriage, 30th April 1663 created Duke of Buccleuch, Earl of Dalkeith and Baron Scott of Whitchester and Eskdale in the Peerage of Scotland with remainder to the heirs male of his body by Anne. She was only thirteen on her marriage. They later went on to have two sons. Their eldest son, Charles born on 24th August 1672 died within the year. Their second son, James, Earl of Dalkeith born on 23rd May 1674 went on to marry Henrietta, daughter of Laurence Hyde, 1st Earl of Rochester. He died of a stroke, aged thirty, on 14th March 1704/5 leaving a son, Francis Scott.

Duke James followed a military career supported by various grants and a pension from the Crown. In the late 1670s there was a move by various anti-catholic groups to have James recognised as the legitimate heir to the throne rather than his uncle James, Duke of York. This claim to legitimacy annoyed Charles II who stripped him of his commands and ordered him to leave the country. Attempts by the anti-catholic groups to persuade the public that Charles II had secretly married James's mother, Lucy Walters were vehemently denied by the King. It is highly probable the duke was aware of the plans to assassinate the King and the Duke of York by what was known as the Rye House Plot. After the discovery of the plot the duke went into hiding but he was convicted, in his absence, of high treason and conspiring to bring about the deaths of the King and the Duke of York.

He fled abroad and was in the Netherlands when Charles II died on 6th February 1685. With his supporters he planned an invasion of England and landed at Lyme Regis in June 1685. Although he had some minor success his army was utterly defeated at the Battle of Sedgemoor on 5th July 1685, and the duke left the field disguised as a peasant. He was later captured and taken to London and, having been found guilty of treason, he was executed on Tower Hill on 18th July 1685 and all his English honours were forfeit. However his Scottish honours were not and, on the death of his widow Anne, Duchess of Buccleuch, on 6th February 1731/2, his grandson Francis, son of the late Earl of Dalkeith, succeeded as 2nd Duke of Buccleuch.

Born on 11th January 1694/5, he became a Knight of the Thistle in 1715. In 1742 he and his heirs male were restored to the English titles of Earl of Doncaster and Baron Scott of Tindal but not to the dukedom of Monmouth.

He married firstly on 5th April 1720, Jean daughter of James, 2nd Duke of Queensberry. She died on 31st August 1729 after which, on 4th September 1722 he married Alice, daughter of one James Powell, said to have been a washerwoman at Windsor. Lady Louisa Stuart called him *'a man of mean understanding and meaner habits'*; she said that after his first wife's death *'he plunged into such low amours and lived so entirely with the lowest company that his person was scarcely known to his equals and his character fell into utter contempt'*. He died on 27th April 1751 and was buried *'very meanly'* in Eton College Chapel.

His son, by his first wife, Francis, Earl of Dalkeith, was

born on 19th February 1720/1 and educated at Christ Church, Oxford. He married on 2nd October 1742, Caroline, daughter and co-heir of John 2nd Duke of Argyll. He sat as Member of Parliament for Boroughbridge 1746–50 but predeceased his father by one year, dying on 1st April 1750 from smallpox aged only thirty.

The second duke was therefore succeeded by his four year old grandson Henry, second, but first surviving, son of Francis above (BUC 1). Born on 2nd September 1746 and educated at Eton, he served in the army. He was Captain General of the Royal Company of Archers and raised a regiment in 1778. He was Governor of the Royal Bank of Scotland from 1777 until his death. He was made a Knight of the Thistle in 1767 but resigned the honour in 1794 on being appointed a Knight of the Garter. He was a firm Tory and a strong supporter of William Pitt's ministry. The book-plate of his sister Lady Frances Scott is shown (BUC 2).

Also in 1794, on the death of his mother, he succeeded to the landed property acquired by her father, the Duke of Argyll. In 1810 on the death of his second cousin once removed, William, 4th Duke of Queensberry he succeeded to considerable estates in Dumfriesshire and also to the titles of Duke of Queensberry, Marquess of Dumfriesshire, Earl of Drumlanrig and Sanquhar, Viscount Nith, Torthorwald and Ross and the Baronies of Douglas of Kinmont, Middlebie and Dornock.

The dukedom of Queensberry was created in 1684 for William Douglas, Marquess of Queensberry. His son James, the second duke (BUC 3 and 4) was a prominent Scottish peer who played an important role in the Union of England and Scotland in 1707. In March 1706 he resigned his dukedom of Queensberry and other titles which had been granted to him at the same time (1684) and then, in June 1706, he obtained a novodamus in favour of himself, his second son Charles and others. In Scottish law a novodamus is a fresh grant of land and/or titles to the grantee. It is usually granted to make some change to the tenure already granted. In this case the purpose was to exclude his eldest son James, who was confined, being mentally handicapped, from the succession.

As a result, when James died in 1711 he was succeeded by his second son Charles. Charles the 3rd Duke of Queensberry had two sons who both predeceased him so, on his death in 1778 he was succeeded by his cousin William Douglas son of William Douglas, 2nd Earl of March. This William died, unmarried in 1810 when the dukedom of Queensberry and the associated titles passed to his second cousin once removed, Henry, 3rd Duke of Buccleuch (BUC 5).

Henry had married, by special licence, whilst still a minor, on 2nd May 1767 Elizabeth, only daughter and heir of George Montagu, 1st Duke of Montagu. He died on 11th January 1817 at Dalkeith.

His first son, George, had died aged two months in May 1768 following an inoculation for smallpox so he was succeeded by his second son Charles William Henry Montagu-Scott, Earl of Dalkeith. Born on 21st May 1772 he was educated at Eton and Christ's College, Oxford. He was Member of Parliament for various boroughs until his succession; Lord Lieutenant of Selkirk 1794–8, Dumfriesshire 1798–1812 and Midlothian 1812–19. He was summoned to the House of Lords in his father's lifetime in his father's barony of Tyndall. He was Captain General of the Royal Company of Archers, President of the Highland and Agricultural Society and Grand Master of Freemasons in Scotland.

He married on 24th March 1795, Harriet youngest daughter of Thomas Townshend, 1st Viscount Sydney (BUC 6). She died on 24th August 1814 of 'a putrid sore throat' but not before producing two sons. He died on 20th April 1819 in Lisbon suffering from consumption aged forty-six having held the title for only two years. His eldest son George Henry, usually referred to as Lord Whitchester, died aged ten whilst suffering from measles in 1808.

So, once again, the successor was a second son, thirteen year old Walter Francis Montagu-Douglas-Scott. Born on 25th November 1806 he was educated at Eton and St John's College, Cambridge. In 1822 at his home in Edinburgh, Dalkeith House aged only sixteen, he entertained George IV for fourteen days on his State Visit to Scotland. This was the first visit by the Sovereign to Scotland since the Act of Union in 1707.

The Duke served as Lord Lieutenant of Midlothian from 1828, and of Roxburgh from 1841, until his death. He became a Knight of the Thistle in 1830 but resigned in 1835 on receiving the Garter. At the time of his death (1884) he was the Senior Garter Knight and the only one not appointed by the reigning Sovereign.

He built, at his own cost of over £500,000, the pier and breakwater at Granton on the Forth four miles from Edinburgh which was seven years in the making.

In 1842 he again entertained his sovereign at Dalkeith House, this time Queen Victoria and her Consort Prince Albert. He was President of the Society of Antiquaries

Lady Frances Scott.

BUC 2

BUC 3

1862–73 and Chancellor of the University of Glasgow 1876 until his death. He married on 13th August 1829, Charlotte Anne, youngest daughter of Thomas Thynne, 2nd Marquess of Bath. He died at Bowhill, Selkirk on 16th April 1884.

The sixth duke was his son William Henry Montagu-Douglas-Scott (BUC 7). Born on 9th September 1831 at Montagu House, Whitehall, London he was educated at Eton and Christ Church, Oxford. He served as Lord Lieutenant of Dumfriesshire and, like his father, became a Knight of the Thistle in 1875 only to resign in 1897 on receiving the Garter. He was Captain General of the Royal Company of Archers and was appointed a Privy Counsellor in 1901. He died on 5th November 1914 aged eighty-four.

His eldest son and heir apparent, William Henry, styled Lord Eskdale until 1884 then Earl of Dalkeith, predeceased his father in 1886, being accidentally killed by his own rifle whilst deer stalking. As a result he was succeeded by his second son John Charles Montagu-Douglas-Scott.

BUC 2 **Lady Frances Scott** F26279

An armorial plate in the form of a lozenge, indicating a spinster, dating from the 1770s.

ARMS: Quarterly, 1 and 4, (Buccleuch); 2 and 3, (Scott).

Lady Frances Scott (1750–1817) was the daughter of Francis, 2nd Duke of Buccleuch. In 1783 she married Archibald, 1st Lord Douglas.

BUC 3 **His Grace The Duke of Queensberry Knight of the Most Noble Order of the Garter** F*10

This is a large early armorial plate most probably for the second duke.

ARMS: Quarterly, 1 and 4, argent, a human heart gules imperially crowned or, on a chief azure three mullets of the field (Douglas); 2 and 3, azure, a bend between six cross

65

BUC 4

BUC 5

crosslets fitchee or (Mar); all within a bordure or, charged with the royal tressure of Scotland gules.

CREST: A winged human heart gules imperially crowned or.

SUPPORTERS: Two winged Pegasus rampant argent.

MOTTO: Forward.

BUC 4 The Most Noble James Duke of Queensberry Knight of the Most Noble Order of the Garter 1703

NIF

This is a smaller plate of similar design to BUC 2. James succeeded in 1695 and died in 1711.

BUC 5 Duke of Buccleugh [*sic*] NIF

The armorial of this plate is identical to BUC 1 but the inscription is slightly different stylistically, particularly the *D* of Duke, the *f* of of and the *B* and *b* of Buccleugh. This plate was possibly produced for the 3rd or 4th Duke of Buccleuch.

BUC 6 HKD (Harriet Katherine Dalkeith) F26258

A small bookplate with initials under an earl's coronet. The initials, in cursive script are 'HKD'.

Harriet Katherine Townsend was the daughter of Thomas Townsend, 1st Viscount Sydney. On 24th March 1795 she married Charles Montagu-Scott, Earl of Dalkeith who on 11th January 1812, succeeded his father as the 4th Duke of Buccleuch.

BUC 7 Buccleuch NIF

A late nineteenth century panel armorial probably for William, sixth duke (1884–1914). The arms are those of Scott, the original family name before the 'Montagu' and 'Douglas' were added: or, on a bend azure an estoile between two crescents of the field.

BUC 6

Buccleuch

BUC 7

DEV 1 The Most Noble William Duke of Devonshire Knight of the Most Noble Order of the Garter F5430

A typical early armorial bookplate dating from the first few years of the eighteenth century for William the first duke who died in 1707. It is close cropped as many early bookplates were.

ARMS: Quarterly of six, 1 and 6, sable, three buck's heads caboshed argent attired or (Cavendish); 2, argent, a chevron gules between three cross crosslets sable; 3, argent, a chevron between three lion's paws erased sable; 4, argent, a saltire engrailed azure, on a chief of the second three roses of the first (Hardwick); 5, argent, a fess sable (Keighley).

CREST: On a wreath of the colours a serpent nowed proper.

SUPPORTERS: Two bucks rampant proper attired or, wreathed with a chaplet of roses, alternatively argent and azure.

MOTTO: Cavendo tutus – Safe by warning.

Dukes of Devonshire

FAMILY NAME: Cavendish

CREATION OF DUKEDOM: 12th May 1694

COURTESY TITLE OF ELDEST SON: Marquess of Hartington

COURTESY TITLE OF GRANDSON AND HEIR: Earl of Burlington

PRINCIPAL RESIDENCE: Chatsworth House, Derbyshire

The earldom of Devon was first created in 1141 for Baldwin De Riviers. It was recreated in 1603 for Charles Blount, Baron Mountjoy K.G. but he died three years later without issue when the earldom, again, became extinct. It was recreated a third time in 1618 for William Cavendish, son of Sir William Cavendish of Hardwicke by his third wife, Elizabeth, afterwards Countess of Shrewsbury (Bess of Hardwicke).

William was born on 27th December 1552 the twelfth child of his father and the fourth of his mother. Educated at Eton and Gray's Inn he served as Member of Parliament for Liverpool and later for Newport. He was Sheriff of Derby 1595/6. He succeeded to his mother's titles on her death in 1607 aged eighty-seven. Two years earlier he had been created Baron Cavendish of Hardwicke. In 1616 he succeeded to his elder brother's estate of Chatsworth and other estates. He was created Earl of Devonshire in 1618 and so the family fortunes were firmly established. He died in 1626 at the age of seventy-four years and was succeeded by his eldest son also William.

The second earl had a short life and a merry one. Born in 1590 he married, in 1608, Christina the twelve year old daughter of Edward, 1st Lord Kinloss. His extravagant life style forced him to sell off some of his estates in order to survive and he died in 1628 from *an indulgence in good living*.

He did manage to leave one son, another William, who succeeded to his father's remaining estates and honours becoming the third earl at the age of eleven years. He lived through the turbulent years of the Civil War and the Commonwealth. He entertained, for one night only, on 13th October 1645, Charles I at his home, Latimers, in Buckinghamshire. He was a founder Fellow of the Royal Society. He lived on through the reign of Charles II dying in 1684 when his son, yet another William, became fourth earl (DEV 2).

The fourth earl led an active political and military life close to the Sovereign's court. He was train bearer to Charles II at his coronation in 1661 and cup bearer to the Queen at the coronation of James II in 1685. However he was opposed to a catholic monarchy and his was one of the seven signatures on the document inviting the protestant William of Orange and his wife, Mary, daughter of James II to come and rule England. He was one of the first to take up arms on William's behalf and as a result of this support he received the eighth of the nine dukedoms which William III created in the first six years of his reign. On 12th May 1694 he became Marquess of Hartington and Duke of Devonshire (DEV 1, 3 and 4). He was the builder of the present Chatsworth, the family seat in Derbyshire, which he started in 1687.

He was appointed one of the Lords Justices to whom, after the death of Queen Mary in 1693, the government of the country was entrusted from 1695–1701 during the King's absences abroad for some months each year. He married in 1662 Mary, second daughter of James, 1st Duke of Ormonde.

About 1700 Bishop Burnet wrote of him *'He was the finest and handsomest gentleman of his time; loved the ladies and plays, keeps a noble house and equipage, is tall, well-made and of a princely behaviour; of nice honour in everything but the paying of his tradesmen'*.

He died *'of the stone'* in 1707 at his London home, Devonshire House in Piccadilly. Once again he was succeeded by a William, his second son, his first son having predeceased him.

The second duke (DEV 5), like his father, had a political and military career. He served as Member of Parliament for various constituencies. He was a Privy Counsellor to Queen Anne and George I and Lord Steward of the Household to both sovereigns. He married in 1688, at the age of sixteen, Rachel sister of the 2nd Duke of Bedford and daughter of

William, Lord Russell (see Bedford). She allegedly brought him £25,000 a year.

He was a great supporter of the Whig Party being, as Lord Walgrave observed '*a man of strict honour, true courage and unaffected affability. He was sincere, humane, generous, plain in his manners, negligent in his dress, had sense learning and modesty with solid rather than showy parts*'. However Dean Swift said of him '*he had a very poor understanding*' but he also made the same remark about his father the first duke.

The second duke died in 1749 and was succeeded by William, his first born son and heir. Born in 1698 he was educated at New College, Oxford, supported the Whig party and was Member of Parliament for Lostwithiel and later for Grampound and Huntingdon. Rather unusually he married out of the peerage when, in 1718, he married Catherine the daughter of John Hoskins, Steward to the Duke of Bedford. He was elected a Privy Counsellor and was Lord Steward of the Household at various times. He was one of the Justices of the Realm during the King's absences abroad and Lord Lieutenant of Ireland 1737–45. He became a Fellow of the Royal Society in 1747. He died in 1755 having been duke for just six years.

William, the fourth duke, was born in 1720 and in 1751 was summoned to Parliament in his own right, using his father's lower title of Baron Cavendish of Hardwicke, four years before he succeeded to the dukedom. He was elected a Privy Councillor in the same year and later Lord Chamberlain of the Household. He was given the Garter in 1756.

He held numerous other offices under the crown including Lord Lieutenant of Ireland. However, during the negotiations for the Treaty of Paris in 1763 at the end of the Seven Years War he refused to attend the Council Board when summoned and as a result was dismissed from his office as Lord Chamberlain and the new King, George III, personally erased his name from the list of Privy Councillors on 3rd November 1762.

He married, in March 1748, Charlotte Elizabeth, daughter and heir of Richard, Earl of Burlington. She was 'suo jure' Baroness Clifford. She brought him Bolton Abbey and numerous estates in Yorkshire and Derbyshire and also Chiswick House in Middlesex and Burlington House, Piccadilly in London. As a result his political importance was greatly increased.

He died in Spa, Germany in 1764 and was succeeded, as fifth duke, by his eldest son, inevitably another William (DEV 6). Born in 1748 he had succeeded to his mother's barony of Clifford in 1754 at the age of six and became duke when only sixteen. Like the rest of his family he was a firm supporter of the Whig party.

The fifth duke is perhaps best remembered for his matrimonial machinations. He married twice. Firstly, in 1774, to Georgiana, eldest daughter of John, 1st Earl Spencer, who died in 1806 from '*an abscess on the liver*'. However he had lived in a ménage a trois for the previous twenty years with his wife and his wife's close friend and confidante a young widow, Lady Elizabeth Foster, daughter of Henry, 4th Earl of Bristol (the Earl Bishop of Derry). Lady Elizabeth bore him two illegitimate children before he finally married her, in 1809, after Georgiana's death. It was, apparently, an amicable arrangement for all three. He died only two years later from '*water on the chest*', – pulmonary oedema.

He was succeeded by his only legitimate son, by his first wife Georgiana, William George who thus became the 6th Duke of Devonshire (DEV 7), Marquess of Hartington, Earl of Devonshire, Baron Cavendish of Hardwicke and Baron Clifford.

Educated at Harrow and Trinity College, Cambridge he went on to become Ambassador Extraordinary to St Petersburg and attended the coronation of Czar Nicholas I in 1826. Later, somewhat lavishly, the Czar bestowed on him three Russian knighthoods, Knight of St Andrew, St Alexander and St Anne.

He became a Privy Councillor in 1827 and in the same year, like all his predecessors, he was given the Garter. It was he who employed the famous Joseph Paxton as estate manager at Chatsworth who created for him the magnificent conservatory which covered over an acre of ground. Unfortunately it had to be demolished in 1920. The Duke was President of the Horticultural Society from 1838–58 and at Queen Victoria's coronation in 1838 he carried the Curtana – sword of mercy.

He was described by the 9th Duke of Argyll as '*the model of the old English nobleman of his time; very tall, very benignant, full of poetic spirit, delighting in doing good, full of schemes for the improvement of the people on his immense estates and generous almost to a fault. To his own kith and kin, however remote, he was an earthly providence.*'

He died, unmarried, in 1858 when the barony of Clifford fell into abeyance. All his other titles and estates devolved on his cousin William Cavendish 2nd Earl of Burlington. The seventh duke (DEV 8, 9 and 10) was the son of Colonel William Cavendish (1783–1812) who was the son of George Augustus Henry Cavendish, younger brother of the

5th Duke of Devonshire who had been created 1st Lord Burlington in 1831.

The seventh duke was born in 1808, educated at Eton and Trinity College, Cambridge. He succeeded his grandfather as 2nd Lord Burlington in 1834. He went on to hold many offices; Chancellor of the University of London 1836–56, Chancellor of the University of Cambridge 1861–91, President of the Iron and Steel Institute, President of the Royal Agricultural Society and a Trustee of the British Museum. He was largely responsible for developing the spa town of Buxton in Derbyshire in the 1870s complete with opera house and a town house for himself.

In 1829 he married his cousin, Blanche Georgiana, fourth daughter of George Howard, 6th Earl of Carlisle and his wife Georgiana, sister and co-heir of the 6th Duke of Devonshire. He died in 1891 aged eighty-three years and, his eldest son having died as an infant, was succeeded by his second son Spencer Compton as eighth duke (DEV 11).

The new duke followed very much in his father's footsteps. Educated privately and at Trinity College, Cambridge he served as Member of Parliament for various constituencies, Secretary of State for War, Secretary of State for India, Postmaster General, Chancellor of the University of Cambridge and Chancellor of the University of Manchester. He was given the Garter in 1892, the eighth Duke of Devonshire in succession to be so honoured, and he was made a Knight Grand Cross of the Royal Victorian Order in 1907.

It is said that P.G. Wodehouse modelled his famous Lord Emsworth on the eighth duke who was a somewhat vague character who liked casual and baggy clothes and was passionate about pig breeding. On one occasion, whilst attending a debate in the House of Lords, when a speaker was holding forth about the 'greatest moments in life' the duke remarked to his neighbour *'My greatest moment was when my pig won first prize at the Skipton Fair,'*

He married, in 1892, Louisa Frederick Augusta, widow of William, 7th Duke of Manchester, and second daughter of Karl Franz, Count Von Alten of Hanover. He died without issue in 1908 and was succeeded by his nephew Victor Christian William Cavendish, as ninth duke.

Victor was the son of Lord Edward Cavendish younger brother of the eighth duke. Born in 1868 and educated at Eton and Trinity College, Cambridge he went on to become Governor General of Canada 1916–21 and Secretary of State for the Colonies 1922–4. He was High Steward of the University of Cambridge in 1923 the year his bookplate (DEV 12) was commissioned.

He married Lady Evelyn Fitzmaurice, elder daughter of the 5th Marquess of Landsdowne and they had seven children. He died on 6th May 1938 and was succeeded by his eldest son, Edward.

Edward William Spencer Cavendish, the tenth duke (DEV 13), was born on 6th May 1895 and educated at Eton and Trinity College, Cambridge. In 1917 he married Lady Mary Gascoyne-Cecil, the granddaughter of Robert Gascoyne-Cecil, 3rd Marquess of Salisbury. Edward's sister, Lady Dorothy Cavendish, married the politician and prime minister, Harold Macmillan, later Earl of Stockton.

The duke died suddenly, of a heart attack, at the early age of fifty-five, in November 1950. His unexpected early death caused his estate to suffer 80% death duties. In order to meet the commitment Haddon Hall, in Derbyshire, was transferred to the National Trust and thousands of acres of land and many works of art and rare books had to be sold.

DEV 5 **The Right Honorable William Lord Marquess of Hartington Eldest Son to his Grace the Duke of Devonshire** F5436

An early armorial (pre 1707) for William son and heir to the first duke. It shows the arms of Cavendish with supporters under a marquess's coronet.

DEV 6 DEVONSHIRE F5431

A mid-eighteenth century armorial plate, possibly for William, fifth duke who succeeded in 1764.

ARMS: Quarterly, 1 and 4, per bend sinister embattled argent and gules, 2 and 3 sable, three buck's heads caboshed argent attired or (Cavendish).

DEV 7 Anonymous F5434

A small crest bookplate for the sixth duke showing the crest surrounded by the Order of the Garter and the Order of St Andrew (Russia) and surmounted by a duke's coronet. The sixth duke, who succeeded in 1811, was Ambassador Extraordinary to the Court at St Petersburg. He attended the coronation of Czar Nicholas I in 1826 and was subsequently made a Knight of the Russian Order of St. Andrew. He was installed a Knight of the Garter in 1827.

DEV 8 William VII Duke of Devonshire KG CHATSWORTH F5435

A simple full armorial bookplate for the seventh duke, who succeeded in 1858, for the Chatsworth Library complete with spaces for inserting bookcase and shelf identification details.

DEV 5

DEV 6

DEV 7

DEV 8

Arms: Quarterly of 6, 1 and 6, sable, three buck's heads caboshed argent, attired or (Cavendish); 2, argent, a saltire engrailed azure, on a chief of the second three roses of the first (Hardwick); 3, argent, a fess sable (Keighley); 4, per bend embattled gules and argent (Boyle); 5. chequey, argent and azure, a fess gules (Clifford).

Dev 9 CHATSWORTH NIF

A simple book label, probably for the 7th duke, for use at Chatsworth. Within a border the crest is shown beneath a duke's coronet and below spaces for inserting the bookcase and shelf location.

DEV 9

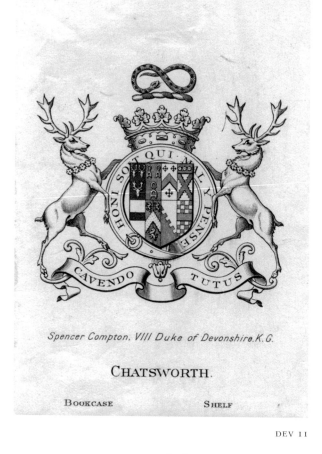

CHATSWORTH.

BOOKCASE   SHELF

Dev 10 THE DEVONSHIRE COLLECTION DERBY FREE LIBRARY presented by His Grace The DUKE OF DEVONSHIRE. K.G. NIF

An interesting presentation plate showing the gift of books to the Derby Free Library by William, 7th Duke of Devonshire in 1881 and later. The Cavendish arms and motto under a duke's coronet with the crest above are shown within a circlet inscribed 'THE DEVONSHIRE COLLECTION ESTAB'D 1881'. There is space below for the press mark and date.

EDWARD WILLIAM SPENCER CAVENDISH, K.G.

XTH DUKE OF DEVONSHIRE

DEV 13

DEV 11 Spencer Compton, VIII Duke of Devonshire K.G. – CHATSWORTH NIF

This armorial plate is known in three sizes all identical in design.

ARMS: Quarterly of eight with Cavendish in the 1st quarter are shown surrounded by the Garter and motto beneath a duke's coronet with crest above the supporters stand on a ribbon carrying the family motto. At the bottom is space for bookcase and shelf number.

DEV 12 VICTOR CHRISTIAN WILLIAM CAVENDISH, K.G. IXTH Duke of Devonshire NIF

A nice panel armorial bookplate made by Robert Osmond, for WPB, in 1923 for the ninth duke, who succeeded in 1908.

ARMS: Quarterly of 8; 1 and 6, sable, three buck's heads caboshed argent, attired or (Cavendish); 2. Argent, a saltire engrailed azure, on a chief of the second three roses of the first (Hardwick); 3. argent, a fess sable (Keighley); 4. ermine,

a chevron or between three lions rampant; 5. per bend embattled gules and argent (Boyle); 6. chequey, argent and azure, a fess gules, 7. sable, a lion passant guardant in fess between three knights helms, 8. argent, on a bend sable three owls proper (Saville).

DEV 13 EDWARD WILLIAM SPENCER CAVENDISH, K.G. Xth DUKE OF DEVONSHIRE NIF

A modern armorial bookplate, the supporters standing on a ribbon which carries the family motto. The shield is surrounded by the collar, badge and motto of the Order of the Garter. Every Duke of Devonshire from the first to the eleventh has been invested as a Knight of the Garter.

GRA 1 Aug^s Henry Duke of Grafton. 1769 F10715

A mid-eighteenth century plate, for Augustus Henry, third duke, dated 1769, in a mixture of baroque and rococo styles depicting the shield with supporters under a duke's coronet.

ARMS: Grand quarters: I and IV, quarterly, 1 and 4, azure, three fleur-de-lys (France); 2 and 3, gules, three lions passant guardant in pale or (England); II, or, a lion rampant with a double tressure flory counter flory gules (Scotland); III, azure, a harp or stringed argent (Ireland); overall a baton in bend sinister company of ten argent and purpure.

CREST: On a chapeau gules turned up ermine a lion statant guardant or crowned with a ducal coronet azure gorged with a collar company argent and azure (not shown).

SUPPORTERS: Dexter, a lion rampant guardant or crowned with a ducal crown azure and gorged with a collar company azure and ermine; sinister, a greyhound rampant argent gorged as the lion.

MOTTO: Et decus et pretium recti – Both the glory and the reward of worth.

Dukes of Grafton

FAMILY NAME: Fitzroy

CREATION OF DUKEDOM: 11th September 1675

COURTESY TITLE OF ELDEST SON: Earl of Euston

COURTESY TITLE OF GRANDSON AND HEIR:
Viscount Ipswich

PRINCIPAL RESIDENCE: Euston Hall, Suffolk

Henry Fitzroy, born on 2nd September 1663, is believed to be the second of three illegitimate sons of Barbara Castlemaine, wife of Roger Palmer, Earl of Castlemaine, by Charles II although, for a long time the King refused to own him and his parentage appeared doubtful.

He was married in 1672 when only nine years of age to Isabella only child of Henry, 1st Earl of Arlington of Euston Hall, Suffolk she being five years old at the time. They were remarried seven years later when the diarist John Evelyn, who was present at both marriages, commented that the bride *'appears to have been sacrificed to a boy that has been rudely born.'*

In consequence of his marriage he was created, in August 1672, Baron Sudbury, Viscount Ipswich and Earl of Euston with special remainder, failing heirs male of his body, to his brother George, the third illegitimate son of Barbara Castlemaine by Charles II. Three years later in 1675 he was created Duke of Grafton so Charles II finally came to accept him as his son. He was given the Garter in 1680.

He rose to high rank in the army and navy becoming a Brigadier General and Vice Admiral of England. He distinguished himself by suppressing the rebellion of the Duke of Monmouth in 1685 and was one of the first to support the landing of William of Orange against his uncle, James II.

His wife, Isabella, who on the death of her father became 'suo jure' Countess of Arlington, Viscountess Ipswich and Baroness Arlington, inherited Euston Hall in Suffolk which became the main family seat of the Dukes of Grafton.

Henry was mortally wounded at the Siege of Cork in September 1690 and died a week later aged only twenty-seven. Following his earlier remark John Evelyn commented on him *'exceedingly handsome, by far surpassing any of the King's other natural issue'* and added *'were he polished he would be a tolerable person … he had great natural bravery, was very sincere but rough as the sea of which he was fond and whereon he lived.'*

He was succeeded, as second duke, by his seven year old son and heir, Charles, born in 1683 (GRA 2). At his baptism Charles II, William of Orange and the future Queen Anne were his godparents. He was styled Earl of Euston before inheriting the dukedom. He entered the army in 1703 aged twenty. He held various offices under the Crown, was a Privy Counsellor, Viceroy of Ireland 1720–4, Recorder of Coventry and Lord Lieutenant of Suffolk 1705–57.

On the death of his mother in 1722 he became Earl of Arlington, Viscount Thetford and Baron Arlington. He was Lord Chamberlain of the Household to both George I and George II and also a Fellow of the Royal Society.

He married, in 1713, Henrietta, sister of the 2nd Duke of Beaufort and daughter of Charles Somerset, Marquess of Worcester and son of the 1st Duke of Beaufort. Unfortunately she died in childbed in 1726 aged only thirty-six.

The second duke was very fond of hunting and continued until he was seventy when he had a fall from his horse which confined him to his room for the rest of his life. He died in 1757 aged seventy-three years.

His first son, Charles Henry, died as an infant. His second son, George, born in 1715 was educated at Eton and became Member of Parliament for Coventry 1737–47. Styled Earl of Euston he married, in 1741, Dorothy, daughter and co-heir of Robert Boyle, 4th Earl of Cork and 3rd Earl of Burlington. Within the year she died of smallpox whilst not yet eighteen. He died in 1747, without issue, in the lifetime of his father.

The third son of the second duke, Lord Augustus Fitzroy, was born in 1716. He entered the navy and was Captain of a man-of-war. He commanded the Orford at the Siege of Carthagena in February 1740/41 where he succumbed to a fever and died in May 1740/41 in the lifetime of his father. His second son was Charles Fitzroy (1737–97) (GRA 3).

The third duke was, therefore, Augustus Henry Fitzroy (GRA 1, 4, and 5) grandson and heir of the second duke, being the second, but first surviving, son of Lord Augustus Fitzroy (see above). He was born in 1735 and styled Earl of Euston 1747–57. He was educated at Westminster School and Peterhouse, Cambridge. He succeeded his grandfather as Lord Lieutenant of Suffolk. He went into politics and held high office becoming Lord of the Treasury 1766–70. It would appear that he was somewhat of a rackety character being described as: *'Unsteady, capricious and indolent, he had hardly any quality for a statesman ... he owed his elevation partly to accident, partly to his great rank and fortune, qualifications which have always had too much weight with the Whig Party.'* It was further said of him that he was *'a man of weak will, admirable purpose and common intellect ... it is true that the country looked to him for salvation but it is also true that the country looked in vain ... for politics he had not the smallest talent.'*

He married twice. Firstly, in 1756, Anne, daughter of Lord Ravensworth but they separated in 1765 and the marriage was dissolved by Act of Parliament in March 1769. He married again three months later, Elizabeth, daughter of the Reverend Sir Richard Wrottesley Bt., Dean of Worcester. Between his two wives he had sixteen children, eight of them sons. He also seems to have been very fond of bookplates having at least three including one jointly with his second wife (GRA 5). He died at Euston Hall, Suffolk in March 1811 aged seventy-five.

He was succeeded as fourth duke by his first son by his first wife, his heir George Henry Fitzroy. He was born in 1760 and educated at Harrow and Trinity College, Cambridge. He followed his father and great-grandfather as Lord Lieutenant of Suffolk. He was the bearer of St Edward's Crown at the coronation of William IV in 1831 and was created a Knight of the Garter in 1834.

He married, in 1784, Charlotte, daughter of James, 2nd Earl Waldegrave. She died of *'a bilious fever'* in 1808 aged forty-eight. He lived on until 1844 when he died at Euston Hall aged eighty-four.

He was succeeded as fifth duke by his eldest son and heir Henry Fitzroy, born 1790, known as Viscount Ipswich until 1811 and then as Earl of Euston. Educated at Harrow and Trinity College, Cambridge he became Member of Parliament for Bury St Edmunds and later Thetford.

He married, in 1812 at Lisbon, Mary Caroline, third daughter of Admiral the Honourable Sir George Berkeley G.C.B. He died, aged seventy-four, in March 1863 at his second country seat Wakefield Lodge, Whittlebury Forest in Northamptonshire (GRA 6).

The sixth duke was his son and heir William Henry Fitzroy, born on 4th August 1819. Styled as Viscount Ipswich until 1844 then as Earl of Euston, he was educated at Harrow; he had a spell in the Diplomatic Service and was Attaché to the British Legation at Naples in 1841. Later he was Member of Parliament for Thetford 1847–63.

He married, in 1858 Maria Anne Louise, daughter of Francis, 3rd Lord Ashburton. He died, without issue, aged sixty-two, in May 1882 from typhoid fever.

He was succeeded, as seventh duke, by his brother Augustus Charles Lennox Fitzroy who was born in June 1821. Educated at Harrow he joined the 60th Rifles and later the Coldstream Guards becoming Lieutenant Colonel in 1854. He served in the Crimean Campaign, being severely wounded at the Battle of Inkerman. He retired from the army as an Honorary General in 1881. He was Equerry to Queen Victoria 1849–82 and given the Garter in 1883. At the coronation of Edward VII in 1902 he carried the Curtana – Sword of Mercy.

He married, in June 1847, Anna, youngest daughter of James Balfour. He lived a long and fruitful life dying, after a week's illness, in December 1918 at Wakefield Lodge aged ninety-seven.

He was succeeded by his son the eighth duke (GRA 7). He married twice. Firstly Margaret Rose, third daughter of Eric Carrington-Smith of Stonewick Sussex who died in 1913 and secondly in 1916 Susana Mary (GRA 8), the daughter of Sir Mark McTaggart-Stewart Bt.

GRA 2 The Right Noble Charles Fitz-Roy Duke of Grafton, Earl of Euston Viscount Ipswich and Baron of Sudbury 1705 F*6

A small early armorial for Charles, 2nd Duke of Grafton showing the royal arms debruised by a baton sinister compony of five argent and purpure – the first duke was an illegitimate son of Charles I. Charles succeeded to the dukedom in 1690 when he was only seven years old.

GRA 3

GRA 3 **Charles Fitz-Roy Lord Southampton** F10719

A plain armorial with the supporters standing on a ribbon carrying the family motto, the arms under a baron's coronet surmounted by the crest. The arms carry, for difference, a baton sinister compony of seven argent and azure. Note the change of tinctures and number of divisions compared to the ducal arms. The plate is signed under the motto 'Darling sc. Newport St.'.

Charles Fitzroy (1737–97) was the second son of Lord Augustus Fitzroy and grandson of the second duke. He joined the army and fought in the Seven Years war, rising to the rank of Lieutenant Colonel in 1758. He served as Member of Parliament at various times between 1768 and 1780 for Orford, Bury St. Edmonds and Thetford; starting as a Whig supporter, switching to Tory and then back to Whig again. He was Vice Chamberlain to Queen Charlotte and was raised to the peerage as Lord Southampton in 1780.

GRA 4 **Aug^s Henry, Duke of Grafton** F10716

Arms with supporters and coronet set within a wreath. Remnants of the baroque style can be seen in the compartment on which the supporters stand. There is a reference number inscribed in ink in the top right hand corner '14.4'. This plate is for Henry the third duke who succeeded his grandfather to the title in 1757.

GRA 4

81

GRA 5

GRA 6

GRA 5 **Anonymous** F10717

A mid-eighteenth century plain armorial for the third duke and his second wife, Elizabeth Wrottesley whom he married in 1769. The two shields are shown accollee, the duke's to the right surrounded by the Garter and garter motto and his wife's to the left: or, three piles in chief sable, a canton ermine in dexter chief (Wrottesley). The reason for the separation is that the Order of the Garter applies only to the husband.

GRA 6 **Wakefield Lodge** NIF

A small crest plate with the Grafton crest within the Garter and motto under a duke's coronet.

This is a nineteenth century plate for the duke's Wakefield estate in Northamptonshire. This was a very large and fruitful estate the income from which, in the eighteenth century, was three times that of his Norfolk and Suffolk estates combined. The family used the house as hunting lodge.

GRA 7 **Alfred William Duke of Grafton 1918** NIF

A large full armorial bookplate showing the ducal arms impaling those of McTaggart-Stewart (see above). Alfred the eighth duke was born in 1850 and succeeded his ninety-seven year old father in 1918, the year of this plate. He died in 1930.

GRA 8 **SUSANNA MARY, DUCHESS OF GRAFTON** NIF

A fine pictorial armorial bookplate for Susanna, the wife of the 8th Duke of Grafton. There is a framed view of Euston Hall, the family seat in Suffolk, with the arms and family supporters arranged gracefully below.

ARMS: Fitzroy impaling: or, a fess chequey argent and azure, overall a bend purpure, surrounded by a tressure flory counter flory gules, a buckle proper in sinister chief (Stewart).

It is initialed in the left hand corner 'A S sc.'

Susana Mary McTaggart-Stewart was the daughter of Sir Mark McTaggart-Stewart Bt.. She married, in 1916, as his second wife Alfred William Fitzroy then Earl of Euston. He succeeded to his father's dukedom two years later.

Alfred William — *Duke of Grafton.*

1918

SUSANNA MARY,
DUCHESS OF GRAFTON.

HAM 1 **Anonymous** F13513

A mid-eighteenth century bookplate in the rococo style probably for Douglas, 8th Duke of Hamilton (1756–99). It is signed 'Austin Sculp" and attributed to Richard Austin.

ARMS: Grand quarters: I, quarterly, 1 and 4, gules, three cinquefoils pierced ermine (Hamilton); 2 and 3, argent, a lymphad sable, sails furled proper, flagged gules (Arran); II, argent, a heart gules ensigned with an imperial crown proper, on a chief azure three mullets argent (Douglas); III, argent, a saltire gules (Gerard); IV, quarterly, argent and gules, in the second and third quarters a fret or, overall on a bend sable three escallops of the first (Spencer).

CRESTS:
1. Out of a ducal coronet or an oak fructed and perforated transversely in the main stem by a frame saw proper, the frame or. The blade bearing the motto 'Through' (Hamilton). The coronet here is shown incorrectly as a duke's coronet rather than a ducal coronet. The artist, no doubt, trying 'to kill two birds with one stone'.
2. On a chapeau gules turned up ermine a salamander in flames proper (Douglas) (not shown).

SUPPORTERS: Two antelopes argent, armed, ducally gorged, chained and hoofed or.

MOTTOES: 'Through' (Hamilton).
Jamais arriere – Never behind (Douglas) (not shown).

Dukes of Hamilton

FAMILY NAME: Hamilton, Douglas Hamilton

CREATION OF DUKEDOM: 12th April 1643

COURTESY TITLE OF ELDEST SON: Marquess of Douglas and Clydesdale

COURTESY TITLE OF GRANDSON AND HEIR: Earl of Angus

PRINCIPAL RESIDENCE: Hamilton Palace, Lanarkshire

The dukedom of Hamilton was created by Charles I for James Hamilton, Marquess of Hamilton, Earl of Arran, Baron Hamilton and Baron Aberbrothwick on 12th April 1643 with special remainder, failing heirs male of his body to his brother William and the heirs male of his body with special remainder, failing heirs male, to James's eldest daughter, Anne, and the heirs male of her body; presumably in an attempt to cover all eventualities.

James was born on 16th June 1606 at Hamilton in Lanarkshire. The son of James Hamilton, Marquess of Hamilton he was styled Earl of Arran. Educated at Exeter College, Oxford he was the bearer of the Curtana – sword of mercy at the coronation of Charles I in 1625 and installed as a Knight of the Garter in 1630. In 1631, aged twenty-five he was General of an army of seven thousand men sent to Germany to assist the King of Sweden to recover the Palatinate. He was made a Privy Counsellor in both England and Scotland in the same year and was Chancellor of the University of Glasgow 1642–9.

He was married, in 1620, at the age of fourteen to Margaret, daughter of William Fielding, 1st Earl of Denbigh, she being aged only seven at the time.

In 1648 he headed the Scottish forces which came into England to support Charles I but was defeated at Preston by an army under Cromwell to whom he surrendered at Uttoxeter on 25th August 1648. He was indicted for invading England, tried and sentenced to death by the High Court. He was beheaded in Palace Yard, Westminster on 9th March 1648/9 a few weeks after the King's execution in Whitehall.

His only son predeceased him, aged ten, in 1640 so under the special remainder the dukedom fell to his brother William. William was born in 1616 and studied at the University of Glasgow. In 1638 he married a rich heiress Elizabeth, daughter and co-heir of James Maxwell, Earl of Dirletoun. In 1639, aged twenty-three, he was created Earl of Lanark in his own right. He was Member of Parliament for Portsmouth in 1640 and made a Privy Counsellor in the same year. In 1648 he commanded the King's army in Scotland and in 1649, following the King's execution, he joined the exiled Prince of Wales in the Hague. A year later he was back in Scotland as a Lieutenant General in the Scottish army supporting the monarchy. He was fatally wounded at the Battle of Worcester on 3rd September 1651 and died on the 12th, aged thirty-four.

On his death a number of his dignities became extinct or dormant but the dukedom of Hamilton and the titles created with it devolved under the special remainder to his niece Anne, eldest surviving daughter of the first duke, James. She became, suo jure, Duchess of Hamilton. In April 1656 she married William Douglas, Earl of Selkirk. Lord William Douglas, fourth son of William, 1st Marquess of Douglas, had been created Earl of Selkirk in 1646. Following the restoration of the monarchy in 1660 he was, on the petition of his wife, created Duke of Hamilton for life only.

He served intermittently as a Privy Counsellor under Charles II and James II but was one of the first to desert James and become President of the Convention at Edinburgh on 14th March 1688/9 which declared the throne vacant. He served under William and Mary 1689–94 and died on 18th April 1694.

On his death his life peerage as Duke of Hamilton ceased but his wife continued as Duchess of Hamilton in her own right along with her other titles. On the 9th July 1698 she resigned those titles in favour of her eldest son James.

James, the fourth duke, was born in 1658 and styled Earl of Arran until succeeding to the dukedom. After attending Glasgow University he had a military career serving in various regiments including the Royal Horse Guards. He was one of the eight original Knights of the Thistle created by

James II when he revived the Order in 1688. He supported James II, in 1688, against his own father. He became a Lieutenant General in 1693.

When his mother resigned her titles in his favour in 1698 he received a novodamus to the titles in his favour from the King. As he had been a firm opponent of William III this mark of royal favour surprised many people. He also opposed the Union of England and Scotland in the early eighteenth century. Because of this opposition he was under suspicion for high treason but no evidence could be obtained which justified putting him on trial.

In an essay on the Union written by Lord Rosebery in 1871 he expressed the view that: '*his great estates in England deterred him from risking his all for Scotland, the Dukedoms , the Garter and the Thistle seem but to have corrupted and unnerved him as indeed they have relaxed stronger fibres than his.*'

On the 10th September 1711 he was created Duke of Brandon and Baron Dutton in the peerage of Great Britain. He was the second Scottish duke to be so honoured the first being the Duke of Queensberry who was created Duke of Dover in May 1708.

James married, in 1686, Anne, daughter of Robert, 2nd Earl of Sunderland. She died in 1690 without producing a male heir. He married again in 1698 Elizabeth, daughter of Digby, 1st Lord Gerard, this was to be a fruitful union.

He was appointed ambassador to Paris in August 1712 but was killed in a dual in Hyde Park on 15th November 1712 before he had taken up the post.

His eldest son, James, the fifth duke (HAM 2), was only ten years old at the time of his succession and a pupil at Winchester. He later went on to Christ Church, Oxford. He used the title Marquis of Clydesdale until he inherited. He became a Captain General in the Royal Company of Archers and was a Tory in his politics although he intrigued with the Jacobites. The 1st Earl of Egremont recorded in his diary, '*The Duke of Hamilton has embarked with the Jacobite Party but having secretly offered to be with the Court if the King will make him an hereditary English peer; the Jacobites who have learnt of this have renounced him as a man unsettled, but all for his own interests. The King recalled him from Rome where he was too busy with the Jacobite Party*'. Nevertheless he was made a Knight of the Thistle by George I in 1726. He also became a Fellow of the Royal Society.

He married first, in 1723, Ann, daughter of Charles, 4th Earl of Dundonald, who died the following year in childbed aged only eighteen. The child, a boy, survived. He married secondly, in 1727, Elizabeth, daughter of Thomas Strangeways of Melbury Stamford in Dorset. She died without issue

'*on the road from Bath*' on 3rd November 1729. He married finally, in 1737, Anne daughter and co-heir of Edward Spencer of Rendlesham in Suffolk. She had a fortune of £70,000. He died five years later in Bath, in 1742 of jaundice and palsy aged forty.

The sixth duke was his son by his first wife. Born on 5th July 1724 he was educated at Winchester and St Mary's Hall, Oxford. He married, in 1752, Elizabeth, second daughter of Colonel John Gunning, and one of the three celebrated Gunning sisters renowned for their beauty. He died young aged only thirty-four in 1758 from a cold caught whilst out hunting in Oxfordshire. His widow later married John Campbell, 5th Duke of Argyll.

The seventh duke, his eldest son, yet another James, was only three when he succeeded. He was six when, on the death of Archibald Douglas, Duke of Douglas in 1761, he succeeded to the marquessate of Douglas. Unlike his father and grandfather he was educated at Eton but he died of a fever in July 1769 in his fifteenth year.

He was succeeded, as eighth duke, by his only brother, Douglas (HAM 1) who, having been born in 1756, was only thirteen. He too was educated at Eton and then spent five years on the Continent, 1772–6, in the care of his tutor, Dr. Moore, father of the celebrated Sir John Moore of Corunna. Returning to England he petitioned the King for his summons to Parliament as a British peer and was summoned as the Duke of Brandon on 11th June 1782. He was created a Knight of the Thistle in 1785.

He married in 1778 Elizabeth Ann, daughter of Peter Russell of Langley Park, Beckenham, Kent and sister of Peter, 1st Lord Gwidir. She divorced him by Act of Parliament in 1794 and he died without leaving legitimate offspring 2nd August 1799. He is reported in the Farington diaries to have '*left all the property he could to the child (a daughter) which he had by a Mrs Eston*'. He also left all his personal property for the same purpose including the pictures and furniture at Hamilton Palace. His successor later bought these back from Mrs Eston at valuation.

The ninth duke (HAM 3) was his uncle, Archibald, being the second son of James, the fifth duke. Born in 1740 and educated at Eton he inherited the Suffolk estates from his mother. He was Member of Parliament for Lancaster 1768–72 and Lord Lieutenant of Lancashire from 1799–1802. In 1768 he married Harriet, daughter of Alexander Stewart, 6th Earl of Galloway. She died in Bath in 1788 and he died in 1819 aged seventy-eight.

His son and heir Alexander, the tenth duke (HAM 4), was

born in 1767 and educated at Harrow and Christ Church, Oxford. Known as Marquess of Douglas and Clydesdale before he inherited he was a supporter of the Whig party but it was said of him *'timidity and variableness of temperament prevented his rendering much service to, or being much relied on by his party; with a great predisposition to over estimate the importance of ancient birth he well deserved to be considered the proudest man in England.'*

He served as Member of Parliament for Lancaster 1802–06 and Lord Lieutenant of Lancashire 1802–52. He was summoned to Parliament in the lifetime of his father in his father's title as Lord Dutton. He was Grand Master of Freemasons (Scotland), President of the Highland and Agricultural Society and a Trustee of the British Museum. He was the bearer of St Edward's crown at the coronations of both William IV and Queen Victoria. He was created a Knight of the Garter in 1836.

He married, in 1810, Susan Euphemia (HAM 5), daughter of William Beckford of Fonthill, Wiltshire. William Beckford was one of the richest men in the country at that time and very keen to form an association with the peerage. He gave his daughter and son-in-law a dinner service made at the Worcester factory as a wedding present The tenth duke died in 1852 aged eighty-four and was buried in the mausoleum which he had had built at Hamilton Palace.

His son, William, the eleventh duke, was born 19th February 1811 and educated at Eton and Christ Church, Oxford. He was styled Marquis of Douglas until his succession. He followed in his ancestors' footsteps becoming Grand Master of Freemasons (Scotland), Lord Lieutenant of Lancashire 1852–63 and President of the Highland and Agricultural Society 1857–8.

In 1843 he married, in the ducal palace at Mannheim, the Princess Marie Amelie Elizabeth of Baden, the youngest daughter of Karl Ludwig Freidrich, Duke of Baden and had a family including sons. He died from a fall after supper on the 15th July 1863 and was succeeded by his eldest son, William, as twelfth duke. (HAM 6, 7, 8 and 9)

Born in 1845 William, like his father, was styled Marquess of Douglas and educated at Eton and Christ Church, Oxford He was later responsible for selling off two large collections of books. His own library, collected whilst he was still Marquess of Douglas, sold in May 1884 for £12,892 and in 1889 he sold the library of his grandmother the tenth duchess who had inherited the Fonthill library from her father William Beckford on his death in 1844. It realised the staggering sum of £173,551.

By a decree of the Emperor Napoleon II he was, on 20th April 1864, maintained and confirmed in the title of Duc de Chatellerault which his predecessors had used and which had been created in 1548 in favour of James Hamilton, Earl of Arran. This was rather odd as the confirmation was in favour of one who was neither the heir male nor heir of the line to the original grantee. Consequently this should be regarded as a new creation of a French dukedom.

He married, on 10th December 1873 at Kimbolton Castle in Huntingdonshire Mary Elizabeth, eldest daughter of William, 7th Duke of Manchester. He died in Algiers in 1895 without leaving a son. As a result he was succeeded as thirteenth duke by a distant cousin, Alfred Douglas Hamilton being the only son and heir of Captain Charles Henry Hamilton R.N.

HAM 2 **Anonymous** F13417

A mid-eighteenth century bookplate for James, 5th Duke of Hamilton, on laid paper showing the ducal arms surrounded by the motto of the Order of the Thistle. The duke was given the Order in 1726. He succeeded to the title, whilst a pupil at Winchester, aged only ten in 1712. He married three times but left only one child, a son and heir by his first wife. He died aged forty in 1742.

HAM 2

JAMAIS·ARRIERE

THROUGH

Hamilton

HAM 9

His Grace the Duke of Hamilton & Brandon.

HAM 10

HAM 9 **Hamilton** NIF

A fine armorial plate showing grand quarters, without tincture lines, double crest and supporters.

ARMS: Grand quarters: I and IV, quarterly, 1 and 4, gules three cinquefoils pierced, ermine (Hamilton); 2 and 3, argent, a lymphad sails furled sable (Arran); II and III, quarterly, 1, azure, a lion rampant argent [ducally crowned or] (Galloway); 2, or, a lion rampant gules debruised by a bendlet sable (Abernethy); 3, argent, three piles gules (Wishart); 4, or, a fess chequey azure and argent surmounted by a bend gules charged with three buckles of the first (Stewart). On an escutcheon of pretence over the last four coats – argent, a heart gules ensigned with an imperial crown proper, on a chief azure three mullets argent (Douglas).

CRESTS:
1. Out of a ducal coronet or an oak fructed and penetrated transversely in the trunk by a framesaw proper the frame or, the blade inscribed with the word 'Through' (Hamilton);
2. On a chapeau gules turned up ermine a salamander in flames proper (Douglas).

SUPPORTERS: Two antelopes argent, armed, ducally gorged, chained and hoofed or.

The date of the plate is probably late nineteenth or early twentieth century. Possibly for William, twelfth duke, or Alfred, thirteenth duke.

HAM 10 **His Grace the Duke of Hamilton & Brandon** F13416

A full armorial with supporters in front of a draped cloak with crest above.

ARMS: Grand quarters: I and IV, quarterly, 1 and 4, gules three cinquefoils pierced, ermine (Hamilton); 2 and 3, argent, a lymphad sails furled sable (Arran); II ??, III, argent, a heart gules ensigned with an imperial crown proper (Douglas).

It is not known for which duke this plate was made.

Ken 1 **HENRY DUKE OF KENT 1713** F12828

A very fine armorial bookplate in the baroque style for
Henry, Duke of Kent. It is a strong bold design showing
the shield surrounded by the Garter motto, with
supporters standing on an architectural plinth all under a
duke's coronet. He was installed as a Knight of the Garter
in 1713, the year of this bookplate.

ARMS: Barry of six argent and azure.

CREST: On a chapeau gules turned up
ermine a wyvern statant (not shown).

SUPPORTERS: Two wyverns rampant.

MOTTO: Stat relegione parentum – Stands in the religion of
parents.

Duke of Kent

FAMILY NAME: Grey

CREATION OF DUKEDOM: 28th April 1710

COURTESY TITLE OF ELDEST SON: Earl of Harrold

PRINCIPAL RESIDENCE: Wrest Park Bedfordshire

Since the end of the eighteenth century the dukedom of Kent has been a royal dukedom. However there was one previous commoner Duke of Kent when Henry Grey, Earl of Kent was raised to that dignity in 1710.

There had been previous earldoms of Kent all of which became extinct, due to the failure of the male line, before Edmund Grey, Lord Grey of Ruthin, was created Earl of Kent in 1465. He had, two years earlier, been appointed Lord High Treasurer by Edward IV.

Edmund Grey was born in 1416 the eldest son and heir of Sir John Grey K.G. and his wife Constance, daughter of John Holland, Duke of Exeter. He succeeded his grandfather to the barony of Ruthin in 1440. He was a Justice of the Peace at various times and places in Bedfordshire, Buckinghamshire, Northamptonshire, Huntingdonshire and Norfolk. He married, c.1458, Catherine, daughter of Henry, 2nd Earl of Northumberland, and had issue. His eldest son, Anthony, predeceased him so, on his death in 1490, he was succeeded by his second son, George, as second earl of that creation. George's son, Richard, died without issue leaving the earldom to his half brother – Sir Henry Grey of Wrest Park, Bedfordshire son of the second earl by his second wife.

Sir Henry did not assume the title of earl it was said, '*by reason of his slender estate*'. The earldom of Kent was suspended by Henry VIII, according to the Heralds '*for want of competent estate to maintain it.*' Although there does not appear to be any proof that this was the case; Sir Henry benefited from the Dissolution of the Monasteries by being given a grant of monastic lands in 1542. He died in London in 1562.

His son, plain Henry Grey because of his father's failure to sustain the earldom, predeceased him so he was succeeded by his grandson Reynold Grey of Wrest Park. In 1571 Reynold petitioned the Queen for recognition and reinstatement as Earl of Kent. This was granted but two years

later he died without issue leaving his brother Henry as 6th Earl of Kent. Henry was a member of the Queen's household, Justice of the Peace and Lord Lieutenant of Bedfordshire and one of the Commissioners at the trial of Mary Queen of Scots. He married Mary, widow of Edward, 3rd Earl of Derby, but died, without issue, in 1615.

He was succeeded by his brother, Charles, who in turn was followed by his son Henry as eighth earl. Henry had married well, Elizabeth daughter and co-heir of Gilbert, 7th Earl of Shrewsbury, but unfortunately this marriage also failed to produce children and, on his death in 1639, the earldom passed, unexpectedly, to a distant cousin.

A letter at the time commenting on the earl's death goes on to say '*…unto whom one succeeds in the Earldom who is a minister and has divers daughters some are married to farmers and some to mercers who will be much troubled to know how to carry themselves like ladies*' another letter gives the information '*the Earl is dead and a clergyman is, by descent, Earl of Kent with which honour there does descend to him only £500 per annum.*'

The new earl, Anthony Grey, was a distant cousin of the eighth earl. He was born in 1557 and later entered the Church. He was Rector of Aston Flauville in Leicestershire for fifty-three years (1590–1643) and was eighty-two years old when he succeeded to the earldom. He was summoned to Parliament in 1640 but never took his seat.

It was said of him: '*He kept an hospitable house for the poor according to his estate, and after his accession to the title he did not distain the society of the Clergy neither did he abate in the constancy of his preaching so long as he was able to be lead to the pulpit. Such was his humility and sanctity that he was truly reverenced by all who knew him.*' He 'enjoyed' his new estate for only four years dying in 1643 at the age of eighty-six.

His son and heir, Henry, not having the reticence of his father, had promptly, but incorrectly, styled himself as Lord Ruthin on the elevation of his father. However, although the earldom had rightly passed to his father as heir male, the Barony of Ruthin devolved to the heir general, a nephew of the eighth earl.

Henry lived through the troubled years of the civil war and the interregnum. He was Member of Parliament for Leicester 1640–3, Lord Lieutenant of Rutland in 1644 and of Bedfordshire in 1646. He was Speaker of the House of Lords in 1645. Although of the Parliamentary Party he took no part in the trial of King Charles or his subsequent execution.

He died in 1651. His eldest son, Henry, had died as an infant so he was succeeded as eleventh earl by his second son, Anthony, who was only six at the time of his accession having been born in 1645. Anthony was educated at Trinity College, Cambridge and took his M.A. in 1661 at the age of sixteen. A year later he married, by licence from the Dean of Westminster, Mary, daughter and heiress of Lord Lucas of Shenfield. They had one son, Henry born in 1671.

Anthony was a pall bearer at the funeral of Queen Mary in 1693 and at the coronation of Queen Anne on 23rd April 1702 he carried the Curtana, one of the three Swords of State. He died suddenly on the bowling green at Tunbridge Wells in August of the same year aged only fifty-seven. His bookplate was made in the year of his death (KEN 2).

He was succeeded, as twelfth earl, by his only son Henry (KEN 3). He had been styled Lord Grey until the death of his father and, his mother also dying in 1702, he also succeeded to her Barony of Lucas of Crudwell. In 1704 he was made a Privy Counsellor and Lord Chamberlain of the Queen's Household; a post he held for six years

In 1706 Henry received further honours being created Viscount Goderich of Hereford, Earl of Harold and Marquess of Kent. Finally, on 28th April 1710 he was created Duke of Kent and in 1713 was given the Garter (KEN 1 and 4). He went on to serve successive sovereigns. He was Lord Steward of the Household to George I, Constable of Windsor Castle and Lord Keeper of the Privy Seal. At the coronation of George II in 1727 he was the bearer of St Edward's Staff.

The duke married twice, firstly, in 1695, Jemima, daughter and co-heir of Thomas, Lord Crew (KEN 5 and 6), who brought him £20,000 and provided him with a son, Anthony (KEN 7 and 8)), who predeceased him in 1723 aged twenty seven. She was to have six children but apart from the last two, both daughters, they all predeceased her. She died in 1727. Henry married, secondly in March 1728, Sophia, daughter of William, 1st Earl of Portland (KEN 9 and 10) and had a second son, George, who died as an infant.

On 19th May 1740, having no surviving male issue, he was created Marquess Grey with special remainder of that dignity, failing heirs male of his body, to his granddaughter Lady Jemima Campbell and the heirs male of her body. The gift came only just in time. Two weeks later on 5th June 1740 he died aged sixty-eight.

With his death the dukedom of Kent (1710), the marquisate of Kent (1706), the earldom of Kent (1465), the earldom of Harold (1706) and the viscountcy of Goderich (1706) all became extinct. The marquisate of Grey and the barony of Lucas of Crudwell both devolved on his granddaughter and co-heir Lady Jemima Campbell.

Lady Jemima was the eldest daughter of John Campbell, 3rd Earl of Breadalbane, and his wife Lady Amabel Grey, daughter of the Duke of Kent by his first marriage. She died in 1727 leaving her daughter Jemima (KEN 11) as the heir to become Marchioness Grey in her own right.

On the 24th April 1799 George III recreated the dukedom of Kent as a royal dukedom for his fourth son Prince Edward Augustus. Edward had only one daughter who, due to the failure of heirs male, became Queen Victoria in 1837. On Edward's death the dukedom again became extinct but was recreated in 1934 by King George V for his fourth son Prince George. The current holder of the title is his son Edward, Duke of Kent.

The Right Hon.ble Anthony Earle of Kent: 1702.

KEN 2

KEN 2 **The Right Hon**ble **Anthony Earle of Kent: 1702**
F12827

This bookplate dated 1702, the year he died, is for Anthony, 11th Earl of Kent and father of Henry, the first duke.

ARMS: Barry of six argent and azure, in chief three roundels gules. The roundels were removed after Henry received the dukedom.

MOTTO: foy est tout – fidelity is everything, may be a corruption of – foy en tout – fidelity in all things which is the Grey family motto given in Boutell's Heraldry. Henry

KEN 3

dropped the Grey motto and assumed his mother's family motto when he inherited her barony of Lucas of Crudwell.

There is a smaller version of this plate in the same design.

KEN 3 **The Right Hon**ble **Henry Earle of Kent: 1702**
F*33

An early armorial, showing a full achievement, for Henry, 12th Earl of Kent, dated the year he inherited the title from his father. He was created Duke of Kent in 1710.

KEN 4 **HENRY DUKE OF KENT 1713** F12829

A smaller version of KEN 1 without the supporters and with a quartered shield.

ARMS: Quarterly, 1 and 4, barry of six argent and azure (Grey); 2 and 3, argent, a fess between six annulets gules (Lucas); on a shield of pretence the arms of Crew.

Henry married, as his first wife, in 1695 Jemima, daughter and co-heir of Thomas Crew, 2nd Baron Crew. She died in 1727.

KEN 5 **JEMIMA DUTCHESS OF KENT.** MDCCX
F12833

This is the first of two plates for the duchess; it is dated 1710 and shows the arms of Grey, with Crew in pretence, accollee with Crew. (Note the three roundels in chief in the Grey arms). Jemima was the duke's first wife; she died in 1727.

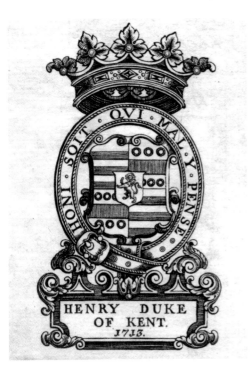

KEN 4

KEN 5

KEN 6

KEN 7

KEN 8

KEN 6 **JEMIMA DUTCHESS OF KENT 1712**
F12834

This is the second plate for the duchess; it is dated 1712 and is similar in design but the three roundels are absent from the Grey arms; the precise reason for their removal is not known. On this plate the tinctures of the Crew arms are correctly shown: azure a lion rampant argent.

KEN 7 **ANTHONY EARL OF HAROLD 1717**
F12835

Anthony was Henry's son by his first wife Jemima. He assumed the courtesy title of Earl of Harold but unfortunately died in 1723, before his father.

ARMS: Quarterly Grey and Lucas with a label of three points, for difference, in the first quarter.

KEN 8 **MARY COUNTESS OF HARROLD 1718**
F12836

A baroque style plate showing the arms accollee below two cherubims under an earl's coronet. The dexter shield: Grey; the sinister shield: sable, an eagle displayed argent (Tufton). Lady Mary Tufton (1701–85) was the daughter and co-heiress of Thomas Tufton, 6th Earl of Thanet. She married Anthony, Earl of Harold in 1718. This dated bookplate is probably commemorating that event. He was son and heir to Henry, 1st Duke of Kent but predeceased his father in 1723.

KEN 9 **HENRY DUKE OF KENT 1733** F12830

A later baroque plate showing the arms of Grey impaling: azure, a cross moline argent (Bentinck). Henry married again in 1728 Sophia, daughter of William Bentinck, 1st Earl of Portland.

KEN 10 **HENRY DUKE OF KENT 1733** F12832

A smaller version of KEN 9 without the supporters.

KEN 9

KEN 10

KEN 11 **Campbell Marchioness Grey** NIF

This is a rococo style bookplate for an unmarried lady showing the arms in a lozenge.

ARMS: Grand Quarters: I, quarterly, 1 and 4, a gyronny of eight sable and or (Campbell); 2, argent a lymphad sable (Lorne), 3, or a fess chequey argent and azure (Stewart); II, barry of six argent and azure (Grey); III, argent, a fess between six annulets gules (Lucas); IV, azure a lion rampant argent (Crew).

Lady Jemima Campbell was the daughter of John Campbell, 3rd Earl of Breadalbane and his wife, Lady Amabelle Grey, daughter of Henry Duke of Kent and his first wife. Under the special remainder she inherited the marquisate of Grey in her own right on the death of her grandfather, the duke, in 1740.

KEN 11

KEN 12

KEN 12 Thomas Philip, 2nd Earl de Grey,
WREST PARK F25232

This bookplate, which is in a mid-eighteenth century style, dates from the second quarter of the nineteenth century post 1833. It shows the arms with supporters under an earl's coronet. It is signed 'Eng^d by F. Ortner, 3 St James St.'.

ARMS: Quarterly of six; 1 and 6, barry of six argent and azure (Grey); 2, vert, a chevron between three stags trippant or (Robinson); 3, argent, a cross saltire pierced in the centre azure (Yorke); 4, a gyronny of eight, sable and or (Campbell); 5, argent, a fess between six annulets gules (Lucas).

Thomas Philip Robinson was the eldest son of Thomas Robinson, 2nd Lord Grantham, and his wife Mary, daughter of Jemima Yorke, 2nd Marchioness Grey, great-granddaughter of the Duke of Kent and younger sister of Amabelle Hume-Campbell, 1st Countess Grey. He succeeded his father as 3rd Lord Grantham in 1786 when he was only five years old. He succeeded his aunt as 2nd Earl de Grey in 1833 and he also inherited the Wrest Park estate in Silsoe, Bedfordshire. He was a Tory politician and statesman, Privy Counsellor and a Knight of the Garter. In 1805 he married Lady Henrietta Cole, daughter of William Cole, 1st Earl of Enniskillen. He died in 1859.

The Right Noble Thomas Duke of Leeds, Marquis of Carmarthen, Earl of Danby, Viscount Latimer & Dumblan, Baron Osborne of Kiveton and Knight of ye most Noble Order of ye Garter. 1701

LEE 1. **The Right Noble Thomas Duke of Leeds, Marquis of Carmarthen, Earl of Danby, Viscount Latimer & Dumblan, Baron Osborne of Kiveton and Knight of ye most Noble Order of ye Garter. 1701**
F22435

A rather fine dated early armorial bookplate for Thomas Osborne, 1st Duke of Leeds. Born in 1631 he succeeded to his father's baronetcy in 1647. In the 1670s he rose rapidly through the peerage collecting the Garter (1676) on the way until finally being given a dukedom by William III in 1694. He died in 1712 aged eighty-one.

ARMS: Quarterly of 8: 1, quarterly, ermine and azure, overall a cross of St George or (Osborne); 2, argent, two bars gules, on a canton of the second a cross of the field (Broughton); 3, argent, a chevron vert between three annulets gules (Secroft); 4, azure, on a fess fimbriated with fleur-de-lys between three horses 2 and 1 argent, three rooks sable (Hewit); 5, gules, a chevron between three owls argent (Hewit); 6, gules, on a chief ermine two bezants (Walmesley); 7, gules, a chevron or between three estoiles argent (Danvers); 8, gules, a cross saltire argent charged with a pellet (Nevill).

CREST: 1. An heraldic tiger passant or, tufted and manned sable (Osborne).

SUPPORTERS: Dexter, a griffin or; Sinister, an heraldic tiger argent, each gorged with a ducal coronet azure.

MOTTO: Pax in bello – Peace in war.

Dukes of Leeds

FAMILY NAME: Osborne, D'Arcy Osborne.

CREATION OF DUKEDOM: 4th May 1694

COURTESY TITLE OF ELDEST SON: Marquess of Carmarthen

COURTESY TITLE OF GRANDSON AND HEIR: Viscount Osborne

PRINCIPAL RESIDENCES: Kiveton (demolished 1811), Hornby Castle, Bedale, Yorkshire.

Each age in our history has made a contribution to the growth of the peerage. As each family has risen in status and wealth it has claimed its perquisites and among them, if they have been fortunate and in favour, has often been a coronet. The Osbornes were a family of merchants in London and first came to prominence when Edward Osborne was knighted on becoming Lord Mayor of the City of London in 1583. From then on they did not lack a title in any generation and the Lord Mayor's great-grandson became the first Duke of Leeds. This particular ascent started when Edward Osborne from Kiveton in Yorkshire was created a baronet by James I in 1620. His second, but first surviving, son Thomas, who was born in February 1631, succeeded to his father's baronetcy in 1647. He rapidly rose to prominence becoming Member of Parliament for the City of York and High Sheriff of Yorkshire in 1661. He was Treasurer of the navy 1671–3 and raised to the peerage as Viscount Osborne of Dunblane in 1672. Thereafter various other honours followed, Baron Osborne of Kiveton and Viscount Latimer of Danby, both in Yorkshire, in 1673 with a grant of twenty marks per annum. He chose the latter title because his mother was descended from the former Lords Latimer of Corby through Elizabeth Latimer who married John Nevill, Earl of Westmoreland, who was later recreated Lord Latimer.

The following year, 1674, he was created Earl of Danby with a grant of £20 per annum. He became Lord Lieutenant of West Yorkshire, Governor of Kingston-Upon-Hull and a Privy Counsellor. In 1676 he became a Knight of the Garter.

Then, in 1679, there came a major hiccough when he was accused by the House of Commons of high treason and sent to the Tower of London for five years, being released in 1684 when he promptly took an active part in bringing about the Glorious Revolution. He was one of the seven signatories inviting William of Orange to take the English throne with his wife, Princess Mary. Needless to say he was rewarded accordingly becoming Marquess of Carmarthen in 1689, although he owned no land in that county, and finally, in 1694 he was created Duke of Leeds (LEE 1 and 2).

This was the sixth of nine dukedoms created by William III. It was originally proposed that he be given the title Duke of Pontefract but there was already a Barony of Pontefract vested in George, Duke of Northumberland. As to the title 'Leeds' the duke himself said at the end of his life *'that it was an honour to himself not the town of Leeds, that he was dignified with that title, it being the most considerable place for trade and York already being appropriated by the Royal Family.'* He was the owner of ground rents in Leeds and his vast estates were almost entirely in Yorkshire.

In 1690 an attempt had been made to try to revive the earlier impeachment and, in 1695, an action was begun for receiving bribes in particular the sum of £6,000 from the French Court to secure his support for the East India Charter. That it did not proceed was no doubt related to the fact that his sovereign, William III, had received a similar sum from the same source for the same purpose.

The duke had married, in 1653, Bridget, daughter of Montagu, 2nd Earl of Lindsay, who by some accounts was a very peculiar lady. Thomas, Earl of Ailsbury, said of her *'She had certainly great defects in her brain. She was always dressed in a very odd manner. Most frequently she had fits of raving and her passions were unlimited, but the worst part of her was her itch to meddle in public affairs.'* Nevertheless she bore him three sons.

The duke died on 26th July 1712 in his eighty-first year and was buried at Harthill in Yorkshire. Like most successful men of his generation he was a survivor being constantly alert to the changing political fortunes and dynastic successions.

He was succeeded as second duke by his third son, Peregrine, his first two sons having predeceased him.

Peregrine was born in 1659 and assumed different titles as his father rose through the ranks of the peerage. He was styled Viscount Osborne in 1674, Earl of Danby 1689–94 and Marquess of Carmarthen 1694–1712. He was summoned to Parliament in his father's lifetime, in his father's title of Viscount Osborne.

On 25th April 1682 he married Bridget only daughter of Sir Thomas Hyde and went on to have a successful naval career becoming Vice Admiral of the Red in 1702.

Originally, he, together with his father and elder brother were supporters of William of Orange but during the Jacobite Rising of 1715 expressed regret at the abdication of James II. Writing at the time he said *'I can take God to witness that I had not a thought when I engaged in it, and I am sure my father neither, that the Prince of Orange's landing would end in deposing the King.'* It would appear that although sympathetic to the Jacobite cause he took no active part in the Rising.

It was said of him, in his fifties, that *'He is of low stature but very well shaped and strong made tho' thin; fair complexion; is very rakish and extravagant in his manner of living, otherwise he would have risen quicker; he is strong and active with an abundance of fire and does not want for wit; he is bold enough to undertake anything and understands all the parts of a sailor well. He contrived to build a ship called the 'Royal Transport' which proved so good a sailor that it shews his knowledge of that part of navigation also.'*

He died on 25th June 1729 in needy circumstances, in receipt of an annuity, the arrears of which were paid to his natural son James Osborne, then serving as a midshipman.

His eldest son William having died of the smallpox in 1711 aged twenty-one he was succeeded, as third duke, by his second son, Peregrine, who was born on 11th November 1671. He had been summoned to Parliament in his father's lifetime in his courtesy title of Viscount Osborne where he sat as a Tory.

He was a much married individual. His first wife was Elizabeth, daughter of Robert Harley, Earl of Oxford. She died in childbed in the first year of marriage. His second wife was Anne, daughter of Charles, 6th Duke of Somerset, who also died in childbed after three years of marriage. Finally he married Julianna, daughter and co-heir of Roger Hele of Halewell in Devon. The third duke died on 9th May 1731, having held the title for less than a year, whereupon his widow promptly married Charles, 2nd Earl of Portmore, although she continued to style herself Dowager Duchess of

Leeds for the rest of her life dying at the age of eighty-nine in 1794.

Although dying in childbed his first wife, Elizabeth, had given birth to a son, Thomas, who survived her and succeeded as 4th Duke of Leeds (LEE 3 and 4). Born on 6th November 1713 he was educated at Westminster School and Christ Church, Oxford . He became Lord of the Bedchamber to George II, Chief Justice in Eyre South of the Trent 1748–56 and Chief Justice in Eyre North of the Trent 1761–74. He was installed as a Knight of the Garter in 1750 and made a Privy Counsellor in 1757.

On 26th June 1740 he married Mary, younger daughter and co-heir of Francis, 2nd Earl of Godolphin, whose wife Henrietta was suo jure Duchess of Marlborough being the eldest daughter of John, 1st Duke of Marlborough (see Marlborough). Mary's elder sister and co-heir, Henrietta, had married Thomas, Duke of Newcastle, in 1717.

Mary died suddenly, of apoplexy (a stroke), whilst at dinner on 3rd August 1764. The fourth duke died on 23rd March 1789. His eldest son and heir apparent, Thomas, had died of the smallpox aged thirteen in 1761 so his successor was his younger son Lord Francis Osborne.

Born in 1750, he was educated, like his father before him, at Westminster School and Christ Church, Oxford. He served a short period as Member of Parliament for Eye and then for Helston 1774–5 before being summoned to Parliament, by Writ, in his father's lifetime, as Lord Osborne on 15th May 1776. He became a Privy Counsellor in 1777 and Lord Lieutenant of the East Riding of Yorkshire 1778–80. He was dismissed from this post for having supported a Yorkshire petition against Lord North's Government but was reinstated in 1782 and continued to serve until his death. He was Ambassador to Paris in 1783 and Foreign Secretary 1783–91. He was also Governor of the Scilly Isles from 1785 until his death. A year after he became duke he was nominated for the Garter but was never installed.

He married first, on 29th November 1773, Amelia daughter of Robert D'Arcy, 4th Earl of Holderness. She later eloped from her husband who subsequently divorced her by Act of Parliament in May 1779. A few days later she married a John Byron who, by a second wife, was the father of Lord Byron, the poet.

The fifth duke, married a second time on 11th October 1788, Catherine, daughter of Thomas Anguish one of the Masters in Chancery. He died, of erysipelas on 31st January 1799 aged forty-eight.

It was said of him, by Horace Walpole, that *'He was a*

light variable young man of very moderate parts and less principles'. Although another view of him, found in Wraxell's Memoirs, was *'He was highly accomplished, of the most pleasing manners and of very elegant deportment.'*

The sixth duke, George (LEE 5 and 6), was his son and heir by his first wife. Born in 1775, George III was one of his sponsors at his baptism. On the death of his mother, in 1784, he succeeded to the Baronies of D'Arcy and Conyers and was accordingly summoned to Parliament as Lord Conyers in May 1798. He did not take his seat as Duke of Leeds until November 1801.

He was Governor of the Scilly Isles from 1801 till his death and Lord Lieutenant of the North Riding of Yorkshire from 1802. He was elected a Privy Counsellor in 1827 and made a Knight of the Garter the same year.

He married in August 1797, Charlotte, daughter of George, 1st Marquess Townshend. He was a prominent patron of the Turf. In 1811 he demolished the ancient family seat at Kiveton and went to live in the more magnificent Hornby Castle near Bedale, Yorkshire. He died in London in July 1838.

He was succeeded by his elder son Francis. His younger son, Conyers, was accidentally killed in a wrestling bout at Christ Church, Oxford in 1831.

Francis was born in 1798 and matriculated from Christ Church, Oxford before spending ten years in the army. He was Member of Parliament for Helston, Cornwall from 1826–30. In April 1828 he married an American, Catherine, daughter of Richard Caton, a Baltimore merchant.

He was an anti-catholic Tory but at the insistence of Lord Melbourne he was summoned to Parliament in his father's barony of Osborne on 2nd July 1838 after which he voted with the Liberals. Eight days later, on the death of his father, he succeeded to the dukedom. In 1849 he took the name of D'Arcy before that of Osborne by Royal Licence.

He died of diphtheria in May 1859 leaving no children. At his death the baronies of D'Arcy and Conyers devolved on his sister's son, his nephew Sackville George Lane-Fox. His dukedom and other titles fell to his cousin George Godolphin Osborne son of Francis Godolphin Osborne, created 1st Baron Godolphin in 1832, who was the second son of the fifth duke.

George was born in July 1802 at Gog Magog Hills near Stapleford, Cambridge. Educated at Christ Church, Oxford, he went on to marry Harriet, the illegitimate daughter of Granville Leveson-Gower, 1st Earl Granville by Henrietta, Lady Bessborough daughter of John, 1st Earl Spencer. Lady Bessborough had already had a large family with her husband before meeting Lord Granville, a much younger man, in 1794. George succeeded to his father's Barony of Godolphin in 1850.

The eighth duke died in 1872 and was succeeded by his son and namesake George Godolphin Osborne who was born in Paris in 1828. He married, in January 1861, Frances Georgiana, second daughter of George, 4th Baron Rivers. He died of bronchitis on 23rd December 1895 at Hornby Castle.

The dukedom of Leeds became extinct, due to lack of a male heir, in 1964 on the death of the twelfth duke, Francis D'Arcy Godolphin Osborne. Born in 1884 and known in his adult life as Sir D'Arcy Osborne, he inherited the dukedom from a second cousin in 1963 but died a year later.

LEE 2 The Right Noble Thomas Duke of Leeds, Marquis of Carmarthen, Earl of Danby, Viscount Latimer, Baron Osborne of Kiveton, & Knight of the most Noble Order of the Garter 1701 F*21

A nice early full armorial for Thomas, 1st Duke of Leeds.

ARMS: Quarterly, 1, quarterly ermine and azure, a cross or (Osborne), 2. barry of five argent and gules, on a canton gules a cross of St George or, 3. argent, a chevron vert between three annulets gules, 4. azure, on a fess fimbriated

LEE 2

LEE 3

with fleur de lys, between three horses, 2 and 1, argent, three rooks sable.

CREST: An heraldic tiger passant or, tufted and maned sable (Osborne).

SUPPORTERS: Dexter – a griffin rampant or; sinister an heraldic tiger rampant argent, both ducally gorged azure.

MOTTO: PAX IN BELLO – Peace in war.

LEE 3 **Anonymous** NIF

A mid-eighteenth century armorial possibly for Thomas Osborne, 4th Duke of Leeds showing arms and supporters upon a compartment bearing a motto, all under a duke's coronet. The plate is signed in the bottom right hand corner – 'T. Spendelowe Sculp^t.'

ARMS: Quarterly ermine and azure, overall a cross or.

SUPPORTERS: Dexter, a griffin or, sinister an heraldic tiger argent, both gorged with a ducal coronet.

MOTTO: Pax in bello – Peace in war.

LEE 4 **Osborne Duke of Leeds** NIF

A fine classical mid-eighteenth century rococo bookplate for Thomas, the fourth duke. It is signed bottom right, 'B. Clowes Inv. and Sculp.'. Born in 1713 Thomas succeeded to the dukedom in 1731 and was installed as a Knight of the Garter in 1750. As this is not shown on the bookplate it is likely the plate was made between these two dates. He was made a Privy Counsellor in 1757 and died in 1789.

LEE 5 **LEEDS** NIF

An early nineteenth century plate for the sixth duke showing the shield with supporters under a duke's coronet.

ARMS: Osborne, quarterly, 1 and 4, quarterly ermine and azure, over all a cross or (Osborne); 2 and 3, azure, three mullets, 2 and 1 between nine cross crosslets 3, 3 and 3 argent (D'Arcy); impaling Townshend, quarterly 1 and 4, azure, a chevron ermine between three escallops argent (Townshend); 2 and 3, quarterly gules and or, in the first quarter a mullet argent (Vere).

The sixth duke married, in 1797, Charlotte, daughter of George, 1st Marquess Townshend.

LEE 6 **Leeds** F22436

A nineteenth century ducal crest bookplate possibly for George, the sixth duke, or his son Francis the seventh duke. Under a duke's coronet it shows two crests, one for Osborne, an heraldic tiger passant or tufted and maned sable and the other for Godolphin, a dolphin embowed sable. The fourth duke, Thomas, married, in 1740, Mary, younger daughter and co-heir of Francis, 2nd Earl of Godolphin, on whose death the daughters inherited the family arms and passed them on to their children.

LEE 4

LEE 5

LEE 6

The Right Honble Charles Montagu Earl of Manchester Viscount Mandevile and Baron Montagu of Kimbolton 1704

MAN 1 The Right Honble Charles Montagu Earl of Manchester Viscount Mandevile and Baron Montagu of Kimbolton 1704
F20872

An early armorial for Charles 4th Earl of Manchester dated 1704. The achievement is on a ribbon but no motto is shown. He succeeded to the earldom in 1682 and in 1719 was created Duke of Manchester by George I.

ARMS: Quarterly 1 and 4, argent, three lozenges conjoined in fess gules, within a bordure sable (Montagu); 2 and 3, or, an eagle displayed vert, beaked and membered gules (Monthermer).

CREST: A griffin's head or between two wings sable collared argent charged with three lozenges gules.

SUPPORTERS: Dexter, an heraldic antelope or armed tufted and unguled argent; sinister, a griffin or collared as the crest.

MOTTO: Disponendo me, non mutando me – By disposing not by changing me (not shown).

Dukes of Manchester

FAMILY NAME: Montagu

CREATION OF DUKEDOM: 28th April 1719

COURTESY TITLE OF ELDEST SON: Viscount Mandeville

COURTESY TITLE OF GRANDSON: Lord Kimbolton

PRINCIPAL RESIDENCE: Kimbolton Castle, Bedfordshire (until 1950)

Henry Montagu, second son of Sir Edward Montagu of Boughton, Northamptonshire, was born *c*.1563. He was educated at Christ's College, Cambridge becoming a barrister (Middle Temple) and Member of Parliament for Hingham Ferrers. He was later Recorder of London and Lord High Treasurer. He was created Viscount Mandeville and Baron Kimbolton on 19th December 1620. He went on to become Earl of Manchester on 5th February 1625/6. He held numerous Government posts and was High Steward of Cambridge University.

He married firstly, on 1st June 1601, Catherine, daughter of Sir William Spencer. She died on 7th December 1612 whereafter he married Anne, widow of Sir Leonard Halliday, Lord Mayor of London. She also died at a date unknown whereupon he married thirdly on 26th April 1620, Margaret, widow of John Hare. Henry died on 7th November 1642 thought to be aged about eighty and buried at Kimbolton.

He was succeeded by his eldest son, by his first wife, Edward, born in 1602 and educated at Sidney Sussex College, Cambridge. He was styled variously Viscount Mandeville, a courtesy title, or Lord Kimbolton which he was by right having been summoned to Parliament in his father's lifetime under his father's barony of Kimbolton 22nd May 1626. He was a royalist supporter, Lord Lieutenant of Huntingdonshire and Colonel of a Regiment of Foot which he commanded at the Battle of Edge Hill on 23rd October 1642. He was Commander-in-Chief at the Battle of Marston Moor on 2nd July 1644 and later was one of the few peers to find favour with Oliver Cromwell and the Commonwealth. He took an active part in bringing about the restoration of the monarchy in 1660 and was given the Garter on 15th April 1661.

He married no less than five times. After the death of each wife he remarried within the year. His last wife was Margaret, widow of James Hay, Earl of Carlisle and daughter of Francis Russell, 4th Earl of Bedford. He died suddenly, of the colic on 7th May 1671. Although he was buried in the family vault at Kimbolton, his widow, who died on 1st December 1676, was buried in the Russell family vault at Chenies in Buckinghamshire.

He was succeeded as third earl by Robert his eldest son, by his second wife, who was baptised on 25th April 1634. He was styled as Viscount Mandeville after his father inherited the earldom. He was a Whig supporter and Member of Parliament for Huntingdonshire 1660–71. He was one of six lords in the deputation to The Hague sent by Parliament on 7th May 1660 to invite the return of Charles II. He followed his father as High Steward of Cambridge University and was Lord Lieutenant of Huntingdonshire, 1671–81. He served as a captain in the Duke of Monmouth's Regiment of Foot before taking his seat in the Lords on 4th February 1672/3.

He married, on 27th June 1655, Anne, daughter of Sir Christopher Yelverton Bt. They had three sons, but two predeceased him, and three daughters. He died at Montpelier, France on 14th March 1682/3 and was brought home and buried in the family tomb at Kimbolton.

He was succeeded as fourth earl by his third son, Charles. Born *c*.1662 he was educated at St Paul's School and Trinity College, Cambridge. He went on the Grand Tour with his friend, Peregrine Bertie, in 1686. He was a strong supporter of the Glorious Revolution and was the bearer of St Edward's Staff at the coronation of William and Mary on 11th April 1689. He fought at the Battle of the Boyne in 1689. He was Lord Lieutenant of Huntingdonshire and followed his father as High Steward of Cambridge University. On 28th April 1719 he was created Duke of Manchester by George I (MAN 1).

He married, on 26th February 1690/1, Dodington, (she was named after her maternal grandfather, John Dodington) second and youngest daughter of Robert Greville, 4th Lord Brooke. She died on 6th February 1720/1 at Kimbolton and he died on 20th January 1721/2 of the colic but, for

MAR 1 **Anonymous** NIF

ARMS: Quarterly with the pronomal arms in the first quarter, sable, a lion rampant argent, on a canton of the last a cross of St. George gules (Churchill), As an honourable augmentation, in centre point an escutcheon of France, azure three fleur-de-lys or.

CRESTS:
1. On a wreath of the colours a lion couchant guardant argent supporting in the dexter paw a banner gules charged with a dexter hand appaumee of the first, staff or (Churchill).

2. Out of a ducal coronet or a griffin's head between two wings expanded argent, gorged with a bar gemelles and armed gules (Spencer) (neither shown).

SUPPORTERS: Two wyverns gules.

MOTTO: Fiel pero desdichado – Faithful though unfortunate.

As the 1st, 3rd and 4th dukes were all given the Garter, this plate could have belonged to any one of them.

Dukes of Marlborough

FAMILY NAME: Churchill, Spencer-Churchill

CREATION OF DUKEDOM: 14th December 1702

COURTESY TITLE OF ELDEST SON: Marquess of Blandford

COURTESY TITLE OF GRANDSON AND HEIR: (from 1733) Earl of Sunderland

PRINCIPAL RESIDENCE: Blenheim Palace, Woodstock, Oxfordshire

John Churchill (1650–1722) was the second son of Sir Winston Churchill an ardent royalist. So much so that in December 1661 the new King, Charles II, ordered a grant of augmentation to the Churchill arms in the form of a St George's cross gules on a canton argent for services to the late King (Charles I) as Captain of Horse and for his present loyalty as a member of the House of Commons.

John was born on 24th June 1650 at Ashe in Devon and educated at St Paul's School, London before entering the army in 1667 serving under the Duke of Monmouth. During the reign of Charles II he served in the Household of James, Duke of York. In 1682 he was created Baron Churchill of Eyemouth in Berwickshire, and became Colonel of the Royal Regiment of Dragoons.

On the accession of James II in 1685 he was made Ambassador to Paris and later Gentleman of the Bedchamber to the King. He was created Baron Churchill of Sandridge, Hertfordshire, one of only ten peerages created by James II. He was Governor of the Hudson Bay Company 1685–91 and served continuously in several Foot Regiments being made Lieutenant General in 1688. However, he turned against his benefactor, King James, giving as his reason his hatred of Popery, and supported the accession of Princess Mary and her husband, William of Orange as King and Queen.

As a result, two days before their coronation he was created Earl of Marlborough, in Wiltshire. Apparently this particular title was chosen because of a remote family connection with a previous holder of the title, James Ley, 1st Earl of Marlborough of an earlier creation (1625).

He became a Privy Counsellor, Gentleman of the Bedchamber to William III and Commander of the English forces in the Netherlands (1690). However he seems to have been something of a double turncoat because he was dismissed from these three posts in 1691 on well-founded suspicions of intrigues with the exiled James II. By 1698 he was back in favour with William III, restored as a Privy Counsellor and became a Cabinet Minister.

In 1701 he became Commander-in-Chief of the English and Dutch forces in the Netherlands and on the accession of Queen Anne he was given the Garter and became Ambassador to The Hague. War having been declared against France and Spain he became Supreme General of the Allied Forces and Master General of Ordnance. He was a successful commander and was rewarded in 1702 by being created Marquess of Blandford and Duke of Marlborough with a grant of £5,000 a year during the Queen's lifetime. In August 1704 he won a crushing defeat over the French at Blenheim but at a cost of four thousand, five hundred killed and seven thousand, five hundred wounded on his own side and forty thousand killed and wounded and eleven thousand taken prisoner on the French side.

His reward for this was a grant of around twenty-two thousand acres of land at Woodstock and Wootton in Oxfordshire, the site of the future Blenheim Palace. He continued with a further series of victories against the French at Ramillies, Oudenarde and Malplaquet.

By 1706 he had no male issue surviving so he obtained a complicated Act of Parliament which declared that his honours, failing heirs male of his body were to devolve on his eldest daughter, Harriet, wife of Francis Godolphin, son and heir apparent of Sidney, Lord Godolphin and the heirs male of her body and in default of which to his second daughter, Anne, wife of Charles Earl of Sunderland and the heirs male of her body and in default of which to his third daughter, Elizabeth wife of Scrope, Earl of Bridgewater and the heirs male of her body and, finally, in default of which to his youngest daughter, Mary, wife of John Montagu, son and heir apparent of Ralph, Duke of Montagu, and the heirs male of her body. It became even more complicated because the Act goes on to say that failing heirs male of any of his daughters the honours shall fall to their daughters in order of precedence and to the heirs male of their bodies and failing that the heirs female. It was the intention that the honours of the first duke *'shall continue, remain and be invested in all the issue of the said Duke so long as any such issue, male or female, shall continue'*.

It would appear that the duke was much taken with receiving bribes for various reasons. So much so that in 1711 he was dismissed from all his lucrative offices. However he was restored to many of them after the accession of George I in 1714. He was a Tory until 1705 but thereafter supported the Whigs who in turn supported the new Hanoverian monarchy. He was probably little different from many who held high office at that time, being sure to always end up on the winning side and to take advantage of opportunities offered.

In 1678 he married Sarah, second daughter and co-heir of Richard Jennings of Sandridge in Hertfordshire. She went on to become a close confidant of Queen Anne and famous in her own right. She was Groom of the Stole, Keeper of the Privy Purse and Mistress of the Robes to the Queen and also Ranger of Windsor Park.

The duke died in 1722 aged seventy-two leaving no living male issue. His son, John, had died of smallpox at Kings College, Cambridge in 1702. Therefore, in accordance with the Act of Parliament, the 1st duke was succeeded by his eldest daughter, Henrietta, wife of Francis, 2nd Earl Godolphin, suo jure Duchess of Marlborough, Marchioness of Blandford etc. She died in 1733 without any living male issue when her Churchill honours devolved on her nephew, Charles Spencer, being the third, but only surviving, son of Charles Spencer, 3rd Earl of Sunderland and his wife, Anne, second daughter of the 1st Duke of Marlborough.

Charles was born in 1706, educated at Eton and succeeded his brother as 5th Earl of Sunderland in 1729. He had a successful military career, distinguishing himself at the Battle of Dettingen in 1743 and being knighted on the field of battle by the King, George II. The last time an English Monarch took an active part in the battlefield. The new duke went on to hold high office in Government being Lord Privy Seal in 1755 and Lord Steward of the Household 1749–55. He had been given the Garter in 1740.

He married, in 1732, Elizabeth, daughter and heir of Thomas, 2nd Lord Trevor. She brought him £20,000 on marriage. He died of a fever whilst in camp at Munster in Westphalia in 1758 in his fifty-second year.

He was succeeded as fourth duke by his son, George Spencer, born on 26th January 1738/9 and also educated at Eton before entering the army. He became Lord Lieutenant of Oxfordshire at the age of twenty-one and held the post for the rest of his life. He was the bearer of the sceptre at the coronation of George III in 1761. He was Lord Chamberlain of the Household, Lord Privy Seal and elected a Privy Counsellor in 1762. He was installed as a Knight of the Garter in 1768.

On 23rd August 1762 he married Caroline, daughter of John Russell, 4th Duke of Bedford. She had been one of the ten train bearers at the marriage of Queen Charlotte to George III. In later life the Queen described her as *'the proudest woman in England'*

The fourth duke died on 8th January 1817 at Blenheim Palace and was succeeded by his son George Spencer (MAR 2). Born 6th March 1766 he was educated at Eton and Christ Church, Oxford before going on to become a Member of Parliament. He sat as a Whig supporter for Oxford 1790–6 and then changed sides and sat as the Member for Tregony as a Tory supporter. He was a Lord of the Treasury 1804–06 and was summoned to Parliament in 1806 in his father's subsidiary title as Baron Spencer. In 1817 he took the surname of Churchill after that of Spencer by Royal Licence.

He had married, in 1791, Susan, second daughter of John Stewart, 7th Earl of Galloway (MAR 3). He built up a considerable library at great expense including a copy of Boccaccio's Decamerone published in 1471 and bought for £2,260 in 1812. He later sold it on to Earl Spencer, in 1819, for only 875 guineas. In fact, due to his extravagance, the whole of his library had to be disposed of in his lifetime in four thousand, seven hundred and one lots realising considerably less than the duke had paid for them. He spent his declining years in seclusion in one small corner of his vast palace at Woodstock and died there on 5th March 1840.

The sixth duke, born on 27th December 1793, was his son and heir George Spencer-Churchill. Like his father he was educated at Eton and Christ Church, Oxford. He sat as Member of Parliament for Chippenham, as a Tory, 1818–20, and then for Woodstock three times between 1821 and 1840 when he became duke.

He married three times. His first wife, whom he married in 1819, was his cousin Jane, daughter of his maternal uncle George Stewart, 8th Earl of Galloway. She died in 1844. He then married, in 1846, Charlotte Augusta, fifth daughter of Henry, 4th Viscount Ashbrook. She too died four years later and after a year he entered his third marriage, this time to another cousin Jane, daughter of the Honourable Edward Stewart younger brother of George, 8th Earl of Galloway. The sixth duke died on 1st July 1857 at Blenheim aged sixty-three and was succeeded by his son.

John Winston Spencer Churchill, the seventh duke was born in June 1822 and styled Earl of Sunderland and later Marquess of Blandford. He was educated at Eton and Oriel College, Oxford before becoming Conservative Member of Parliament for Woodstock 1844–57 and Lord Lieutenant of Oxfordshire from 1857 until his death.

He married, in 1843, Frances Anne, daughter of Charles, 3rd Marquess of Londonderry. He became a Privy Counsellor in 1866 and was given the Garter in 1868. He was Viceroy of Ireland (as Lord Lieutenant) 1876–80. His administration was popular as he endeavoured to benefit the trade of that country. His wife instituted a famine relief fund which raised over £100,000 which was spent on seed potatoes, food and clothing.

During his tenure of the dukedom he began a series of sales of the family collections. A collection of jewellery, sold in one lot, raised £10,000 in 1875, the Sunderland Library went for nearly £60,000 in 1882/3 (MAR 4), the Blenheim Collection of enamels raised over £73,000 and in 1884/5 eleven pictures were sold; nine of them went abroad but two, a Raphael (£70,000) and Vandyke's equestrian portrait of Charles I (£17,500) were purchased for the nation.

He died suddenly, from heart disease, being found dead in his bed on the 5th July 1883 and was succeeded by his son George Charles Spencer-Churchill. Born in 1844 and educated at Eton he became an officer in the Horse Guards 1863–9. In the latter year he married Albertha, daughter of James, 1st Duke of Abercorn. She had the marriage dissolved by decree nisi in 1883 because of her husband's proven adultery with the Countess of Aylsford.

He married again in June 1888 Lilian, daughter of Cicero Price Commander of the U.S.A. navy and widow of Louis Hammersley of New York. He died, suddenly, aged forty-eight in November 1892 leaving an estate valued at over £350,000, more than double that left by his predecessor.

The ninth duke was his son, Charles, by his first wife. He was born in Simla India on 13th November 1871. Educated at Winchester and Trinity College, Cambridge he served in numerous high offices; Pay Master General 1899–1902, Under Secretary of State for the Colonies 1903–05, Privy Counsellor 1894. He also served in the Great War 1914–18

as Lieutenant Colonel on the General Staff. He became a Knight of the Garter in 1902.

He married on 6th November 1896, in New York, Consuela daughter of William Vanderbilt a wealthy American financier. He was one of a number of peers who were marrying rich American heiresses at that time partly in an attempt to restore their family fortunes. In 1902, whilst on a trip to St Petersburg, the duke commissioned from Carl Faberge one of his magnificent gold and enamelled Easter Eggs in the form of a band clock as a present for the duchess. The marriage, however, was not a particularly happy one and ended in 1921 with Consuela petitioning for and obtaining a divorce.

MAR 2 **Marquis of Blandford Ch. Ch.** F5842

A late eighteenth century plate showing the arms of Spencer quartering Churchill with supporters, coronet and crest.

George Spencer, son of the fourth duke, was born in 1766 and would have been attending Christ Church Oxford in the 1780s when he commissioned this bookplate. He succeeded as fifth duke in 1817. He built up a considerable library which he later had to sell to pay his debts. He died in reduced circumstances in 1840.

MAR 2

MAR 3 The Right Honble the Earl of Galloway F28127

A mid-eighteenth century armorial bookplate for Alexander Stewart, 6th Earl of Galloway showing the arms of Stewart: or, a fess argent and azure overall a bend engrailed gules within a bordure flory counter flory gules.

There was a close relationship between the Spencer-Churchill family and the Stewarts. The fifth duke married Susan, daughter of John, 7th Earl of Galloway in 1791. The sixth duke married firstly, Jane, daughter of George, the eighth earl, in 1819 and then married thirdly Jane, daughter of the Honourable Edward Stewart, younger brother of the eighth earl.

MAR 4 From the Sunderland Library Blenheim Palace NIF

A small seal type armorial bookplate possibly commissioned by the seventh duke to be inserted into books from the Sunderland Library which he sold in 1882. The Sunderland Library had come into the Marlborough family in 1733 when Charles 5th Earl of Sunderland inherited the dukedom. The arms are those of Spencer under an earl's coronet.

MAR 5 Blenheim Palace

A small pictorial bookplate depicting a view of Blenheim Palace under conjoined 'M's' and a duke's coronet.

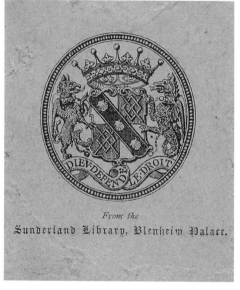

JOHN CHURCHILL, DUKE of MARLBOROUGH

London Published as the Act directs May 30.th 1801 by J.Wilkes

John Churchill, 1st Duke of Marlborough, 1650–1722. A military man and statesman whose life spanned the reign of five monarchs. For his many services to his country and success in battles, Queen Anne created him 1st Duke of Marlborough in 1702.

NEW 1 **The Most Noble John Duke of Newcastle Marquis & Earl of Clare Baron Haughton of Haughton and Knight of yᵉ Most Noble Order of the Garter**

(second creation 1694) F15108

An early armorial bookplate for John Holles, son of Gilbert, 3rd Earl of Clare. He succeeded to his father's earldom in 1689 and in the same year he married Margaret Cavendish third daughter and co-heir of Henry Cavendish, 2nd Duke of Newcastle (first creation) As a result of his marriage he was created Duke of Newcastle (second creation) in 1694. He received the Garter in 1698 and died in 1711 when the dukedom again became extinct.

ARMS: Quarterly of twelve with the arms of Holles, ermine, two piles in chief sable, in the pronomal quarter. The arms of Cavendish, sable, three bucks heads caboshed or, are in pretence.

CREST: On a chapeau gules turned up ermine a boar azure charged with a crescent argent.

SUPPORTERS: Dexter, a lion rampant; sinister, a wolf rampant.

MOTTO: Spes audaces audiuvat – Hope assists the brave (Holles).

116

Dukes of Newcastle

FAMILY NAME: Cavendish, Pelham-Holles, Pelham-Clinton

CREATIONS OF DUKEDOMS OF NEWCASTLE-ON-TYNE: first, 16th March 1664; second, 14th May 1694; third, 11th August 1715.

COURTESY TITLE OF ELDEST SON: Earl of Ogle

CREATION OF DUKEDOM OF NEWCASTLE-UNDER-LYME: 17th November 1756

COURTESY TITLE OF ELDEST SON: Earl of Lincoln

PRINCIPAL RESIDENCE: Clumber Park, Ollerton, Nottinghamshire.

The dukedom of Newcastle was bestowed, in the seventeenth century, upon a branch of the Cavendish family, earls and dukes of Devonshire.

William Cavendish was the son and heir of Sir Charles Cavendish of Welbeck Abbey, Nottinghamshire, younger brother of William, 1st Earl of Devonshire. Born in 1593 he was educated at St John's College, Cambridge. He was made a Knight of the Bath in 1610 and sat as Member of Parliament for East Retford, Nottinghamshire. He succeeded his father in 1617 and two years later entertained the King, James I, at Welbeck Abbey.

He was created Viscount Mansfield in 1620. The reason for this would appear to be that he was executor of the estate of his uncle by marriage, Gilbert, Earl of Shrewsbury, who died in 1616. There was some dispute over the Will and one John Woodford noted in 1620 – *'In order to settle the dispute between the heirs of the late Earl of Shrewsbury and Sir William Cavendish … to whom the Countess of Shrewsbury, prisoner in the Tower, gave some of the lands, it is determined to create Cavendish Viscount Mansfield.'* Exactly how this resolved the dispute is not explained.

The new viscount served as Lord Lieutenant of Nottinghamshire 1626–42 and also, during the minority of the Earl of Devonshire, for Derbyshire 1628–38. In 1627 he was made Baron Cavendish and Earl of Newcastle-on-Tyne. He entertained the King a second time at Welbeck Abbey in 1633, this time Charles I on his way to Scotland. He acted as governor and tutor to the young Prince Charles (Charles II).

With the outbreak of the Civil War he raised the King's Standard in the North and, leading his troops, fought valiantly and with considerable success over the whole of the north east of England from the Humber northwards. In 1643 he was further honoured becoming Marquess of Newcastle-on-Tyne.

Following the disastrous Battle of Marston Moor in July 1644 he left England for the Continent, firstly to Hamburg then Paris where he joined the young Prince, the future King Charles II, in exile. He was a great equestrian and whilst on the Continent set up a riding school and wrote a definitive treatise on horsemanship. He was nominated as a Knight of the Garter, 12th January 1649 but for obvious reasons not installed until after the Restoration, 15th April 1661.

Finally, as a reward for all his losses in the royal cause, particularly financially, he was created, 16th March 1664, Earl of Ogle and Duke of Newcastle-on-Tyne. (It was estimated, by his wife, that his total financial losses amounted to a staggering £941,303). In the patent creating him duke the king said *'We shall always retain a sense of those good principles he instilled unto us.'* Amongst those principles were: *'a man cannot be too civil to a woman'* and *'a too devout man may be a bad King.'*

He married firstly, c.1618, Elizabeth, widow of the Honourable Henry Howard, who bore him four sons and after her death, in 1643, he married again, in Paris in 1645, Margaret, sister of John, 1st Lord Lucas.

She was thought to be a somewhat odd lady and certainly ahead of her time. She wrote several books on natural philosophy and even challenged the thinking of members of the Royal Society. She had been a lady of the court of Queen Henrietta Maria where she was regarded as a natural fool. She became known as Mad Madge. Following the Restoration, the Marquess had to leave his wife in Paris as a security for his bad debts and had some difficulty in raising the money to redeem her.

The Loyal Duke, as he was called latterly died at Welbeck Abbey on 25th December 1676. His first three sons having predeceased him he was succeeded as second duke by his fourth son Henry, born 24th June 1630, styled in his early years, Viscount Mansfield and later Earl of Ogle.

Henry was Member of Parliament for Derby in 1660 and for Northumberland 1661–76 and Lord Lieutenant of the same county 1670–88. He had a commission to raise a Regiment of Foot for James II in 1688 and opposed the settlement of the crown on William and Mary. After their accession he refused to take the Oath of Allegiance and retired from public life resigning all offices. He died on 26th July 1691 without male issue, but leaving three daughters,when all his titles, except the Barony of Ogle, became extinct. However, the Dukedom of Newcastle-on-Tyne was recreated, three years later for his son-in-law, John Holles, the 4th Earl of Clare (NEW 1, 2 and 3).

John Holles, Earl of Clare and Baron Haughton was son and heir of Gilbert, 3rd Earl of Clare. He succeeded to his father's earldom in 1689. Being a strong supporter of the ruling Whig Party he was, in consequence of his marriage in 1689 to his first cousin Margaret, third daughter and co-heir to the 2nd Duke of Newcastle-on-Tyne, created, in 1694, Marquess of Clare and Duke of Newcastle-on-Tyne. Unfortunately this marriage also was not productive of a male heir so when he died, as the result of falling from his horse on 15th July 1711, aged forty-nine, all his honours became extinct. His daughter Henrietta (NEW 4) married Edward Harley, 1st Earl of Oxford.

What nature failed to provide the King was able to recreate and the dukedom of Newcastle-on-Tyne was recreated a third time in 1715, this was for the late duke's nephew, son of his sister, Grace, wife of Thomas, 1st Lord Pelham. This nephew, Thomas, was born on 1st July 1693 and educated at Westminster School and Clare College, Cambridge. He inherited the Holles Estate on the death of his uncle, the third duke and at the same time took the name of Holles in addition to that of Pelham.

Being also a strong supporter of the Whigs and the Hanoverian Succession he was in favour and created Viscount Haughton and Earl of Clare in 1714 with special remainder, failing heirs male, to his brother Henry Pelham. Henry was a key figure in mid-eighteenth century political life. He served as 1st Lord of the Treasury, i.e. Prime Minister, from 1743 till his death in 1754.

Within the year Thomas had been further elevated as Marquess of Clare and Duke of Newcastle-on-Tyne with similar special remainder. He held, in succession, numerous Lord Lieutenancies and was appointed Steward of Sherwood Forest and Lord Chamberlain of the Household. He was Chancellor of the University of Cambridge 1748–68.

He married, in 1717, Henrietta, elder daughter and co-heir of Francis, Earl Godolphin. Her younger sister and co-heir, Mary, married Thomas, 4th Duke of Leeds, in 1740.

His brother, Henry, having died in 1754 and Thomas having at that time no male issue he persuaded the King to create two new honours for him, Duke of Newcastle-under-Lyme in 1756 (the only commoner dukedom that George II created) and Baron Pelham of Stanmer in 1762 with specific but different remainders in both cases.

He died in 1768 aged seventy-five still with no direct male heir. As a result all his honours, except the two last mentioned, became extinct. Under the special remainder the Dukedom of Newcastle-under-Lyme fell to Henry Clinton, 9th Earl of Lincoln (NEW 5, 6 and 7), and his heirs male by his wife, Catherine, who was a niece of the deceased duke Thomas.

Henry had been born in 1720 and educated at Eton and Clare College, Cambridge. He succeeded to the earldom of Lincoln when he was only ten years old, on the death of his elder brother in 1730. In adult life he held multiple offices under the Crown and in the Royal Household. He married his cousin Catherine, daughter of the Prime Minister, Henry Pelham, in 1744 and succeeded his paternal (and his wife's maternal) uncle as 2nd Duke of Newcastle-under-Lyne in 1768. He also took the name of Pelham before that of Clinton by Royal Licence.

It would appear that he was somewhat of a rake in his youth and later Horace Walpole said of him – *'he was the adopted heir of the Duke of Newcastle and the mimic of his fulsome fondness and follies, but with more honour and more pride. As the Duke, his uncle was a political weathercock he was a political weatherglass, his quicksilver being always up at insolence or down at despair.'*

He died on 22nd February 1794 'of paralysis' and, his two elder sons having predeceased him, was succeeded by his third son, Thomas, as 3rd Duke of Newcastle-under-Lyme and 10th Earl of Lincoln.

Thomas was born on 28th July 1751 and educated at Eton. He entered the army as was the lot of many third sons at that time. Before succeeding to the title he had risen to the rank of Major General. He was later Steward of Sherwood Forest and Lord Lieutenant of Nottinghamshire. He married, after his succession, on 5th May 1782 Anna Maria, fifth and youngest daughter of William, 2nd Earl of Harrington. He died at a young age, only forty-three, in 1795 and his death was said to be due to '*the violent operation of an emetic which he had taken for whooping cough*'. It sounds as though he choked to death.

He was succeeded, as fourth duke, by his ten year old son Henry Pelham-Clinton, Earl of Lincoln. He was educated at Eton, given the Garter in 1812, and went on to fill his father's roles as Steward of Sherwood Forest and Lord Lieutenant of Nottinghamshire 1809–39. He was dismissed from these offices by the Government for his violent objection to a Whig Dissenter being appointed a magistrate. When he appealed to the Duke of Wellington he was told he deserved his fate.

It was said of the fourth duke that he was not a wise man. He was very aristocratic and conservative in his politics. When criticised for ejecting tenants from some of his properties in Newark he famously replied '*Shall I not do what I like with my own?*' This so inflamed the local mob that they burnt down his mansion in Nottingham Castle.

He married, in 1807, Georgiana, second daughter of Edward Mundy of Shipley, a wealthy heiress who had landed estates worth £12,000 and a dowry of £190,000. They were to have thirteen children and she died in child bed at the family home Clumber Park, Nottinghamshire on 26th September 1822 aged only thirty-three years. The duke died in 1851 when he was succeeded by his eldest son and heir, Henry. (NEW 8 is for either father or son.)

Henry Pelham-Clinton, 5th Duke of Newcastle-under-Lyme, was born in 1811 and educated at Eton and Christ Church, Oxford. He had a political career, was Member of Parliament for South Nottinghamshire, Lord of the Treasury 1834–5 and Secretary of State for the Colonies 1852–6. He was given the Garter in 1860 and was Provincial Grand Master of the Nottinghamshire Freemasons. He married in 1832 Susan Harriet, only daughter of Alexander, 10th Duke of Hamilton, but divorced her in 1850. He died at Clumber Park in 1864 aged fifty-three.

The sixth duke was his son Henry Alexander, born on 25th June 1834 and educated at Eton and Christ Church, Oxford. Unusually, for a peer, he married a girl who was illegitimate. On 11th February 1861, in Paris, he married Adela Hope, the illegitimate daughter and testamentary heiress of Henry Thomas Hope of Deepdene. Having fathered two sons, who succeeded him, he died suddenly aged forty-five on 27th February 1879.

Henry Archibald Pelham-Clinton-Hope, the seventh duke (NEW 9 and 10) was born on 28th September 1864 and educated at Eton and Magdalene College, Oxford. He married, on 20th February 1889, Kathleen daughter of Henry Candy, a Major in the 9th Lancers. He died, without issue, on 30th May 1928 and was succeeded as eighth duke by his brother Henry Francis Pelham-Clinton-Hope.

The dukedom became extinct in 1988 on the death of the twelfth duke, Edward Charles Pelham-Clinton, due to lack of a male heir.

NEW 2 **The Most Noble John Duke of Newcastle Marquis & Earl of Clare Baron Haughton of Haughton and Knight of ye Most Noble Order of the Garter** F15109

A smaller version of NEW 1 with only the pronomal arms shown and the arms of Cavendish in pretence. As the motto of the Garter is shown in both cases the plates date after 1698 and before the duke's death in 1711.

NEW 2

NEW 3 The Most Noble John Duke of Newcastle Marquis & Earl of Clare Baron Haughton of Haughton and Knight of yᵉ Most Noble Order of the Garter 1702 FI5I08

A similar plate to NEW I but by a totally different hand. The most obvious differences are in the mantling and the fact that this plate is dated. The boar in the crest is less well endowed than in NEW I.

John Holles, 4th Earl of Clare, married, 1689, his cousin Margaret, co-heir of Henry, 2nd Duke of Newcastle. The Duke died in 1691 and three years later his son-in-law was created Duke of Newcastle, 2nd creation. He died, without leaving a male heir, in 1711 when the dukedom again became extinct.

NEW 4 Henrietta Cavendish Holles Oxford and Mortimer. Given me by NIF

This well-known bookplate dating from the second quarter of the eighteenth century shows a library interior with symbols of the arts and sciences in a baroque framework with titling below.

Lady Henrietta Cavendish Holles was born on 11th February 1711 the only child of John Holles, Duke of Newcastle on Tyne. She married Edward Harley, 1st Earl of Oxford.

NEW 5 **Anonymous** F6116

A mid-eighteenth century armorial bookplate showing the shield and supporters under an earl's coronet enclosed in a mantle. The shield is surrounded by the Garter motto.

ARMS: Quarterly of six with the Clinton arms: argent, six cross crosslets fitchee sable, 3,2 and 1; on a chief azure two mullets or pierced gules in the pronomal quarter The arms of Pelham are shown in pretence, quarterly 1 and 4, azure, three pelicans vulning themselves proper, 2 and 3, gules, two demi belts with buckles argent, the buckles in chief.

Henry Clinton, born in 1720, succeeded to the earldom of Lincoln, when only ten years old, on the death of his elder brother in 1730. In 1744 he married his cousin, Catherine, daughter of the then Prime Minister Henry Pelham. In 1768 on the death of his paternal uncle (and his wife's maternal uncle), Thomas, 1st Duke of Newcastle under Lyme he succeeded as second duke and took the name of Pelham before that of Clinton by Royal Licence.

NEW 6 **Anonymous** F6117

A simple, mid-eighteenth century armorial consisting of the arms surrounded by a garter bearing the family motto and surmounted by an earl's coronet.

ARMS: Grand quarters, I and IV, argent, six cross crosslets fitchee, 3,2 and 1, on a chief azure two mullets or pierced

gules (Clinton); II and III quarterly 1 and 4, azure, three pelicans argent vulning themselves proper (Pelham); 2 and 3 gules, two demi belts in pale with buckles argent in chief (Reputedly an augmentation of honour in memory of Sir William Pelham taking King John of France prisoner at Poitiers in 1356).

MOTTO: Loyaute n'a honte – Loyalty is not ashamed.

Henry Clinton was born in 1720. His father, the seventh earl died in 1728 and his elder brother, the eighth earl, died in 1730 when Henry, aged ten, succeeded as ninth earl. He married his cousin Catherine Pelham, daughter of his uncle Henry Pelham in 1744 when he took the name and arms of Clinton by Licence. He was given the Garter in 1752, this plate pre-dates that event (see NEW 7).

NEW 7 **Anonymous** F6114

This is a similar plate to NEW 6 but not an altered version; there are many variations in the detail. In addition the Garter now bears the garter motto and the coronet has become that of a duke.

Henry Pelham-Clinton, 9th Earl of Lincoln, succeeded to the dukedom, in 1768, on the death of his wife's uncle the first duke, under the special remainder granted with the title. The second duke died in 1794.

NEW 6

NEW 7

NEW 8

NEW 9

NEW 8 **Anonymous** NIF

A small armorial bookplate showing the shield surrounded by the Garter motto and supporters, with two crests and a duke's coronet above and the family motto – Loyaulte n'a honte – on a ribbon below.

ARMS: Clinton quartering Pelham and the crests – 1. Out of a ducal crown gules, a plume of five ostrich feathers argent banded with a line chevron wise azure (Clinton) 2. On a wreath of the colours a peacock in his pride proper (Pelham).

This bookplate is either for Henry Pelham-Clinton, the fourth duke or Henry Pelham-Clinton, the fifth duke who were both given the Garter, in 1812 and 1860 respectively.

NEW 9 **HENRY PELHAM ARCHIBALD DOUGLAS VII DUKE OF NEWCASTLE**
NIF

A nice late nineteenth century panel armorial for the seventh duke who succeeded in 1879. It shows the full achievement with the arms of Clinton quartering Pelham and the two crested helms above upon a duke's coronet.

Although Henry married, in 1889, Kathleen, daughter of Henry Candy he died childless in 1928 and was succeeded by his brother Henry Francis Pelham-Clinton-Hope as eighth duke.

NEW 10 **HENRY PELHAM ARCHIBALD DOUGLAS Seventh Duke of Newcastle** NIF

A fine pictorial bookplate showing a panelled interior with the ducal arms above the fireplace and repeated in the stained glass windows. The arms of Eton College are shown to the right of the fireplace. A hound sleeps before the fire and on the table are some books, a plate camera and tripod no doubt reflecting the duke's interests. The plate is signed 'W.P.B.'09'. It was engraved by Robert Osmond.

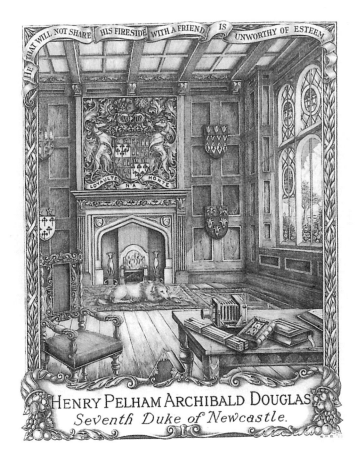

NEW 10

Stafford, Duke of Buckingham. He died at Kenninghall, Norfolk in 1554 aged eighty.

His son and heir apparent, by his second wife, was Henry Earl of Surrey who did not survive his father. He was indicted on a charge of high treason (quartering the arms of Edward the Confessor – see above) found guilty and executed on Tower Hill 19th January 1546/7 aged about thirty. This shows the considerable importance attached to armorial bearings, particularly those of the monarch, in those days.

He had married, in 1532, Frances daughter of John, Earl of Oxford who bore him a son, Thomas, who succeeded to his grandfather's titles and estates but not those of his father. As the fourth duke, Thomas went on to hold high office under Queen Elizabeth. Unfortunately he was ill advised enough to attempt to marry Mary, Queen of Scots, and place her on the throne. As a result he was charged with high treason. He was found guilty and attainted, all his honours were forfeited and he was sentenced to death. He was beheaded on Tower Hill on 2nd June 1572.

The duke had been married three times and had a son, Philip, by his first marriage to Mary daughter and sole heiress of Henry FitzAlan, Earl of Arundel. On the death of his maternal grandfather in 1580 Philip succeeded to the earldom of Arundel. In 1584 he converted to the catholic faith, which was risky in a protestant country. Whilst trying to leave England without a licence, he was arrested and imprisoned in the Tower of London where he remained until his death in 1595. In 1589 he had been attainted on a charge of high treason and all his honours were forfeited.

He had a son, Thomas born in 1585 who was educated at Westminster School and Trinity College, Cambridge. By Act of Parliament, 18th April 1604, he was 'restored to the blood' and to the titles of Earl of Arundel and Earl of Surrey and to such baronies as his grandfather, the late Duke of Norfolk, had possessed but not to the dukedom. He went on to hold high office under James I, was installed as a Knight of the Garter in 1611, made a Privy Counsellor in 1515 and, in 1621, was made Earl Marshal of England for life (this office only became hereditary in this family in 1672).

In 1627 he obtained an Act of Parliament 'For the annexing of the Castle, honour, manor and lordship of Arundel and the titles and dignitaries of the baronies of FitzAlan, Clun and Oswaldestre and Maltravers, settling the same on him and the heirs male of his body.' In 1641 he presented a petition to the King, signed by sixteen peers, praying to be restored to his grandfather's title as Duke of Norfolk. In reply the King, Charles I, created him, in June 1644, Earl of Norfolk. He died at Padua on 4th October 1646 aged sixty-one and was buried at Arundel, possessed of three earldoms, three baronies but no dukedom.

He was followed by Henry his second son, his first son having predeceased him, who, in turn, was followed by his son Thomas born in 1626. Thomas had been with his grandfather in Padua in 1645 when he had suffered 'a brain fever' which had severely affected his mental faculties. He remained in Padua under care and supervision supported by his relations. He was described as 'unapproachable, an incurable maniac' and 'with all the marks imaginable of lunacy'

Nevertheless, on the petition of a large number of his relatives and a number of other peers totalling ninety-one in all, he had restored to him, by Act of Parliament dated 29th December 1660, the dukedom of Norfolk. He never returned to England and died, unmarried, in Padua in 1677.

He was succeeded, as sixth duke, by his younger brother, Henry Howard, who was a staunch catholic. Born in 1628 he spent a large part of his early life abroad in Europe. He was back in London in 1666 when he was made a Fellow of the Royal Society on the 28th November. Pepys wrote in his diary 'Here is Mr Henry Howard that will, hereafter be Duke of Norfolk, who is admitted this day to the Society, who being a very proud man and one that values himself upon his family, writes his name as he do everywhere, Henry Howard of Norfolke'

In 1669, whilst still Mr Howard, he had been created Baron Howard of Castle Rising and in 1672 he was created Earl of Norwich and Earl Marshal of England entailed on the heirs male of his body.

In 1652 he had married Anne daughter of Edward Somerset, Marquess of Worcester. She died in 1662 and fifteen years later he married his mistress Jane Bickerton. John Evelyn wrote in his diary that the Duke had 'newly declared his marriage to his concubine, whom he promised me he would never marry'. He died at Arundel in 1683.

He was succeeded by his son by his first wife, Henry who was born in 1654 and educated at Magdalene College, Oxford. He was summoned to Parliament in his father's lifetime in his father's barony as Lord Mowbray. He served as Lord Lieutenant of Berkshire, Surrey and Norfolk and as Constable of Windsor Castle. He was installed as a Knight of the Garter in July 1685, the first knight nominated by James II. As Earl Marshal he was ordered by the King to conduct the Marshal's Court (Court of Chivalry) from time to time to hear causes, abuses having gone unenforced by discontinuance of the court since the Civil War started in 1641.

He married, in 1677, Mary, daughter of Henry Mordaunt, 2nd Earl of Peterborough. He separated from her in 1685 due to her misconduct and divorced her in 1700. He died, childless, in 1701.

His heir was his nephew, Thomas Howard, son of his brother Lord Thomas Howard. He was seventeen at the time of his succession as eighth duke (NORF 1). He married, in 1709, Maria daughter of Sir Nicholas Shireburn. She, aged sixteen on marriage, had a fortune of over £30,000. He died, again without issue, after a long illness in 1732 when he was succeeded, as ninth duke, by his brother, Edward. Another, younger, brother was Philip Howard of whose bookplate (NORF 2) a number of copies are to be found in the library at Arundel Castle.

Edward (NORF 3 and 4) had taken part in the Jacobite Rising of 1715 and, as a result, was tried for high treason. However due to the influence of his brother, the eighth duke, and the fact that no witnesses appeared against him he was acquitted. In 1722 he was again arrested on suspicion of partaking in a plot *'for dethroning the King and restoring the Pretender'*. He was never tried and was released on bail after six months imprisonment.

He married, in 1727 Mary, daughter of Edward Blount of Blagden in Devon. They had no children and when he died, in 1777, aged ninety-one the earldom of Norwich and the barony of Castle Rising became extinct. The dukedom and earldom of Norfolk, the earldoms of Arundel and Surrey and the baronies attached to them devolved on his cousin and heir, Charles Howard, who was the son of Henry Howard (NORF 5) and grandson of Lord Charles Howard, younger brother of Thomas the mentally ill 5th Duke of Norfolk

Born in 1720 Charles Howard, 10th Duke of Norfolk, had married, in 1739, Katherine, daughter and co-heiress of John Brockholes. They had one son, Charles, who on his father's death in 1786 became the eleventh duke. He was Member of Parliament for Carlisle 1780–6, Deputy Earl Marshal, before succeeding to the title, and Lord Lieutenant of the West Riding of Yorkshire. He married twice but he too died childless in 1815 when the dukedom fell to a third cousin, Bernard Edward Howard, who was a lineal descendent of the fifth duke, Thomas.

Bernard, the twelfth duke (NORF 6), was born in 1765 in Sheffield. He, too, was a staunch catholic but, following his succession, an Act of Parliament in 1824 empowered him

and his heirs and successors to exercise the office of Earl Marshal of England in spite of being of the Roman Catholic faith. He took his seat in the House of Lords for the first time in 1829 and became a Privy Counsellor in 1830. He was given the Garter in 1834.

In 1789 he had married Elizabeth, third daughter of Henry, Earl Fauconberg, but they were divorced by Act of Parliament in 1794 because of her infidelity with the Honourable Richard Bingham whom she married within days of the divorce. She had apparently been in love with him before her marriage to the duke which had been forced on her by her father. The duke died in London in March 1842 aged seventy-six and was succeeded by his only son Henry.

Henry, the thirteenth duke (NORF 7 and 8), was born in 1791 and styled Earl of Surrey after his father's succession in 1815. He was a Liberal Member of Parliament for Horsham 1829–32 and for West Sussex 1832–41. He was appointed a Privy Counsellor in 1837 and was Treasurer of the Household in the early years of Queen Victoria's reign. The inevitable K.G. was bestowed on him in 1848.

He married, in 1814, Charlotte, eldest daughter of George, 1st Duke of Sutherland (NORF 9). He died in 1856 and was succeeded, as the fourteenth duke, by his son also Henry, born in 1815, the year of his grandfather's succession. He was known as Lord Fitzalan in his grandfather's lifetime and then as Earl of Surrey. Henry was educated at Eton and Trinity College, Cambridge before entering the Royal Horse Guards. He was Liberal Member of Parliament for Arundel 1837–51 and for Limerick 1851–2. By Royal Warrant, in 1842, he and his brothers and sisters took the name of Fitzalan before that of Howard. He was offered the Garter by the Prime Minister, Lord Palmerston, but refused it because he disapproved of his policies.

He married, in July 1839, Augusta youngest daughter of Edmund, Lord Lyons. Disraeli commented at the time *'Lord Fitzalan, who was sent to Greece because he would marry a Miss Pitt, has returned engaged to Miss Lyons, daughter of our minister there. It is said that he escaped from the Pitt to fall into the Lyons mouth.'*

The duke was an ardent catholic and, when he succeeded to the dukedom, his wife converted to the Roman Catholic faith. He only held the dukedom for four years before dying in 1860 from what was termed *'congestion of the liver'*, he was forty-six.

He was succeeded by his son, Henry Fitzalan Howard who, being born in 1847, was only thirteen at the time of his succession. He went on to receive the Garter in 1886, become a Privy Counsellor in 1895 and Post Master General

1895–1900. He served in the South African War and was Lord Lieutenant of Sussex 1905–17.

He married twice. Firstly in 1877 Flora, daughter of Charles, 1st Lord Donington (NORF 10), she died in 1887, and secondly in 1904 Gwendoline daughter of Marmaduke, Lord Herries. He died, of *'gastric influenza'*, in February 1917.

NORF 2 Philip Howard of Norfolk F15530

A simple baroque type shield without accessories showing the arms of Howard quartering Brotherton, Warren and Fitzalan, an annulet for difference in the centre point denoting a fifth son.

Philip Howard of Buckenham was the fifth son of Lord Thomas Howard younger son of Henry, 7th Duke of Norfolk. Two of Philip's elder brothers were respectively eighth and ninth dukes. A number of books bearing Philip's bookplate are to be found in the ducal library at Arundel.

NORF 3 Edward Duke of Norfolk Earle Marshall of England F15479

This is the identical plate to NORF 1 but has had the name altered from Thomas to Edward. Fortunately both names have the same number of letters so the substitution would have been simple. Edward succeeded his brother Thomas as ninth duke in 1732.

NORF 4 Belonging to the Library bequeathed by the Will of Edward Duke of Norfolk to remain in his family. Henry Howard & Thoˢ Eyre Esqʳˢ Executors
NIF

This label, the inscription on which is self explanatory, was produced in 1777 the year of the duke's death. It was attached to those books bequeathed to the family in the duke's will. There are a number of variations of the label known but the message conveyed is the same.

NORF 2

NORF 3

NORF 4

NORF 5

NORF 7 **Henry Charles Earl of Surrey** NIF

A simple armorial plate with typical 'dog-eared' shield dating from the first half of the nineteenth century with an earl's coronet above surmounted by the Howard crest.

Henry Charles Howard (1791–1856) was the son and heir of Bernard, 12th Duke of Norfolk. He was styled Earl of Surrey from 1815 to 1842 when he succeeded his father as thirteenth duke (see NORF 8). He married, in 1814, Lady Charlotte Leveson-Gower, daughter of George, 1st Duke of Sutherland (see NORF 9). He served as Member of Parliament for Horsham and later West Sussex from 1829–1841. He was elected a Privy Counsellor in 1837 on Queen Victoria's accession and given the Garter in 1848.

NORF 5 **Henry Charles Howard of Greystock in Cumberland Esqr** F15516

A baroque style plate from the first half of the eighteenth century.

ARMS: Howard quartering 2, Brotherton, 3, Warren and 4, Fitzalan.

The plate is known in two sizes of which this is the smaller.

Henry Howard was a nephew of Henry, sixth duke and the father of Charles, tenth duke.

NORF 6 **Bernard Edward Duke of Norfolk** NIF

A plain and simple book label, an unusual plate for a duke. Bernard Howard of Glossop was a third cousin of Charles, eleventh duke whom he succeeded in 1815. Like many of his family he was a staunch catholic and it required a special Act of Parliament in 1824 to allow him to perform the office of Earl Marshal.

NORF 7

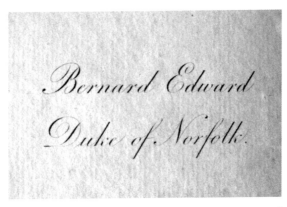

NORF 6

NORF 8

NORF 9

NORF 8 henry charles duke of norfolk F15481

An early seal type armorial bookplate for the thirteenth duke made sometime between 1848, when he received the Garter, and his death in 1856. It shows good design and balance with the arms well displayed.

NORF 9 Charlotte Duchess of Norfolk NIF

A simple shield above two olive branches surmounted by a duchess's coronet.

ARMS: Howard impaling, quarterly, 1 and 4, barry of eight or

and gules, overall a cross flory sable (Gower); 2 and 3, azure, three laurel leaves or (Leveson).

Lady Charlotte Leveson-Gower (1788–1870) was the daughter of George, 1st Duke of Sutherland. In 1814 she married Henry Charles Howard later 13th Duke of Norfolk. They had three sons and two daughters. She was a very accomplished lady. Between 1811 and 1823 she put together a collection of songs and piano pieces by famous composers such as Mozart, Arne and Handel which she translated into five languages.

NORF 10 FLORA DUCHESS OF NORFOLK
F15483

A nice circular seal type armorial from the late nineteenth century inscribed around the base 'G.A.LEE DEL. MONEY-PENNY SC.' The arms are Howard impaling Hastings below a duchess's coronet.

Lady Flora Hastings (1854–87) was the daughter of Charles Abney-Hastings, 1st Lord Donnington and his wife Edith Rawdon Hastings, 10th Countess of Loudon. She married in 1877, as his first wife, Henry Fitzalan Howard, 15th Duke of Norfolk. They had one son who predeceased his father. The duke married a second time in 1904, Gwendoline, his first cousin once removed, the daughter of Marmaduke Constable-Maxwell, 11th Lord Herries. He was fifty-six and she was twenty-seven. They had a further four children one of whom, Bernard, succeeded as sixteenth duke.

NORF 10

NORF 11 **EX LIBRIS MILES FRANCIS STAPLETON DUKE OF NORFOLK** NIF

A twentieth century simple armorial ex libris for the seventeenth duke designed by Rodney Dennys, Arundel herald . Born in 1915 the Duke had a military career, serving in World War II and being awarded the Military Cross. He retired from the army in 1967 with the rank of Major General. He succeeded to the dukedom in 1975 on the death of a distant cousin and was one of only two peers to retain his seat without having to seek election when the House of Lords was reformed in 1999. He died on 24th June 2002.

NORF 12 **Book Label for Arundel Castle** NIF

A fascinating and amusing little book label by Eric Gill and inscribed 'THIS BOOK COMES FROM A BEDROOM IN ARUNDEL CASTLE'. It would seem that even ducal visitors had to be reminded should they, inadvertently or otherwise, find a spare book in their luggage on their return home.

The author is grateful to His Grace the Duke of Norfolk for permission to reproduce NORF 11 and 12.

NORF 11

NORF 12

Nor 1 **1899 Anonymous** NIF

A large and magnificent full panel armorial bookplate created by C.W. Sherborn for Henry George Percy, 7th Duke of Northumberland who succeeded to the title on 2nd January 1899 and received the Garter later in that year. The plate may have been made in celebration of this honour, the collar and badge of which surrounds the shield with the date under the badge.

ARMS: Grand quarters, I and IV, quarterly, 1 and 4, quarterly, or, a lion rampant azure (Ancient arms of Duke of Brabant); 2 and 3, gules, three lucies hauriant argent (Lucy); 2 and 3, azure, five fusils conjoined in fess or

(Percy). II and III, quarterly 1 and 4, or, three bars wavy gules (Drummond); 2 and 3, or, a lion's head erased within a double tressure flory counter flory gules (Drummond augmentation).

CREST: On a chapeau gules turned up ermine a lion statant azure the tail extended.

SUPPORTERS: Dexter, a lion rampant azure; sinister, a lion rampant guardant or ducally crowned of the last gorged with a collar gobony argent and azure.

MOTTO: Esperance en Dieu – Hope in God.

Dukes of Northumberland

FAMILY NAME: Percy

CREATION OF DUKEDOM: 17th October 1766

COURTESY TITLE OF ELDEST SON: Earl Percy

COURTESY TITLE OF GRANDSON AND HEIR:
Lord Lovaine

PRINCIPAL RESIDENCE: Alnwick Castle, Northumberland

The earldom of Northumberland has a long and chequered history having been created first in 1139 for Henry, Earl of Huntingdon, the only son and heir of King David I, king of Scotland. It became extinct and was recreated by Richard II, at his coronation, and conferred upon the 4th Lord Percy of Alnwick. It came and went in various families as male lines failed and new creations were made. It had been extinct for some time when Charles II recreated it again this time for one of his illegitimate sons, George Fitzroy, third and youngest son by Barbara Villiers, Countess of Castlemaine.

George was born on 28th December 1665, '*in a Fellow's chamber at Merton College, Oxford.*' At the age of eight he was created Baron Pontefract, Viscount Falmouth and Earl of Northumberland. Later in his eighteenth year he was made Duke of Northumberland and the following year a Knight of the Garter. He had a military career as well as enjoying various Royal perks such as, Constable of Windsor Castle and Ranger of Windsor Forest. He married twice but both marriages were childless. He died, without issue, in 1716 when all his honours once again became extinct.

In 1749 George II revived the earldom for Algernon Seymour who, the year before, had succeeded to his father's dukedom of Somerset. Algernon's mother, Elizabeth was the daughter of Joceline, 5th Earl of Northumberland, and had succeeded to her father's vast estates on his death and the barony of Percy but the earldom became extinct. So it was recreated for Elizabeth's son, Anthony, with special remainder to Anthony's son-in-law, Sir Hugh Smithson failing male heirs. He died later the following year leaving no male heir when most of his titles became extinct (see Somerset). However under the special remainder the earldom of Northumberland and the barony of Warkworth devolved on his son-in-law Sir Hugh Smithson Bt. who had married the earl's only daughter, Elizabeth and thus, as it turned out, had made a very advantageous marriage. (NOR 2, 3 and 4)

The Smithsons were a Yorkshire family. In 1660 Hugh Smithson was created a baronet by King Charles II for services to the royalist cause during the Civil War. It was his great great grandson also Hugh, the third baronet, who married the Northumberland heiress and rose rapidly through the ranks of the peerage. He was born on 19th December 1714, succeeded his grandfather in 1733 and his father-in-law in 1750. He took his seat in the House of Lords in March 1750 and a month later, by Act of Parliament, took the name of Percy in lieu of Smithson.

He held numerous posts politically, militarily and within the Royal Household. He became a Knight of the Garter in 1756. He was socially and politically avaricious and ambitious and felt because of his great wealth and estates he deserved a higher status. Eventually, on 17th October 1766, he was created Earl Percy and Duke of Northumberland (NOR 5). He died at Syon House, Middlesex in June 1786 and was buried in Westminster Abbey.

He was succeeded by his son Hugh, who, following Eton, had a career in the army. He commanded a brigade in North America at the time of the Civil War there, eventually reaching the rank of general. He was popular and much admired by his troops, so much so that the 5th Regiment of Foot claimed the right to be known as the Northumberland Fusiliers.

He married first, in 1764, Anne, third daughter of John, 3rd Earl of Bute, whom he divorced, childless, in 1779. He married, secondly, Frances Julia, daughter of Peter Burrell of Langley Park in Kent, by whom he had children. He died at Northumberland House in the Strand, London in July 1817 and he too was buried in Westminster Abbey.

His eldest son having predeceased him he was succeeded as third duke by his second son Hugh (1785–1847). He was educated at Eton and St. John's College, Cambridge and followed his father in various public offices including Lord

Lieutenant and Vice Admiral of Northumberland. He was a trustee of the British Museum and Chancellor of the University of Cambridge 1840–7.

He married, in 1817, Charlotte Florentia, second daughter of Edward, Earl of Powis (NOR 6). She was a governess to the young Princess Victoria. The couple were described as follows in Greville's Memoirs 1829: '*He is a very good sort of man, with a very narrow understanding; an eternal talker and a prodigious bore. The Duchess is a more sensible woman and amiable and good humoured.*' He died at Alnwick Castle in 1847 without leaving a male heir and was succeeded by his younger brother Algernon.

Lord Algernon Percy was born in 1792 and, following Eton, he entered the navy in 1805 aged thirteen. He rose to be Rear Admiral of the Blue by 1850. He was a Fellow of the Royal Society and the Society of Antiquaries and was given an LL.D. by Cambridge in 1835 and a D.C.L. by Oxford in 1841. He was President of the Royal Institution.

On 25th August 1842 he married Eleanor, the elder daughter of Richard Grosvenor, 2nd Marquess of Westminster (NOR 7). Like his older brother he left no male issue and when he died, of the gout in 1865, he was succeeded, as fifth duke, by his cousin, George Percy, 2nd Earl of Beverley the son of Algernon, 1st Earl of Beverley who was the second son of Hugh, 3rd Duke of Northumberland.

George, who was born in 1778 and educated at Eton and St John's College, Cambridge, inherited his father's earldom in 1830 and was eighty-six years old when he inherited the dukedom. He had married, in 1801, Louisa, third daughter of the Honourable James Archibald Stuart-Wortley-Mackenzie the younger son of John, 3rd Earl of Bute. George died in 1867 in his ninetieth year. His elder two sons having predeceased him he was succeeded, as sixth duke, by his third son Algernon (NOR 8, 9, 10 and 11).

Algernon, born in 1810 and educated at Eton and St John's College, Cambridge had been styled as Earl Percy since his father's succession to the dukedom. He had previously had an army career and was later Member of Parliament for North Northumberland, 1852–65. He was a Privy Counsellor and Vice-President of the Board of Trade. He was Provincial Grand Master of the Northumberland Freemasons 1865–86; President of the Royal Institute 1873–99. He was given the Garter in 1886. In 1845 he had married Louisa, eldest daughter and co-heir of Henry Drummond of Aldbury Park, Surrey (NOR 12). He died on 2nd January 1899 at Alnwick and is buried in Westminster

Abbey. His second son Lord Algernon Malcolm Arthur Percy's bookplate is shown (NOR 13).

He was succeeded as seventh duke by his eldest son Henry George who was born 29th May 1846 and educated at Christ Church, Oxford. He was a Trustee of the British Museum and Lord Lieutenant of Northumberland; President of the Royal Institute and a Fellow of the Royal Society. He was given the Garter in the year of his succession, 1899. He had married, 28th December 1868, Edith, eldest daughter of George Douglas Campbell, 8th Duke of Argyll. He died suddenly, of apoplexy, at Alnwick Castle on 14th May 1918 and was succeeded by his fourth, but first surviving son, Lord Alan Percy as eighth duke (NOR 14).

NOR 2 DUTCHESS OF NORTHUMBERLAND. Northumberland House F23303

A small crest plate, showing the Percy crest, for the use of the duchess in their London home, Northumberland House in the Strand. Lady Elizabeth Seymour was the daughter of Algernon Seymour, 7th Duke of Somerset and Earl of Northumberland, who married Hugh Smithson 1st Duke of Northumberland.

NOR 3 DUTCHESS OF NORTHUMBERLAND. Syon House F23304

A similar plate to NOR 2 but for use in Syon House by the river Thames in Middlesex. Somewhat unusually although titled 'Dutchess of Northumberland' it displays the Seymour crest of her father.

NOR 4 DUTCHESS OF NORTHUMBERLAND. Alnwick Castle NIF

Small oval plate showing one of the Percy badges, a crescent, within a pair of olive branches below a duchess's coronet. It dates from the late eighteenth century and is possibly for Elizabeth, the first duchess, who had a number of these small plates for her various residences (see NOR 2 and 3).

NOR 5 Anonymous F23295

A small badge plate in the rococo style for Hugh Percy, 1st Duke of Northumberland, depicting one of the Percy badges, a crescent, within the motto of the Garter under a duke's coronet and surrounded by a rococo framework.

NOR 2

NOR 3

NOR 4

NOR 5

NOR 6

NOR 6 **C.F. Northumberland** F23305

An armorial bookplate for Charlotte wife of the third duke. It shows the ducal arms surrounded by the Garter accollee with the ducal arms impaling those of Clive, Earl of Powis. Charlotte Florentia was the second daughter of Edward Clive, 1st Earl of Powis. She married Hugh Percy, 3rd Duke of Northumberland in 1817. She was governess to the young Princess Victoria before she became Queen.

NOR 7 **EEN 1864** F23306

This monogram bookplate shows two entwined Es within an N with a Percy badge, a crescent, in the centre all under a duke's coronet and is dated 1864.

Eleanor, daughter of Richard Grosvenor, 2nd Marquess of Westminster, married Algernon, 4th Duke of Northumberland in 1842. The duke died the year after this plate was made.

NOR 7

NOR 8

NOR 9

NOR 10

NOR 11

NOR 8 **Anonymous 1867** F23296

A small bookplate showing one of the Percy badges surrounded by the family motto under a duke's coronet and dated 1867 the year the sixth duke succeeded to the title.

NOR 9 **Anonymous** F23298

A similar plate to NOR 8 but is undated and the badge is surrounded by the Garter motto. The duke received the Garter in 1886. It is signed 'E. ORTNER SC. 3 ST JAMES ST.'.

NOR 10 **Anonymous. 1886** F23302

This plate shows another of the Percy badges – a lion rampant standing in a crescent surrounded by the Garter motto under a duke's coronet and dated 1886.

NOR 11 **ALGERNON GEORGE DUKE OF NORTHUMBERLAND** F23301

A seal type armorial bookplate by C.W. Sherborn made in 1887 for the sixth duke the year after he received the Garter. It is signed and dated at the bottom.

NOR 12 **LN** F23307

This bookplate shows the ducal arms with those of Drummond in pretence surrounded by the family motto under a duke's coronet. Either side of the shield are the letters L and N for Louisa Northumberland. Louisa, the daughter and co-heir of Henry Drummond, married Algernon, 6th Duke of Northumberland in 1842.

NOR 12

NOR 13 **AM AP** NIF

A panel armorial bookplate showing the arms of Percy under the family crest and surrounded by the family motto. Two of the family badges are featured in the top corners and in the bottom the initials 'AM' and 'AP' which stand for Algernon Malcolm Arthur Percy.

He was the second son of Algernon George Percy, 6th Duke of Northumberland and his wife Louisa. Born in 1851 and educated at Eton and Christ Church, Oxford he went on to have a military career. Between 1872 and 1895 he served in the Grenadier Guards, the Royal Berkshire Regiment and the Northumberland Fusiliers. He was Member of Parliament for Westminster 1882–5 and for St Georges, Hanover Square 1885–7. In 1840 he married Lady Victoria Edgecombe the daughter of the 4th Earl of Mount Edgecombe. He was Aide de Campe to Edward VII from 1902–10 and to George, Viscount Ipswich, from 1910–20. He died in 1933.

NOR 14 **ALAN IAN DUKE OF NORTHUMBERLAND** MCMXVIII NIF

A very fine seal armorial for Alan, 8th Duke of Northumberland, by J.A.C. Harrison. The plate is dated 1918 and was probably made for the duke's succession in that year. It is a full armorial displaying a single coat – or, a lion rampant azure with the crescent badge of the Percy's below all within a circular border. The plate is known in two sizes.

NOR 13

NOR 14

Por 1 **WILLIAM ARTHUR SIXTH DUKE OF PORTLAND K.G.** NIF

A large panel armorial bookplate for William Arthur, 6th Duke of Portland signed 'INV. W.P.B. 1900' in the bottom right hand corner. It was designed by James Scott and engraved by J.A.C. Harrison. A first state of this plate is known with the coronet above the helmet producing a rather squashed appearance which was later corrected (see POR 1a) The sixth duke (1857–1943) succeeded in 1879.

ARMS: Quarterly, 1 and 4, azure, a cross Moline argent (Bentinck); 2 and 3, sable, three stags heads caboshed argent (Cavendish).

CRESTS:
1. Out of a ducal coronet or, two arms embowed vested gules, gauntleted or and each holding an ostrich feather argent (Bentinck),
2. On a wreath of the colours a serpent embowed proper (Cavendish).

SUPPORTERS: Two lions rampant double queued, the dexter or the sinister sable (tincture not shown here).

MOTTO: Craignez houte – Dread shame.

Dukes of Portland

FAMILY NAME: Bentinck, Cavendish-Bentinck

CREATION OF DUKEDOM: 6th July 1716

COURTESY TITLE OF ELDEST SON: Marquess of Titchfield

COURTESY TITLE OF GRANDSON AND HEIR: Viscount Woodstock

PRINCIPAL RESIDENCE: Welbeck Abbey, Worksop, Nottinghamshire

The family of this creation are of Dutch descent. Hans Willem Bentinck, fourth son of Bernhard Bentinck, Lord of Diepenheim and Drost of Devanter, was born on 20th July 1649 in Holland. He became a page of honour to William Prince of Orange. He was Colonel of a regiment of Horse Guards in the Dutch army. He was sent as an envoy to England in 1677 to help arrange the marriage of William of Orange to Princess Mary daughter of the Duke of York (James II). He seems to have crossed the water on a regular basis. In 1683 he came to congratulate King Charles II, on the collapse of the Rye House Plot (see Dukes of Bedford), in 1685 he was back again this time to congratulate the king, James II, on his success in defeating the Duke of Monmouth, and finally in 1688 he accompanied William, Prince of Orange and his wife Princess Mary when they came to ascend the British throne.

In April 1689, a few days before the coronation, he was rewarded for his support of the House of Orange by being created by King William, Baron of Cirencester, Viscount Woodstock and Earl of Portland. He continued to support the new king and queen both militarily and politically although he disliked the English and the English way of life. Consequently he was disliked by the natives who saw him as having too much influence at Court. He held numerous offices within the Royal Household and in 1696 was made a Knight of the Garter (POR 2). He saw military service in Ireland and had been present at the Battle of the Boyne in 1688.

He married, firstly, in February 1677 in The Hague, Anne, daughter of Sir Edward Villiers and sister of Edward, 1st Earl of Jersey. They had a family but she died at an early age in 1688. He married, secondly, in May 1700 Jane, the widow of Lord Berkeley of Stratton. He died of pleurisy on 23 November 1709 and is buried in Westminster Abbey.

His eldest son died as a child and so he was succeeded, as 2nd earl, by his second son William Henry who was born in 1682. He was styled Viscount Woodstock 1689–1709. As a young man he did the Grand Tour and then became a Member of Parliament and a Colonel in the Life Guards. The family was further honoured when, on 6th July 1716, he was created Marquess of Titchfield and Duke of Portland by George I. He then became Governor and Vice Admiral of Jamaica 1721–6. He married on 9th June 1704, Elizabeth eldest daughter and co-heir of Wriothesley, 2nd Earl of Gainsborough. He died in 1746 in Jamaica whilst serving as Governor and is buried in Westminster Abbey.

The second duke was his son William born on 1st March 1709. He was educated at Eton and went on to become a Trustee of the British Museum, a Fellow of the Royal Society and an Honorary D.C.L. of the University of Oxford. He was installed as a Knight of the Garter in 1741. He married on 11th July 1734, Margaret Cavendish, the only daughter and heir of Edward Harley, 1st Earl of Oxford, whose wife was Henrietta Cavendish, daughter of John Holles, 1st Duke of Newcastle (see Newcastle). He died in 1762 at the age of fifty-four and, he too, is buried in Westminster Abbey.

The third duke, his son William Henry born in 1738, went on to become an Establishment figure in eighteenth century England, twice serving in the office of Prime Minister. He was educated at Westminster School and Christ Church, Oxford before undertaking the Grand Tour in his early twenties (1757–61). He was Lord Chamberlain of the Household, 1765–6 and Viceroy of Ireland in 1782. He served as First Lord of the Treasury (Prime Minister) for the first time in 1783. He was a Fellow of the Royal Society and Chancellor of the University of Oxford.

He married, on 8th November 1766, Dorothy, only daughter of William Cavendish, 4th Duke of Devonshire.

He had assumed the name of Cavendish before Bentinck

POR 4

POR 4 **H.S.P** F2261

A small initial book label showing the letters 'H.S.P.' under a duchess's coronet. Henrietta was the eldest daughter and co-heir of General John Scott of Balconnie who, in 1795, married William, 4th Duke of Portland. As a consequence of this marriage William took the name of Scott by Royal Licence in addition to Cavendish- Bentinck thus becoming Cavendish-Scott-Bentinck.

POR 5 **Welbeck Abbey** F2258

A large simple armorial, full achievement without tincture lines. The arms are quarterly Bentinck and Cavendish with the crests of Bentinck and Cavendish above. On either side are two Portland badges. Welbeck Abbey is the family's principal seat near Worksop in Nottinghamshire.

Stylistically it dates from the late nineteenth century and was probably made for William the sixth duke who succeeded in 1879.

POR 6 **WINIFRED PORTLAND** F2262

A nice pictorial panel bookplate depicting flowers, books and the lamp of knowledge around a duchess's coronet by C.W. Sherborn. The inscription above reads – '*Here may I read all at my ease. Both of the newe and olde*'.

Winifred was the only daughter of Thomas Dallas-Yorke of Walmsgate, Lincolnshire. In 1889 she married William Arthur, 6th Duke of Portland.

POR 7 **EX LIBRIS CICELY CAVENDISH BENTINCK** NIF

A well known and fine pictorial bookplate showing the owner's interests in the arts and bearing the words MY BOOK AND FRIEND AND THIS IS HAPPINESS. It depicts flowers, books, sheet music and a violin together with the lamp of knowledge. According to a note by J.A.C. Harrison it was designed by Scott and probably engraved by G. Vise for W.P.B.

Cicely Mary Grenfell was the daughter of Charles and Elizabeth Grenfell. In 1897 she married Lieutenant Colonel Lord Charles Cavendish-Bentinck who was the younger half brother of the 6th Duke of Portland. He fought in the Boer War and the first World War and was awarded the D.S.O. Cicely died in 1936.

CRAIGNEZ HONTE

Welbeck Abbey.

POR 5

"Here may I reade all at my ease. Both of the newe & olde."

WINIFRED PORTLAND

POR 6

MY BOOK AND FRIEND AND THIS IS HAPPINESS

EX LIBRIS

CICELY CAVENDISH BENTINCK

POR 7

RIC 1 **Charles Lennox Duke of Richmond, Lennox and Aubigny Knight of yᵉ most noble order of the Garter** F18141

ARMS: Quarterly, 1 and 4, France and England quarterly, 2, Scotland, 3, Ireland all within a bordure compony argent and gules charged with eight roses of the second barbed and seeded proper (Richmond); over all an escutcheon of pretence, gules charged with three buckles, or (Aubigny).

CRESTS: [not shown]
1. On a chapeau gules turned up ermine a lion guardant or ducally crowned and gorged with a collar compony of four pieces argent and gules, charged with two roses of the last,
2. Out of a marquess's coronet or a stag's head and neck affrontee proper attired gold.

SUPPORTERS: [not shown] Dexter, a unicorn argent; sinister, an antelope argent, each gorged with a collar company as in the crest.

MOTTO: En la rose je fleurie– By the rose I flourish (not shown).

Dukes of Richmond and Gordon

FAMILY NAME: Lennox, Gordon-Lennox

CREATION OF DUKEDOM OF RICHMOND: 9th August 1675

COURTESY TITLE OF ELDEST SON: Earl of March

COURTESY TITLE OF GRANDSON AND HEIR: Lord Settrington

RECREATION OF DUKEDOM OF GORDON: 13th June 1876

PRINCIPAL RESIDENCE: Goodwood House, Chichester, Sussex

The dukedom of Richmond was first created in 1525 for Henry Fitzroy the illegitimate son of Henry VIII by Elizabeth Blount, maid of honour to Queen Catherine. He died without issue in 1536 when the honour became extinct.

It was recreated, by James I, in 1623 for his cousin Ludovic, Duke of Lennox, who held it for less than a year before also dying without issue. The English dukedom of Richmond fell into abeyance but his Scottish title, Duke of Lennox, passed to his brother James who was later (1641) also created Duke of Richmond. He was succeeded by his son Esme in 1655 being then only six years old. He died of smallpox, in Paris, in 1660 when all his honours fell to his cousin Charles Stuart who died without issue in 1672 when the dukedoms of Richmond and Lennox again became extinct.

On the 29th July 1672 Louise de Keroualle, spinster and mistress of Charles II, gave birth to his illegitimate son who was christened Charles after his father. Three years later, in 1675 he was created Duke of Richmond, of the third creation, and the following year Duke of Lennox (RIC 2). He also received an annuity of £2,000 per annum plus the duty of a shilling a caldron on all sea coals shipped out of Newcastle.

He became Aide de Campe to William III in 1693, aged twenty-one, and later Lord High Admiral and Grand Master of Freemasons. He spent some time in France and was suspected of Jacobite sympathies but nothing was proven. As befitted his royal association he was bearer of the Sceptre at Queen Anne's coronation and later made Lord of the Bedchamber to George I. In Parliament he was a supporter of the Whig administration.

In June 1692 he married Anne, widow of Lord Belasyse and the sister of the 3rd Earl of Cardigan. In 1720 he bought the Goodwood Estate in Sussex from the Compton family and died there in 1723. He was buried in Westminster Abbey but his body was later removed (1750) to Chichester Cathedral where the Lady Chapel had been granted to the third duke in 1750 as a family mausoleum.

John Evelyn wrote of him and his half brother, the Duke of St. Albans, as '*very pretty boys*' whilst Macky described him as '*good natured to a fault, very well bred and hath many valuable things in him; is an enemy to business, very credulous, well shaped, black complexion much like King Charles.*' On the other hand Thomas Hearne said of him '*He was a man of very little understanding, and tho' the son of so great a king as King Charles, was a man that struck in with everything that was Whiggish and opposite to true monarchical principles.*'

He was succeeded as second duke by his only son Charles, born at Goodwood in 1701 (RIC 1). After being educated privately and undertaking the Grand Tour in 1719–20 he entered the army joining the Horse Guards and followed a military career, serving at the Battle of Dettingen in 1743 and against the Jacobites in Scotland in 1745. Like his father he was a Whig supporter, Grand Master of the Freemasons and Lord of the Bedchamber to George I and George II.

He married on 4th December 1719 at The Hague, Sarah daughter and co-heir of William, 1st Earl of Cadogan, who bore him twelve children. He died on 8th August 1750, reputedly from inflammation of the bladder, at Godalming on his way to Goodwood. His widow, broken hearted at her husband's sudden death, survived him by only a year.

Like his father there seems to have been two sides to him. John, Lord Hervy, said of him '*There never lived a man of a more amiable composition; he was friendly, benevolent, generous, honourable and thoroughly noble in his way of acting, talking and thinking*'. Queen Caroline, wife of George II, on the other hand said '*he is so half witted, so bizarre and so grand Seigneur and so mulish that he is as troublesome from meaning well and comprehending so ill as if he meant as ill as he comprehends'.*

He was succeeded as third duke by his third, but first surviving, son Charles who was born on 22nd February 1734. He was educated at Westminster School and on the Continent, at Leyden, where he graduated in 1753. He followed his father into the army. He took part in the attack at Cherbourg in 1758 and distinguished himself at the Battle of Minden the following year. He rose to the rank of General in 1787 and finally, in 1792, Field Marshal and Colonel of the Royal Regiment of Horse Guards until his death.

He was a founder member of The Society of Arts, elected a Fellow of the Royal Society, Lord of the Bedchamber to George III and Lord Lieutenant of Sussex. He became a Privy Counsellor and, like his father and grandfather before him, was installed as a Knight of the Garter.

He married on 1st April 1757, Mary, third daughter of Charles, 3rd Earl of Ailsbury, (RIC 3). Although he had a number of illegitimate children he had only one daughter by his wife. It is said that he left £50,000 to each of his illegitimate daughters by his housekeeper and the same amount to their mother. One of these daughters lived with the duke and the duchess who was very fond of her. She was even introduced at Court. When he died on 29th December 1806, aged seventy-one, he was succeeded by his nephew Charles only son of his brother Lord George Henry Lennox (RIC 4 and 5) who had died a year earlier.

Charles Lennox, 4th Duke of Richmond, was born on 9th September 1764 and had followed his uncle into the army. Unlike his predecessors the fourth duke was a Tory. He sat as Member of Parliament for Chichester and became Lord Lieutenant of Ireland, 1807–13.

He became notorious when, on 26th May 1789 he fought a dual on Wimbledon Common against H.R.H. The Duke of York when, it is said, the Duke of York received his fire and then coolly fired into the air.

He married Charlotte daughter of Alexander Gordon, 4th Duke of Gordon on 9th September 1789 (RIC 6). She bore him fourteen children, seven sons (RIC 7) and seven daughters. He was given the Garter in 1812 and rose to the rank of General in 1814. Finally he became Governor General of Canada in 1818 and died there, in Ontario, on 28th August 1819 from rabies, having been bitten by a pet fox.

His son and heir Charles , the fifth duke, was born on 3rd August 1791 and educated at Westminster School and Trinity College, Dublin. He had a military career, serving in the Peninsula Wars. He was assistant military aide to the Duke of Wellington 1810–14 and fought at the Battle of Waterloo as Aide de Campe to the Prince of Orange. He sat as Member of Parliament for Chichester 1812–19 whilst still a serving officer

He married, in 1817, Caroline daughter of Henry William, 1st Marquess of Anglesey. On the death in 1836 of his maternal uncle, the fifth, and last, Duke of Gordon, he inherited Gordon Castle and other estates of the Gordon family and, as a result, he took, by Royal Licence, the additional surname of Gordon before that of Lennox although he did not inherit the dukedom of Gordon.

He was installed as a Knight of the Garter in 1829 and made a Privy Counsellor in 1830. He was Post Master General from 1830–4. He was a keen racehorse owner, a Steward of the Jockey Club, and won a number of classic races with various horses.

He was perceived in various ways by his contemporaries. Disraeli said of him, in 1849, *'he is really a working man, has mastered the great questions by reading blue books, and is a fair and improving speaker.'* Earlier, in 1833 Greville had written, *He is utterly incapable, entirely ignorant and his pert smartness, saying sharp things, cheering offensively, have greatly exasperated many people against him in the House of Commons. He has, in fact, that weight which a man can derive from being positive, obstinate, pertinacious and busy but his understanding lies in a nutshell and his information in a pin head. He is however good humoured, a good fellow and personally liked.'*

He died of the dropsy in October 1869 aged sixty-nine when his son, Charles Henry Gordon-Lennox became the sixth duke. Born in 1818 and educated at Westminster School and Christ Church, Oxford he served in the Horse Guards from 1839–44. In November 1843 he married Frances daughter of Algernon Greville, Bath King of Arms. He was Member of Parliament for West Sussex 1841–60 and Aide de Campe to the Duke of Wellington 1842–52. He became a Privy Counsellor in 1859 and in 1867 he was installed as a Knight of the Garter, the sixth duke of his line to be so honoured.

He was Chancellor of the University of Aberdeen from 1861 until his death. He was Leader of the Conservative Party in the House of Lords and Lord President of the Council 1874–80. On 13th June 1876 Queen Victoria raised him to the extinct dukedom of Gordon in recognition of his connection to that family through his grandmother, Charlotte elder sister of George, fifth, and last, Duke of

Gordon and wife of the 4th Duke of Richmond. At the same time she also made him Earl of Kinrara.

The dukedom of Gordon had been created by Charles II in 1684 for George Gordon son and heir of Lewis, 3rd Marquess of Huntley who inherited his father's title as 4th Marquess of Huntley, aged four, in 1653. It passed from eldest son to eldest son through five generations becoming extinct on the death of the fifth Duke in 1836 (RIC 8, 9 and 10).

In August 1879 the Prime Minister, Benjamin Disraeli installed the 6th Duke of Richmond as Lord Lieutenant of Banffshire saying *'though he has four duchies and the Garter he has not been a Lord Lieutenant'* A month later he wrote, *'I am told we lost the Banffshire election because I made him Lord Lieutenant, he is so hated, Why?'*

He died at Gordon Castle in 1903 aged eighty-five.

RIC 2 **Anonymous** NIF

An early armorial for Charles 1st Duke of Richmond and 1st Duke of Lennox, who died in 1716, showing arms and supporters standing on a ribbon bearing the family motto all under a duke's coronet.

ARMS: The Royal arms within a bordure compony argent and gules charged with eight roses of the second barbed and seed proper.

SUPPORTERS: Dexter, a unicorn argent; sinister, an antelope argent both gorged with collar argent and gules.

MOTTO: En la rose je fleurie – By the rose I flourish [©*The British Library Board: Harl.5963*].

RIC 3 **M. Richmond** FI8144

A very neat little book label for Mary wife of Charles, 3rd Duke of Richmond whom she married in 1757. She was the daughter of Charles, 3rd Earl of Ailsbury. The couple only had one daughter but the duke had a number of illegitimate daughters by his housekeeper.

RIC 3

RIC 2

RIC 4

RIC 4 **Lord George Lennox, Stoke, near Chichester Sussex** F18146

A plain armorial dating from the third quarter of the eighteenth century showing arms, supporters, crest and motto.

ARMS: The royal arms within a bordure compony argent and gules charged with eight roses of the second barbed and seeded proper (Richmond), impaling, quarterly, 1 and 4, azure, a sun in splendour or (Lothian); 2 and 3, gules, on a chevron argent three mullets of the first (Jedburgh).

Lord George Lennox, 1737–1805, was the second son of Charles, 2nd Duke of Richmond. He had a military career rising to the rank of General. He married, in 1759, Lady Louisa Ker daughter of William Ker, 4th Marquess of Lothian. They had one son and three daughters. The son, Charles, succeeded his uncle as 4th Duke of Richmond in 1806.

RIC 5 **LORD GEORGE LENNOX** F18147

Another bookplate for George, the second son of Charles 2nd Duke of Richmond, showing a crescent in centre chief denoting a second son.

RIC 5

RIC 6 **C. Richmond** F18143

A small bookplate for Lady Charlotte Gordon, 1768–1842. She was the daughter of Alexander Gordon, 4th Duke of Gordon. She married, in 1789, Charles, 4th Duke of Richmond. They had seven sons and seven daughters. The signature at the top of this plate is that of their eldest son, the fifth duke, George Gordon Lennox. The duchess was famous, amongst other things for hosting the Ball in Brussels attended by the Duke of Wellington before the Battle of Waterloo.

RIC 7 **Lord Arthur Lennox** F18145

A small plate for Arthur Lennox the seventh son of Charles, 4th Duke of Richmond. Born in 1806 he served as Clerk of the Ordnance from 1844 and died in 1864.

RIC 8 **The Arms of Her Grace Henrietta Dutches of Gordon** F12217

An early armorial post dating 1716 for a married lady showing the arms on a lozenge under a duchess's coronet.

ARMS: Quarterly,1, azure, three boars heads couped or (Gordon); 2, or, three lions heads erased gules (Badenoch); 3, or, three crescents within the royal tressure of Scotland gules (Seton), 4, azure, three cinquefoils argent (Fraser); impaling argent, a chevron between three estoiles sable (Mordaunt).

Lady Henrietta Mordaunt, born 1688, was the daughter of Charles Mordaunt, 3rd Earl of Peterborough. In February 1706/7 she married Alexander, Marquess of Huntley who subsequently, in 1716, succeeded his father as 2nd Duke of Gordon. She died on 11th October 1760.

RIC 6

RIC 7

RIC 8

RIC 9

RIC 9 **The Arms of His Grace Cosmo George Duke of
Gordon** NIF

Cosmo George Gordon (1730–52) was the son of the 2nd
Duke of Gordon and was named after his father's close
Jacobite friend Cosimo III de Medici, Grand Duke of
Tuscany. In 1747 he married Lady Catherine Gordon
daughter of William Gordon, 2nd Earl of Aberdeen. He sat
as Scottish representative in the House of Lords 1747–52.

ARMS: Quarterly, 1, azure, three boars heads or (Gordon);
2, or, three lions heads erased gules (Badenoch); 3, or, three
crescents within a tressure flory counter flory gules (Seton);
4, azure, three cinquefoils argent (Fraser).

RIC 10 **His Grace Cosmo George Duke of Gordon**
NIF

RIC 10

A similar but much smaller version of the previous plate.

Charles Gordon Lennox, 5th Duke of Richmond, 1791–1860, from a painting by W. Salter, 1842. A prominent soldier and agriculturalist. His mother was Charlotte, daughter of the 4th Duke of Gordon and, on the death of the 5th Duke of Gordon in 1836, without issue, he inherited vast estates in Scotland but not the dukedom. This was later conferred on his son, the 6th Duke, who became the 1st Duke of Gordon of the second creation.

RUT 1 The Most Noble John Duke of Rutland F19636

A large and very impressive early armorial bookplate for John Manners, 9th
Earl of Rutland who in 1703 was created Duke of Rutland. This plate may well
be in celebration of that creation.

ARMS: Quarterly of thirty two with the arms of Manners in the first quarter ,
or, two bars azure, a chief quarterly azure and gules, in the 1st and 4th quarters
two fleur-de-lys, in the 2nd and 3rd quarters a lion passant guardant all or.

CREST: On a chapeau gules turned up ermine a peacock in his pride proper.

SUPPORTERS: Two unicorns argent.

MOTTO: Pour y parvenir – In order to accomplish.

Dukes of Rutland

FAMILY NAME: Manners

CREATION OF DUKEDOM: 29th March 1703

COURTESY TITLE OF ELDEST SON: Marquess of Granby

COURTESY TITLE OF GRANDSON AND HEIR: Lord Haddon

PRINCIPAL RESIDENCE: Belvoir Castle, Leicestershire

The fortunes of the Manners family were founded by one Thomas Manners. Born sometime before 1492, he was descended on his mother's side from Edward IV. In 1513 he inherited his father's barony of Ros (or Roos). He became Joint Constable of Nottingham Castle and Keeper of Sherwood Forest.

He was a courtier and accompanied the king, Henry VIII, on his visit to France in March 1519/20 to meet Francis I and was present at the Field of the Cloth of Gold in June of that year.

In 1525 he was created Earl of Rutland and given the Garter. To commemorate his descent from the sister of Edward IV the King granted him arms: or, two bars azure, a chief quartered azure and gules, in the 1st and 4th quarters two fleur-de-lys or, in the 2nd and 3rd quarters a lion passant guardant or. He held numerous remunerative offices under the Crown. He benefited considerably from the Dissolution of the Monasteries being granted large areas of land in various parts of the country including Belvoir in Leicestershire which became the main family seat, the other being Haddon Hall in Derbyshire.

He married twice. His first wife, Elizabeth, daughter of Sir Robert Lovell, died without issue. He married secondly Eleanor, daughter of Sir William Paston of Paston in Norfolk. He died in 1543 and was succeeded by his son Henry, born in 1526.

The earldom continued through eight generations to the ninth earl, John, born in 1638. He was the third, but only surviving, son of the eighth earl. He was Member of Parliament for Leicestershire and Lord Lieutenant of that county. In 1679 he was created Baron Manners of Haddon in his own right in the lifetime of his father and summoned to Parliament in that title.

He was one of the chief supporters of the 'Glorious Revolution' of 1688, joining the Earls of Devonshire and Stamford in raising forces for William of Orange in Nottinghamshire. When the future Queen Anne fled from Whitehall she sought shelter in Belvoir Castle the Manners family seat. As Queen she created him Marquess of Granby and Duke of Rutland in 1703 (RUT 1 and 2).

He married three times. Firstly, in 1658, Anne, daughter of Henry, Marquess of Dorchester; she came with a dowry of £10,000. However he obtained a divorce, on the grounds of her adultery in 1666, and her offspring were declared illegitimate. Secondly he married, in 1671, Diana, widow of Sir Seymour Shirley Bt. but she died in childbed the following year. Thirdly, in 1673, he married Katherine, daughter of the 3rd Viscount Campden.

He died in 1710 aged seventy-two years and was succeeded by his second son, by his third wife, his first son, by his second wife having died on the day of his birth.

John Manners, 2nd Duke of Rutland (RUT 3 and 4), was born in 1676. He was styled Lord Roos and then Marquess of Granby after his father's elevation to the dukedom in 1703. He was appointed a Commissioner for the Union of England and Scotland in 1706. He served as Member of Parliament. for various constituencies in Leicestershire and Lincolnshire and was installed as a Knight of the Garter in 1714.

He married twice. Firstly, in 1693, Catherine sister of Wriothesley 2nd Duke of Bedford and youngest daughter of William, Lord Russell, who was beheaded for treason in 1683 (see RUT 5 and Bedford). She brought him £15,000 as a dowry; she also unfortunately died in childbed in 1711. He remarried in 1712, this time to Lucy, sister of the 1st Earl of Harborough. He died of the smallpox in 1720 aged forty-four. One of their sons, Lord Robert Manners married Mary Digges (RUT 6).

The third duke was his son John by his first wife. Born in 1696 and educated at Eton he became Member of Parliament for Rutland and Lord Lieutenant of Leicestershire. Given the Garter in 1722 he was appointed a Privy Counsellor in 1727. He held numerous posts at court and raised a Regiment of Foot against the Jacobites in 1715.

He married, in 1717, Bridget, the eighteen year old daughter and heir of Robert, 2nd Lord Lexington. She died young at the age of thirty-five in 1734 having borne him eleven children in in fourteen years. The duke lived on until the age of eighty-two, dying in 1779. One of their grandsons, Thomas, son of their fifth son Lord George Manners-Sutton, was created Baron Manners in 1807 (RUT 7 and 8).

He was succeeded, as fourth duke, by his twenty-five year old grandson Charles (RUT 9), his son John, Marquess of Granby, having died before his father. Charles was educated at Eton and Trinity College, Cambridge and sat as Member of Parliament for the University. He was Lord Lieutenant of Leicestershire 1779–87 and Lord Lieutenant of Ireland 1784–7.

He married, in 1775, Mary Isabelle daughter of Noel, 4th Duke of Beaufort, and died in 1787.

The fifth duke was his son and heir, John Henry Manners who, born in 1778, followed in his father's footsteps being educated at Eton and Trinity College, Cambridge and becoming Lord Lieutenant of Leicestershire from 1799 until his death.

An account of his coming of age party held at Haddon Hall, Derbyshire in 1799 makes interesting reading. The cost of the celebration was £618. 12s. 6d *'The number of gentlemen that dined was about seventy and a hundred and thirty gentlemen and ladies attended the ballroom in the evening which had a very good effect in promoting harmony and sobriety. The tenants who dined were about two hundred and fifty in number and the populace were computed to be about 10,000 and I believe all who wished to be drunk were so which comprised a considerable number.'*

The year 1799 was a busy one for the duke. As well as coming of age he was made Recorder of Cambridge and also married Elizabeth, daughter of Fredrick, 5th Earl of Carlisle. He later became Recorder for Scarborough and Grantham, served as a Trustee of the British Museum and was given the Garter in 1803.

A disastrous fire at Belvoir Castle, the family seat in Leicestershire, in October 1816 caused considerable damage and the loss of a number of family portraits and other works of art including The Nativity by Reynolds valued at 10,000 guineas. The total loss was estimated to be in excess of £120,000.

The fifth duke died in 1857 at Belvoir and, his two elder sons having died in infancy, he was succeeded by his third son Charles Cecil John Manners. Born in 1815 he followed the family tradition of Eton and Trinity College before becoming Member of Parliament for Stamford 1837–52 and for North Leicestershire 1852–7. At the same time he was Lord Lieutenant of Lincolnshire 1852–7 and of Leicestershire 1857–88.

He died, unmarried, in 1888 and was followed, as sixth duke, by his brother John Robert Manners born in 1818. As the younger son of a duke he was styled as Lord John Manners until he succeeded. Following Eton and Trinity College he had served as Member of Parliament for various constituencies until his succession.

In 1868 he was offered the post of Governor General of Canada but refused it. In 1875 he was offered the post of Viceroy of India but, again, declined it. In recommending him for the latter post the Prime Minister, Disraeli, wrote to Queen Victoria *'He is a man of many admirable qualities and unjustly underrated by the public. He is a statesman with a large practical experience of public affairs; a student as well as a practical statesman; thoroughly versed in all the great political questions of Eastern and European politics; an admirable administrator with a great capacity of labour; a facile pen, brave, firm and a thorough gentleman.'*

He married twice, firstly, in 1851, Catherine daughter of Lieutenant Colonel George Marby. She died in childbed in 1854. In 1862 he married again, this time to Janetta, daughter of Thomas Hughan of Airds, Co. Galway. He died at Belvoir in 1905 aged eighty-seven. Writing in her diary in 1892 Queen Victoria said of him *'Saw the Duke of Rutland who will not, I fear, be able to take office again. He is so kind and amiable and a perfect gentleman and great Seigneur that I shall miss him very much'.*

RUT 2 **The Most Noble John Duke of Rutland**
F19637

A much smaller and simpler plate for John the first
duke showing only a single coat rather than the multiple
quarterings of RUT 1. It dates between 1703 and 1710.

RUT 3 **John Mannors Lord Roos eldest son and
heir apparent to the Right Hon**ble **John Earl of
Rutland ec**t **1700** F19641

An early armorial bookplate, dated 1700, for John
Manners [Mannors], second son and heir to John,
9th Earl of Rutland later,1703, 1st Duke of Rutland.
John was born in 1676 and styled Lord Roos until his
father's elevation to the dukedom after which he was
styled, Marquess of Granby. He succeeded to the
dukedom in 1710.

RUT 4 **John Mannors Lord Roos eldest son and
heir apparent to the Right Hon**ble **John Earl of
Rutland 1700** F19640

A second bookplate of the same style as his father's,
RUT 1, but this time showing the family arms impaling
those of Russell, argent, a lion rampant gules, on a
chief sable three escallops of the first. John married
firstly, in 1693, Catherine youngest daughter of William,
Lord Russell who was executed for treason in 1683
(see Bedford). She died in 1711.

POVR Y PARVENIR

The Right Hon:ble Rachel Mannors Lady Roos .1700

RUT 5

POUR PARVENIR

Y

Lady Robert Manners

RUT 6

RUT 5 The Right Honble Rachel Mannors Lady Roos 1700 F19639

This is a very peculiar early armorial apparently for Rachel, Lady Roos but no such lady existed in 1700. Apart from the name it is identical to RUT 4 and the arms show a marriage between the Manners and Russell families. As stated above John, Lord Roos married, in 1693, <u>Catherine</u> Russell daughter of Lord William Russell and sister of the 2nd Duke of Bedford. Her elder sister <u>Rachel</u> had earlier, in 1688, married William 2nd Duke of Devonshire.

RUT 6 Lady Robert Manners F19647

A simple late eighteenth century armorial plate showing the arms of Manners with Digges in pretence.

Mary Digges (1737–1829) was the daughter and heiress of Colonel Thomas Digges. Her portrait, painted by Allen Ramsay in 1756, is in the National Gallery of Scotland. In 1758 she married Lord Robert Manners (1721–82) who was the son of John, 2nd Duke of Rutland, from his second marriage to Lucy Sherrard. He had a Military career, rising to the rank of General and was Member of Parliament for Kingston upon Hull from 1747 until his death in 1782.

RUT 7 Manners F19643

An uninspiring 'die sinker' bookplate from the first half of the nineteenth century for Sir Thomas Manners-Sutton (1756–1843), a distant relative of the ducal family, who was a lawyer and politician. He was the fifth son of Lord George Manners-Sutton who in turn was the third son of John, 3rd Duke of Rutland. He was created Baron Manners in 1807. The arms shown are those of the Duke and should bear a differencing mark.

RUT 8 **John Thomas, Baron Manners** NIF

This is a nineteenth century bookplate composed in an eighteenth century style for either John Thomas, 2nd Lord Manners (1818–64), or for John Thomas, 3rd Lord Manners (1852–1927). Again it also shows, incorrectly, the undifferenced ducal arms. The plate occurs in black and sepia.

RUT 9 **Charles Lord Roos** F19642

A simple crest armorial within a garland of flowers and titles below.

Charles Manners was the eldest legitimate son of John, Marquess of Granby, son and heir of John, 3rd Duke of Rutland. John died in 1770 before his father; at which point Charles, who had been styled Charles Lord Roos between 1760 and 1770, became Marquess of Granby. On his grandfather's death in 1779 Charles succeeded him as 4th Duke of Rutland.

RUT 8

RUT 7

RUT 9

ST ALB 1 **Anonymous** NIF

A bookplate from the middle of the
eighteenth century in the rococo style
probably for George, the third duke who
succeeded in 1751

ARMS: Grand quarters, I and IV, quarterly,
1 and 4 France, 2 and 3 England, II,
Scotland, III, Ireland, over all a baton
sinister gules charged with three roses
argent.

CREST: On a chapeau gules turned up
ermine a lion guardant or, ducally crowned
per pale argent and gules, and gorged
with a ducal collar gules thereon three roses
argent.

SUPPORTERS: Dexter, an antelope argent;
sinister, a greyhound argent each collared as
the crest.

MOTTO: Auspicium melloris aevi –
The token of a better age.

Dukes of St Albans

FAMILY NAME: Beauclerk

CREATION OF DUKEDOM: 10th January 1683/4

COURTESY TITLE OF ELDEST SON: Earl of Burford

COURTESY TITLE OF GRANDSON AND HEIR: Lord Vere

PRINCIPAL RESIDENCE: Redbourne Hall, Brigg, Lincolnshire.

Charles Beauclerk was an illegitimate son of Charles II by Eleanor (Nell) Gwynne, the elder of his two sons by that lady. Born on the 8th May 1670 at his mother's house in Lincoln's Inn Fields, London he was, aged six, in 1676 created Baron Heddington and Earl of Burford with a special remainder, failing heirs male of his body, to his younger brother James Beauclerk. He was subsequently, on the 10th January 1683/4 created Duke of St. Albans. He took his seat in the House of Lords in 1691.

He was an army officer and served in the Low Countries and accompanied William III when he received Peter the Great at Utrecht in 1697. He was Registrar of the Courts of Chancery (£1,500 p.a.) and granted a pension of £800 p.a. by the Irish Parliament in 1703.

He served as Lord Lieutenant of Berkshire 1714–26, was given the Garter in 1718 and became a Fellow of the Royal Society in 1722.

He married on 17th April 1694 Diana, second daughter of Aubrey de Vere, 20th, and last, Earl of Oxford.

He died on 10th May 1726 in Bath and was buried in Westminster Abbey.

He was succeeded by his eldest son, Charles, born 6th April 1696 and styled Earl of Burford. He was educated at Eton and New College, Oxford and was Member of Parliament for Bodmin 1718–22 and for Windsor 1722–6. He was Governor and Constable of Windsor Castle and Warden of Windsor Forest 1730–51. He was given the Garter in 1741.

He married on 13th December 1722 Lucy, the eldest daughter and co-heir of Sir John Werden, and had one son, George.

He died on 27th July 1751 and was described by John,

Lord Hervy as *'one of the weakest men either of the legitimate or spurious brood of the Stuarts'*.

He was succeeded by his only son, George, who was born on 25th June 1730 (ST ALB 1 and 2). Styled Earl of Burford he was educated at Eton and went on to hold various offices, Hereditary Grand Falconer of England, Hereditary Registrar of the Courts of Chancery and Lord Lieutenant of Berkshire 1751–60.

He married on 23rd October 1752 Jane, daughter of Sir Walter Roberts Bt., and died, without leaving a legitimate heir, in 1786 in Brussels.

He was succeeded by a second cousin George Beauclerk, the son and heir of Lieutenant Colonel Charles Beauclerk, who was the son and heir of Lord William Beauclerk, the second son of the first duke.

He was born on 5th December 1758 at Berwick on Tweed and entered the Foot Guards in 1775 becoming Lieutenant Colonel in 1786. He took his seat in the House of Lords on 13th March 1786 but died, unmarried, after a lingering illness, on 16th February 1787 aged only twenty-eight.

Yet again the title fell to a distant cousin, this time to Aubrey Beauclerk, a grandson of the first duke. His father was Vere Beauclerk, 1st Baron Vere of Hanworth, and the third son of the first duke.

Aubrey, the fifth duke, was born in June 1740 and became Member of Parliament for Thetford in Norfolk and later for Aldborough in Yorkshire. He succeeded to his father's peerage, in 1781, whilst travelling in Italy and to the dukedom in 1787 taking his seat in the House of Lords the following year. He spent the rest of his life in suitable ducal activities.

He married, in August 1763, Catherine, eldest daughter of William Ponsonby, 2nd Earl of Bessborough and granddaughter of the 3rd Duke of Devonshire. She died in 1789 of cancer of the breast and he died in 1802 in his sixty-second year.

The title went to their eldest son Aubrey who, born in 1765, was styled Earl of Burford until his succession (ST ALB 3 and 4). He went into the Foot Guards in 1781 and nine years later was a Lieutenant Colonel. He was Member of Parliament for Kingston-Upon-Hull from 1790–6.

He married firstly, in July 1788, Jane, daughter of John Moss of Hull but she died, without bearing a child, in 1800. He married secondly, in August 1802, Grace Louisa daughter of Louisa, suo jure Countess of Dysart, and her husband John Manners of Grantham. Writing in September 1802 Lady Harriet Cavendish said of the marriage *'She is a very great beauty and, what I confess surprises me, seeming perfectly happy. The Duke is the most hideous, disagreeable little animal I ever met with.'*

The duke died suddenly of apoplexy aged fifty in August 1815. His widow died the following February three hours after the death of her infant son, the seventh duke, who was not then a year old.

The infant duke was succeeded by his uncle, William Beauclerk, the second son of the fifth duke. Born in 1766 and known as Lord William Beauclerk he had entered the navy in 1782.

He married firstly, in July 1791, Charlotte, daughter of the Reverend Robert Thelwall of Redbourne in Lincolnshire. Through this marriage Redbourne Hall near Brigg came into the family and remained the principal seat of the dukes of St Albans until the time of the tenth duke. The duchess died, childless, in 1797 and the duke married again in 1799 this time to Maria Janette, daughter of John Nelthorpe, who produced an heir, William, born in March 1801. She died in 1822 and the duke three years later in 1825 aged fifty-eight.

The ninth duke, William, went as a nobleman scholar to Christ's College, Cambridge being awarded a LL.D. in 1828. He was the bearer of the Sceptre at the coronation of William IV in 1831. Politically he was a Whig supporter and voted in favour of the Reform Bill in 1832.

It is generally understood that marriages within the peerage were made with an eye to the benefits to both families and in the hope of a male heir. This would not seem to be the case with the duke's first marriage. In June 1827 he married Harriet, the childless widow of Thomas Coutts the well-known banker (ST ALB 5). He was twenty-six and she was fifty. She had for many years been on the stage in her younger days. She died ten years later in 1837. He married secondly, in May 1839, Elizabeth Catherine the daughter of Major General Joseph Gubbins, who was young enough to produce an heir which she duly did. The duke died in May 1849 at his house in Piccadilly, London as a result of a fit consequent upon a fall whilst out hunting. His widow later, in 1859, married Lucius, 10th Viscount Falkland but retained her title as Dowager Duchess of St. Albans until her death in 1893.

Her marriage to the duke had produced a son, William, born on 15th April 1840 who succeeded to the title aged only nine years. He was educated at Eton and Trinity College, Cambridge and became an Honorary Colonel in the 1st Nottinghamshire Volunteers. He was later Captain of the Yeoman of the Guard. He was a Privy Counsellor, Lord Lieutenant of Nottinghamshire from 1880 until his death and Provincial Grand Master of Freemasons for Lincolnshire and Nottinghamshire.

He married firstly, in June 1867, Sybil Mary, daughter of General the Honourable Charles Grey and sister of the 4th Earl Grey. She died of puerperal fever in September 1871. The duke married secondly, in January 1874, Grace, the daughter of Ralph Bernal-Osborne of New Anner, County Tipperary. He died in May 1898.

ST ALB 4

ST ALB 6

ST ALB 2 **Anonymous** NIF

This bookplate in the Adam style dates from around 1770. The spade shaped shield is typical of the period. Possibly for George, third duke who succeeded to the title in 1751, died in 1786 childless, and was succeeded by a distant second cousin George Beauclerk.

ST ALB 3 **Anonymous** FI939

A fine neo-classical plate from the third quarter of the eighteenth century showing the royal arms debruised by a baton gules charged with three roses argent with supporters, compartment and motto under a duke's coronet. This was also probably made for George the third duke.

ST ALB 5

ST ALB 4 **Anonymous** NIF

A simple early nineteenth century plate possible for Aubrey, 6th Duke of St Albans.

ARMS: Quarterly,1 and 4, Beauclerk, 2, quarterly gules and or in the first quarter an estoile argent, 3 or, three chevrons and overall in chief a label of three points gules.

Aubrey was born in 1765 and succeeded to the title in 1802. He died in 1815 and was succeeded by his infant son who died before his first birthday when the title passed to his uncle, a younger brother of the sixth duke.

ST ALB 5 **Stratton Street Library. Harriot, Duchess of St Albans** NIF

A small coronet bookplate for the duchess's library at the family's London house in Stratton Street. Notice the mis-spelling of her name. This plate is also known with the superscription 'Holly Lodge Library'.

Harriet was the wife of William, 9th Duke of St. Albans. Theirs was rather an odd marriage. He married her in 1827 when he was twenty-six and she was fifty. She was the widow of Thomas Coutts, the Banker which may have had some bearing on the marriage.

ST ALB 6 **Anonymous** NIF

A monogram and crest plate under a duke's coronet with the family motto on a ribbon below. The large capital 'A' encloses the crest and 'St'. Stylistically this is a late nineteenth century plate either for the ninth or tenth duke.

SOM 1 The Right Noble Charles Duke of Somerset Knight of the most Noble Order of the Garter 1705 F*15

This bookplate for the sixth duke is in the early armorial style and dated 1705. The sixth duke held the title for seventy years, succeeding in 1678, aged sixteen, and dying in 1748 in his eighty-seventh year.

ARMS: Quarterly, 1st and 4th, or, on a pile gules, between six fleur-de-lys azure, three lions of England passant guardant or. (being the augmentation granted by Henry VIII to Edward Seymour, later 1st Duke of Somerset, on Henry's marriage to Lady Jane Seymour Edward's sister), 2nd and 3rd, gules, two wings conjoined in lure or. (Seymour).

CREST: Out of a ducal crown or a phoenix rising from the flames proper.

SUPPORTERS: Dexter, a unicorn argent, ducally gorged per pale azure and or, chained of the last; sinister, a bull azure ducally gorged and chained or.

MOTTO: Foy pour devoir – Fidelity for duty.

Dukes of Somerset

FAMILY NAME: Seymour

CREATION OF DUKEDOM: 16th February 1546/7

COURTESY TITLE OF ELDEST SON: Lord Seymour

GRANDSON AND HEIR: Does not use a courtesy title

RESIDENCES: Bradley House, Maiden Bradley, West Wiltshire; Stover Lodge, Newton Abbot, Devonshire

The dukedom of Somerset has been held by various families over the centuries but the Seymour's tenure dates back to the sixteenth century with an interregnum on the way.

Edward Seymour, brother of Jane Seymour, Queen Consort to Henry VIII, was the second, but first surviving, son of Sir John Seymour of Wolf Hall, Wiltshire. He was born c.1500 and was said to have been educated at both Oxford and Cambridge. He later had a military career.

On 5th June 1536 shortly after his sister's marriage to the king he was created Viscount Beauchamp. On 18th October the following year he was created Earl of Hertford with £20 per annum to support the title. He was made a Knight of the Garter in 1541. He held high office serving as Warden of the Scottish marches, Lord High Admiral and Great Chamberlain of England. On 15th February 1546/7 he was created Baron Seymour and the following day created Duke of Somerset.

He was one of the executors of the will of Henry VIII, on whose death he was appointed Governor of the new boy king, Edward VI, (his nephew) and Protector of the Realm.

In 1550 he was confined to the Tower of London being accused of high treason and felony. At his trial he was only found guilty of felony, nevertheless he was condemned to death and beheaded on Tower Hill on 27th January 1551/2. Shortly afterwards he was posthumously attainted and all his honours forfeited.

The dukedom was in abeyance for over a hundred years until 1660 when William Seymour, great grandson of the first duke had the title restored to him. William was the second, but first surviving, son of Edward Seymour styled Lord Beauchamp. He was born in 1587 and educated at Magdalen College, Oxford. In 1621 he succeeded his grandfather as Earl of Hertford and Baron Beauchamp and, in June 1641, was created Marquess of Hertford.

He was a loyal supporter of the crown and after the Restoration of the Monarchy in 1660 he was, by Act of Parliament on 13th September 1660, restored to his great grandfather's title as Duke of Somerset but died only a month later on 24th October 1660.

He left five sons, the first four predeceased him but the third son, Henry, left a son William, born on 17th April 1652, who succeeded his grandfather as third duke when only eight years old. He died whilst still a minor on 12th December 1671 of 'a maligned fever' and was succeeded by his uncle, John, the fifth and youngest son of the second duke.

John, styled Lord John Seymour until his succession, was born in 1641. As a young man he was continually in debt until a marriage was arranged for him in 1661 to Sarah, widow of George Grimston, and daughter and co-heir of Sir Edward Alston, President of the Royal College of Physicians. She brought him £10,000 on marriage. The marriage was not a happy one and did not produce children. They separated in about 1672 and he died in April 1675 (see SOM 4).

He was succeeded, as fifth duke, by a cousin and heir male Francis Seymour the fourth, but first surviving, son of Charles, 2nd Baron Seymour, whose father, the first baron, was the younger brother of the second duke.

Francis, who was born on 17th January 1657/8 attended both Eton and Harrow and succeeded to his father's barony in 1665 aged seven and to the dukedom aged seventeen. He met a tragic end three years later on a visit to Genoa when, on 20th April 1678, he was shot at his inn door by Horatio Botti, a Genoese nobleman, whose wife the duke and his companions were said to have insulted.

As he died unmarried he was succeeded by his younger brother Charles (SOM 1 and 2) who was born on 13th August 1662 and educated at Harrow and Trinity College, Cambridge. Before, unexpectedly, succeeding to the title he was Lord Lieutenant of the East Riding of Yorkshire and of Somerset. He was Gentleman of the Bedchamber to Charles II and James II and, after his elevation took an active part in the coronations of James II, William and Mary, Queen Anne, George I and George II. He held many prestigious posts under successive monarchs and was largely instrumental, with the 1st Duke of Argyll, in brokering the succession of the House of Hanover in 1714.

He married firstly, on 30th May 1682, Elizabeth, daughter of Joceline, 5th Earl of Northumberland, who, although only sixteen was the childless widow of Thomas Thynne of Longleat. Born on 29th January 1666/7 she became, on her father's death three years later, heir to the vast Percy estates in Northumberland. The marriage produced two sons, the first of whom, Charles, predeceased his father. She died of breast cancer in 1722.

The duke married secondly, in February 1725/6, Charlotte, third daughter of Daniel, 7th Earl of Winchilsea. The duke died in his eighty-seventh year on 2nd December 1748 and was succeeded by Algernon the second son of his first marriage. He was born on 11th November 1684 and after his brother's death was known as the Earl of Hertford until his succession. As earl he served as Member of Parliament for Marlborough 1705–8, and for Northumberland 1708–22, whilst at the same time serving in the war in Flanders and acting as Aide de Campe to the Duke of Marlborough. In 1715 he married Frances daughter and co-heir of the Honourable Henry Thynne.

Shortly after becoming duke in his middle sixties and with no surviving male children, he was created Baron Warkworth and Earl of Northumberland with special remainder, failing heirs male of his body, in favour of his son-in-law Sir Hugh Smithson Bt. (see Northumberland). He died on 7th February 1749/50, having held the dukedom for only fourteen months, when his various titles were dispersed, some becoming extinct. The earldom of Northumberland went to his son-in-law under the special remainder and the dukedom went to Edward Seymour, a lineal descendent of the first duke and a fifth cousin once removed of the seventh, about as far away as one could get.

Edward, born in 1694, was educated at Magdalen College, Oxford and succeeded his father as sixth baronet in 1740. He was Member of Parliament for Salisbury 1741–7 and Lord Lieutenant of Wiltshire and Chief Justice in Eyre North of the Trent 1752–7.

In 1716 he had married Mary, daughter of Daniel Webb of Monckton Farleigh. He died on 12th December 1757 aged sixty-two and was succeeded as ninth duke by his eldest son and heir, Edward, born on 2nd January 1717/18. Educated

at Winchester and Oriel College, Oxford the new duke carried the orb at the coronation of George III in 1761 and was made a Privy Counsellor in 1770.

He never married and was somewhat of a recluse. He had a great fear of the risk of smallpox spreading due to inoculation which was to develop into a mania in later life preventing him from attending crucial divisions in the House of Lords. In 1783 he was granted a pension of £1,200 by the King. A report in the Gentleman's Magazine said 'There are said to be some oddities in his Grace's disposition but he interferes very little in the public transactions of his time, living mostly in his country seats in a private peaceful manner'.

He was lampooned in a satirical work 'Ways and Means' published in 1782 as follows: 'The Wiltshire chimney corner is legible in every lineament of his Grace's features and discoverable in every thread of his habiliments … the furniture within is of a gothic cast wonderfully distinguished for its originality but it scarcely tells you that human policy has held any correspondence with it'.

He died on 2nd January 1792 aged seventy-three and was succeeded by his younger brother Webb. Born in December 1718 he was known as Lord Webb Seymour after the succession of his brother. He married on 11th December 1769, Anna Maria, daughter and heir of John Bonnell of Stanton Harcourt, Oxfordshire. His tenure of the dukedom lasted less than two years as he died on 15th December 1793.

His first two sons, Edward and Webb, had died as infants so he was succeeded as eleventh duke by his third son, Edward Adolphus, born on 24th February 1775. He matriculated from Christ Church, Oxford and became a member of the Royal Society. He was President of three organisations; The Royal Literary Fund, The Royal Institution and The Linnaean Society. He was the bearer of the orb at the coronation of William IV in 1831 and of Queen Victoria in 1838.

He married firstly, on 24th June 1800, Charlotte, second daughter of Archibald, Duke of Hamilton. She died after a long illness in 1827. He married secondly, on 28th July 1836, Margaret (SOM 5), daughter of Sir Michael Shaw-Stewart Bt., and died on 15th August 1855 at Somerset House in the Strand, London aged eighty.

The twelfth duke was his son and heir by his first marriage, Edward Adolphus, born on 20th December 1804 and educated at Eton and Christ Church, Oxford. His politics seem uncertain. He was Tory Member of Parliament for Okehampton 1830–1 and Liberal Member for Totnes 1834–55. He held numerous posts including Metropolitan Commissioner in Lunacy, Secretary to the East India Board,

1st Lord of the Admiralty, Governor of the Royal Naval College, Portsmouth, Lord Lieutenant of Devon and elder Brother of Trinity House.

He married on 10th June 1830, Jane Georgiana, daughter of Thomas Sheridan who was the son of the more famous Sir Richard Brinsley Sheridan, the dramatist. As Lady Seymour she was 'The Queen of Beauty' in the celebrated Eglinton Tournament in 1839. This was the re-enactment of a medieval joust and revel held on 30th August and funded and organised by Archibald, 13th Earl of Eglinton. It took place at Eglinton Castle, Kilwinning, Ayrshire in Scotland. Another distinguished participant was Napoleon III of France. The spectacle took place before a crowd estimated at over one hundred thousand. The duchess was one of three sisters well-known for their beauty and achievements. She died in 1884 and the duke died a year later.

He left no direct surviving male heir. His eldest son, Edward, had an illegitimate son, Major Richard Harold St Maur, who tried unsuccessfully in later life to lay claim to the dukedom declaring he always believed that his parents had married prior to his birth.

The twelfth duke was therefore succeeded by his younger brother Archibald Henry, born on 30th December 1810, known as Lord Archibald Seymour. Educated at Eton he was a supporter of the Liberal Party and High Sheriff of Leicestershire later in life. He died, unmarried on 10th December 1891 when the title went to his younger brother the third son of the eleventh duke.

SOM 2

SOM 2 Seymour, Duke of Somerset NIF

An early armorial for the sixth duke, the arms quarterly as in SOM 1. The helmet is incorrect as it is shown full face with the visor open protected by bars. Such helms are reserved for the Royal Family.

SOM 3 Anonymous NIF

A simple armorial bookplate of somewhat indeterminable date. The shield shape is rather similar to SOM 2 although the general design is freer. It could date from the second half eighteenth century. An attempt has been made to place the helmet correctly facing sideways.

SOM 3

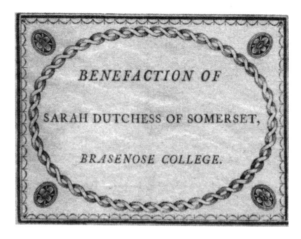

SOM 4 **BENEFACTION OF SARAH DUCHESS OF SOMERSET, BRASENOSE COLLEGE** NIF

This is a bookplate recording the benefaction of the duchess to Brasenose College, Oxford. Sarah (1631–1692) was the daughter and co-heir of Sir Edward Alston and widow of George Grimston, who married in 1652, Lord John Seymour later 4th Duke of Somerset. It was a marriage of convenience. She brought much needed wealth to the family and in return moved up into the aristocracy. The couple were incompatible and eventually separated in 1672, the Duke died in 1675. Her wealth had been protected on marriage to prevent Lord John acquiring all of it. She married a third time Henry, 2nd Baron Coleraine, but she continued to style herself Duchess of Somerset. This marriage too was an unhappy one. Her first marriage to George Grimston a fellow of Brasenose College had been happy and she bore him two children who unfortunately died as infants. In 1680 she gave land in Iver, Buckinghamshire to Brasenose College for the benefit of four scholars, choosing the first four scholars herself. When she died, in 1692, she left further land in Thornhill, Wiltshire to provide Brasenose with further scholarships. This bookplate, which stylistically dates from the late eighteenth century was presumably placed in books purchased out of Sarah's bequests.

SOM 5 **M. Somerset** F26508

A small bookplate, with the owner's name under a duchess's coronet, for Margaret, 11th Duchess of Somerset. Margaret, the daughter of Sir Michael Shaw-Stewart Bt., married Edward, 11th Duke of Somerset in 1836 as his second wife.

Charles Seymour, Duke of Somerset.

From the original of Kneller, in the Collection of

The Right Hon.ble The Earl of Egremont.

Charles Seymour, 6th Duke of Somerset, 1662–1748, from an original painting by Godfrey Kneller. A second son, he inherited the dukedom unexpectedly when his elder brother, the fifth duke was murdered in Italy on 16th April 1678 aged only twenty. The inheritance came without any property. However, four years later, he married a very wealthy heiress, the fifteen year old Lady Elizabeth Percy daughter and sole heiress of Joceline, 11th Earl of Northumberland. He was instrumental along with the Duke of Argyll and the Duke of Shrewsbury in securing the Hanoverian succession.

169

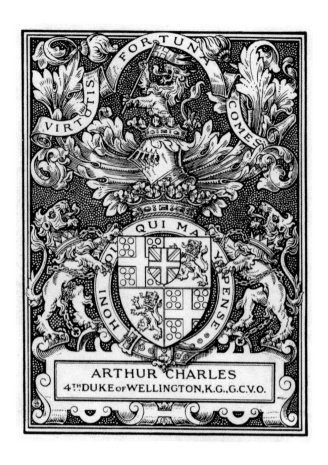

Wel 1 **ARTHUR CHARLES 4ᵗʰ DUKE OF WELLINGTON, K.G., G.C.V.O.** NIF

A large flamboyant panel armorial bookplate, by Harry Soane, for the 4th duke who succeeded in 1900.

ARMS: Quarterly, 1 and 4, gules, a cross argent, in each quarter five plates in saltire (Wellesley); 2 and 3, or, a lion rampant gules ducally gorged or (Colley); and for augmentation, in chief, an escutcheon charged with the Union Flag.

CREST: Out of a ducal coronet or a demi lion gules holding a forked pennon of the last, per pale argent charged with the cross of St George.

SUPPORTERS: Two lions gules, each gorged with an eastern crown and chained or.

MOTTO: Virtutis fortuna comes – Fortune the companion of virtue.

Dukes of Wellington

FAMILY NAME: Wesley, Wellesley

CREATION OF DUKEDOM: 3rd May 1814

COURTESY TITLE OF ELDEST SON: Marquess of Douro

COURTESY TITLE OF GRANDSON AND HEIR: Earl of Mornington

PRINCIPAL RESIDENCE: Stratfieldsaye, Hampshire

This is a further clear case of a rapid rise through the ranks of the peerage in one generation. Arthur Wesley (later Wellesley) was the third son of Garret Wesley, 1st Earl of Mornington, and his wife Anne, daughter of Arthur, 1st Viscount Dungannon.

He was born on 1st May 1769 in Dublin. He was educated at Eton 1781–4 and later on the continent. Whilst in Dublin he met and formed an attachment to Catherine Pakenham daughter of the 2nd Lord Longford. Following many visits to the Longford home in Dublin he made his feelings towards Catherine clear. However the family disapproved as Wellesley was the third son of a very large family and appeared to have little in the way of prospects. Following this rebuff Catherine, fearing that any prospect of marriage to Wellesley was over, became engaged to Galbraith, second son of the Earl of Enniskillin. Learning later that Wellesley still considered himself committed to her she broke off the engagement although the stress of it all sadly affected her health.

Wellesley had joined the army in 1787 at the age of seventeen and, for whatever reason, he changed regiments six times in five years finally joining the 32nd Regiment of Foot in 1792, becoming Major and then Lieutenant Colonel in that regiment. He served in India 1797–1805 taking part in the campaign against Tippoo Sahib and becoming Governor of Seringapatam and Mysore. For his Indian campaign he was made a Knight of the Bath in 1804.

Returning to England in 1806 Wellesley renewed his proposal to Catherine but meeting her again after ten years he realised she had lost much of her youthful beauty. He reputedly said to his brother 'She has grown ugly, by Jove,'

Nevertheless he went ahead with the marriage which was conducted by his brother, the Reverend Gerald Wellesley (WEL 2) on 19th April 1806. Although she bore him two sons the marriage was not a particularly happy one. She died in 1831 aged fifty-eight.

On his return to England Wellesley had combined his military career with a political one becoming Member of Parliament for Rye as a Tory. He served as Chief Secretary to the Lord Lieutenant of Ireland and as Lord of the Treasury. He went back to the army as Commander-in-Chief of the successful Iberian Peninsula Campaign 1808–9 as a result of which he was created Baron Douro of Wellesley, Co. Somerset and Viscount Wellington of Talavera and Wellington also in Somerset. He also received the thanks of Parliament who conferred on him an annuity of £2,000 a year in February 1810 to extend to him and the next two holders of the title.

After receiving various foreign honours he was created Earl of Wellington in February 1812 with an additional annuity of £2,000 on the same terms as previously. Following further military success in Spain he was created Marquess of Wellington in October 1812 with a one off grant of £100,000 for the purchase of lands to descend with the peerage.

He defeated Marshal Jordan at Vittoria in June 1813 and sent the Marshal's baton to the Prince Regent who responded by sending him the baton of a British Field Marshal. He was given the Garter in April 1814 and finally in May of that year he became Marquess of Douro and Duke of Wellington (WEL 3) with a further grant of £400,000 to buy estates to be entailed on the heirs male of his body and failing that the heirs female.

He took his seat in the House of Lords for the first time in June 1814 holding various political appointments until Napoleon's escape from Elba in 1815. Then he was appointed Commander-in-Chief of forces on the continent and what followed was the great victory at Waterloo and the restoration of Louis XVIII to the throne of France. For this victory he received a further £200,000 for the purchase of land for himself and his heirs on tenure of rendering a

Wes 1 HUGH, DUKE OF WESTMINSTER.
EATON. 1884 FI2961

A large, well designed, full panel armorial bookplate engraved by C.W. Sherborn, for the 1st Duke of Westminster, and signed bottom right (see also wes 6). The shield is surrounded by the Garter collar with the St. George insignia dependant from it.

Arms: Quarterly, 1 and 4, azure, a portcullis or, on a chief of the last in pale the arms of King Edward the Confessor between two united roses of York and Lancaster (The City of Westminster, granted as a coat of augmentation); 2 and 3, azure, a garb or (Grosvenor).

Crest: A talbot or.

Supporters: Two talbots regardant or, gorged with a collar azure.

Motto: Virtus non stemma – Virtue not pedigree.

Dukes of Westminster

FAMILY NAME: Grosvenor

CREATION OF DUKEDOM: 27th February 1874

COURTESY TITLE OF ELDEST SON: Earl Grosvenor

COURTESY TITLE OF GRANDSON AND HEIR:
Viscount Belgrave

PRINCIPAL RESIDENCE: Eaton Hall, Chester

Romantic family tradition had it that the family's origins could be traced back to one Hugh Le Gros Venor (translated as Hugh the great or fat huntsman) who came over with William the Conqueror and was created by him Earl of Chester. He had responsibility for preventing the Welsh from raiding the English borders and stealing cattle particularly in Cheshire. So effective was he in this role that he became known as Hugh Lupus, Hugh the Wolf, a name we shall meet in a later descendant of the family.

There is no proof of this origin and the earliest recorded ancestor was, in fact, a great grand nephew of Hugh Le Gros Venor, one Robert Le Grosvenor who was granted land in Cheshire around 1160. The family prospered and a Sir Robert Le Grosvenor was Sheriff of Chester in 1389 and again in 1394.

He was involved in a famous heraldic dispute. He bore as arms 'azure a bend or' but his right to these arms was challenged by the then Lord Treasurer, the 1st Lord Scrope. Scrope's claim was upheld by the Court of Chivalry and, although Sir Robert appealed to the king, Richard II, he endorsed the decision of the court and Sir Robert was liable for the costs. It was further decided that instead of a 'bend or' Sir Robert should bear 'a golden wheat sheaf' on his arms. There is no doubt that this decision annoyed him and his descendants considerably. As late as the nineteenth century the 1st Duke of Westminster named his successful racehorse 'Bend Or' and his son and heir was nicknamed 'Bendor'.

Despite this hiccup the family fortunes prospered both in lands and titles. In 1622 Sir Richard Grosvenor secured a baronetcy and later in the century the third baronet, Sir Thomas (1656–1700), made a very advantageous marriage to one Mary Davies. Her father, Alexander, had inherited considerable land in the area of what is now covered by Oxford Street, Park Lane and Knightsbridge in London, which he bequeathed to his daughter.

With his newly acquired wealth on marriage Sir Thomas commissioned the building of a new house, Eaton Hall, on his estate in Cheshire. Thomas and Mary had a large family, five sons and three daughters. Following the death of Sir Thomas Mary married again but her property remained with the Grosvenors.

Early in the eighteenth century their son, Sir Richard the fourth baronet (WES 2), started to develop his mother's estate by means of selling leases to parcels of land on condition that a house of agreed quality was built on the land. These houses became the property of the freeholder on expiry of the lease, usually after a period of ninety-nine years. Grosvenor Square was built in this way. He was succeded as fifth and sixth (WES 3 and 4) baronets by his two younger brothers.

Another Richard, the seventh baronet, born on 18th June 1731, was created Baron Grosvenor in 1761 on the accession of George III and twenty years later became Viscount Belgrave and Earl Grosvenor. He spent the proceeds from his London estates on acquiring more property, collecting paintings and racing horses. He won the Derby three times in five years.

He married on 19th July 1764, Henrietta, daughter of Henry Vernon but in 1770 he accused her of adultery with H.R.H. the Duke of Cumberland. He obtained a separation and was awarded £10,000 damages. In spite of this he still settled £1,200 per annum on his repudiated wife. He died on 5th August 1802.

The second earl, Robert (1767–1845) (WES 5), continued his father's hobby of collecting paintings and also breeding racehorses. It was very much a case of 'unto them that have more shall be given'. On the accession of William IV in 1830 Robert was created Marquess of Westminster.

He replaced the old family seat, Eaton Hall, with a much larger building more in keeping with his new status. It was an impressive, but to modern eyes unattractive, gothic mansion. It was dark and uncomfortable inside and successive owners did their best to improve the property. Finally it was largely demolished because of its condition, after the second World War following its use (misuse!) by the army. A new modern Eaton Hall has now been erected close by.

As his wealth increased the first marquess acquired more land around the country in Dorset, Hampshire, Hertfordshire and Cheshire. Furthermore he began developing his land in Belgravia and Pimlico. His heir and successor Richard (1795–1869) the second marquess was a much quieter individual preferring family life and the management of his estates to further expansion. He was careful with money both on his own behalf and that of his family. It was said of him that, he lived for the pleasure of making money which he had not the heart to enjoy.

His heir, who had been christened Hugh Lupus, shades of a distant ancestor, succeeded to the marquessate in 1869 and in the same year received the following letter from William Gladstone, the retiring Prime Minister.

> '*My Dear Westminster,*
> *I have received authority from the Queen to place a Dukedom at your disposal and I hope you may accept it, for both you and Lady Westminster will wear it right nobly.*
> *With my dying breath, yours sincerely W.E .Gladstone*'

Needless to say the marquess was not slow to accept his new honour. In his reply the following day he said, '…*I have come to the conclusion that I should not hesitate to accept the step in rank graciously approved by Her Majesty and which your dying breath has strength to convey to us.*'

Although this was probably a political appointment to keep the wealth of the Grosvenors on the side of the Liberal Party it was certainly popular with the Queen. (WES 1 and 6).

This was one of only two non-royal dukedoms in the peerage of the United Kingdom Victoria created during her reign. She had long been a friend of the new duke and his first wife Lady Constance the youngest daughter of the 2nd Duke of Sutherland. They had married in 1852 in one of the grandest Society weddings of Queen Victoria's reign. The Queen insisted that the couple were married in the Chapel Royal opposite St James's Palace, a venue normally used only for royal weddings, and where the Queen's own wedding had taken place. The Queen, Prince Albert and the Duchess of Kent all attended the ceremony. The couple went on to have eleven children and after the duchess's death in 1880 the duke remarried, in 1882, Katherine Cavendish a descendant of the 4th Duke of Devonshire. The duke was fifty-six and

his new bride twenty-four. They had a further four children, two sons and two daughters. The first duke was a credit to his class, doing all the things that good dukes should do and he was widely mourned at his death in 1899.

His eldest son having predeceased him he was succeeded by his grandson Hugh Richard Arthur (1879–1953) (WES 7 and 8). The second duke followed in the tradition set by his grandfather. He played his part in the Boer War and the first World War being awarded a D.S.O. He was a good and caring landlord. In the depression of the 1930s he remitted half of their rents to his tenants and after the second World War remitted rents to all who had suffered damage in the blitz.

His private life was not so successful. He married four times but the only marriage which need concern us here was his third marriage to Loelia, daughter of Sir Fredrick Ponsonby, private secretary to George V. They married in 1930 but separated after five years and were finally divorced in 1947. However, she left us her rather fine bookplate depicting St James's Palace (WES 9).

WES 2

WES 2 S^r. Richard Grosvenor of Eaton in Com. Cheshire, Bar^t F I 2969

A simple early armorial for the fourth baronet dating from the early years of the eighteenth century and may, in fact, be as early as 1700 the year he succeeded to the baronetcy. There is a ribbon to contain a motto but no motto.

WES 3 S^r: Robert Grosvenor of Eaton-Hall, in the County Palatine of Chester; of Swell Court in the County of Somerset, of Halkin-Hall in the County of Flint, and of Millbank Westminster in ye County of Midd^x. BAR^T: F I 2970

The bookplate of Sir Robert Grosvenor who succeeded as sixth baronet in 1733.

The plate is in the baroque style with the Grosvenor arms impaling Warren, Gules, a lion rampant between eight cross crosslets fitchee 3, 2, 3 argent. The oddity is the helmet which is facing sideways with visor closed denoting the arms of a gentleman – not a baronet. However, the error was later corrected, see WES 4.

He was the fifth son of Sir Thomas Grosvenor third baronet whose first two sons predeceased him, the third and fourth served as 4th and 5th baronets but each left no male heirs, hence Robert's succession. Born in 1695 and educated at Eton and Brasenose College, Oxford he married, in 1730, Jane daughter of John Warren of Swell Court in Somerset. In 1733 he was elected Member of Parliament for Chester a post he held until his death in 1755.

WES 4 S^r: Robert Grosvenor of Eaton-Hall, in the County Palatine of Chester; of Swell Court in the County of Somerset, of Halkin-Hall in the County of Flint, and of Millbank Westminster in y^e County of Midd^x. BAR^T: F I 2971

The same plate but the helmet has been redrawn to show it facing forwards with the visor open. This is the correct position for the holder of a baronetcy.

WES 3

WES 4

Belgrave.

WES 5 **Belgrave** NIF

A simple armorial in the neo-classic manner with spade shaped shield. Dating from the third quarter of the eighteenth century it is, almost certainly, the bookplate of Robert, the second earl and used in the lifetime of his father.

WES 6 **HUGH, DUKE OF WESTMINSTER.**
EATON 1884 FI2963

A smaller, less detailed version of WES I, again by C.W. Sherborn, signed with initials in centre base, but omitting the supporters, crest, helmet and mantling. The base and surround of the arms are the same all under a duke's coronet.

WES 7 **HUGH RICHARD ARTHUR DUKE OF WESTMINSTER** 1899 NIF

The family obviously favoured the work of Sherborn. This is another plate by him for the second duke who succeeded in 1899. The plate is signed and dated in the bottom right hand corner, '1906'. It is a full armorial with shield, helmet, crest, coronet, motto and supporters. The date on the inscription obviously refers to the duke's accession.

WES 8 **HUGH RICHARD ARTHUR DUKE OF WESTMINSTER** 1899 NIF

A larger version of WES 7.

WES 9 **Loelia Westminster Ex Libris** NIF

This is a beautiful pictorial plate. Within a floral wreath, topped by a cartouche inscribed 'Loelia Westminster', supported by putti blowing horns and surmounted by a stylised duke's coronet there is a view of the Clock Tower of St James Palace with, in front, a brougham drawn by two horses and followed by a small dog. The cartouche in base reads, 'Ex Libris'.

This bookplate is based on a design by Rex Whistler which was a wedding gift to the Duchess from Victor Cazalet, when she married the second duke as his third wife in February 1930. The original design carried the date of the wedding and a gift inscription. These were amended to produce the bookplate which was engraved by Robert Osmond. The duchess was married in St James Palace as her father, Sir Frederick Ponsonby, who was private secretary to George V, lived there.

Some There Were Who Refused

Attractive and desirable as a dukedom might appear from a distance this does not always seem to have been the case at close quarters. Over the centuries a number of individuals have refused the offer when it has been made to them. There is no doubt that the role of duke was something very special and stood apart even amongst the other ranks of the peerage. They were addressed as 'My Lord' he was addressed as 'Your Grace'. Their status was exceedingly high for over six hundred years

The reasons for refusal were not always clear, but in some cases seems to have been the lack of an heir or a fear that the candidate did not feel himself equal to supporting the dignity and lifestyle of a duke. Usually this was due to the lack of the necessary resources financial and otherwise. In some cases it seems they just did not want the bother as they already had a peerage albeit at a lower level.

In the early eighteenth century when Queen Anne wanted to reward John Churchill, Earl of Marlborough with a dukedom, his wife Sarah, a great friend of Queen Anne at that time, was very much against it. She wrote to her husband begging him to refuse the dukedom on the grounds that being a peer already was sufficient and they had not the wherewithal to sustain a dukedom. Whilst agreeing with the latter point, which he thought could be resolved by a grant from the Crown, he was greatly pleased by the Queen's benevolence towards him and graciously accepted the honour, together with the necessary funds to enable the building of Blenheim Palace.

George II offered dukedoms to Charles Bruce, 3rd Earl of Ailsbury, (1682–1747) (R1) and to James Compton, 5th Earl of Northampton, (1694–1773). In both cases the offer was refused and in each case the reason given was that neither had sons to succeed them.

Phillip, 4th Earl of Chesterfield, (1694–1773) (R2) also refused a dukedom from the same king in 1748 for reasons unstated although the fact that he had no legitimate male heir may have had something to do with his refusal.

In the nineteenth century Queen Victoria met with a number of refusals when she was prepared to offer dukedoms. Henry, 3rd Marquess of Lansdowne, (1780–1863)

(R3) was an eminent Victorian politician, who served in many Offices of State, Chancellor of the Exchequer (when only twenty-seven years old), Home Secretary and Lord President of the Council. He twice refused to become Prime Minister and in 1857 refused a dukedom. This caused the following lines to appear in Punch:

Lord Lansdowne won't be Duke of Kerry.
Lord Lansdowne is a wise man – very.
Punch drinks his health in port and sherry.

In 1827 W.H. Lyttelton wrote of him '*Landsdowne, than whom a more unvenal and, I think, unambitious soul never existed in the breast of a public man; a sagacious counsellor. A courteous and liberal host, a valued friend, cultivated companion and munificent patron.*'

Later in her reign his grandson, Henry Charles, the fifth marquess (1845–1927), also a politician, refused a dukedom on his retiring as Viceroy of India in 1894 because he did not feel he had sufficient wealth to support the advancement in rank. It should be noted that he was already the possessor of nine peerages – Marquess of Lansdowne, Earl of Wycombe, Viscount Calne, Earl of Kerry, Earl of Shelburne, Viscount FitzMaurice, Baron Kerry and Baron Dunkerton. In 1895 he succeeded to his mother's barony of Nairne (Scotland) thus giving him the distinction of holding a peerage in each of the three kingdoms, England, Ireland and Scotland. His daughter, Evelyn, married the 9th Duke of Devonshire.

Benjamin Disraeli, Queen Victoria's favourite Prime Minister, was also offered a dukedom in 1878 following his success at the Congress of Berlin, he too refused feeling no doubt, that having already been given an earldom (Beaconsfield), he had sufficient for his needs.

Perhaps the most persistent refuser of dukedoms was Robert Gascoyne-Cecil, 3rd Marquis of Salisbury (R4), one of Queen Victoria's Prime Ministers. He refused two offers of a dukedom from the Queen, once in 1886 and again in 1892, citing on both occasions the prohibitive cost of the lifestyle dukes were expected to maintain. On the second occasion he did accept the Garter instead.

If one looks at the lifestyle of the marquess it is doubtful if the reason he gave was the right one. As well as the

Hatfield estate in Hertfordshire he owned homes in Lancashire and Wiltshire, a town house in London, a chateau in France and the island of Rum in the Inner Hebrides. He entertained lavishly and frequently. Queen Victoria made a state visit in 1846 and was back again in 1887 as part of her Golden Jubilee celebrations. On that occasion he not only entertained his sovereign but five other reigning kings and queens and five crown princes and their princesses with all their retinues. One could really not have a more lavish and expensive lifestyle than that. A third offer of a dukedom was made by Edward VII on his accession in 1901 but this too was refused.

Edward VII is also reputed to have offered a dukedom to the British-born, American philanthropist Andrew Carnegie (R5). Carnegie refused on the grounds that he had accepted American citizenship and was, therefore, ineligible. This was not true as he was still a British citizen having been born in Scotland and therefore eligible for such an honour. However it is probable that the offer ran counter to his socialist principles.

And finally, the last person to refuse a dukedom was the World War II Prime Minister, Winston Spencer Churchill (R6). It was suggested, more than once, that he should accept a peerage but on each occasion he made light of the possibility and indeed ridiculed it. Exactly why and what went on is not entirely clear but it is probable that one reason for refusal was, that like many before him, he did not feel he had the affluence to support such a life style and possibly he preferred to stay in the Commons. Following his retirement from the House of Commons on 4th April 1955 he had a final audience with the Queen during which it is said the offer of a dukedom was again discussed. Whilst greatly admiring and respecting his sovereign and conscious of the great honour which would be bestowed on him he nevertheless politely refused the suggestion, asking to be forgiven for not accepting it. It is recorded by his private secretary Jack Colville that afterwards Churchill said to him he felt he should die as he had lived – Winston Churchill. He did however, finally, accept the Garter having previously refused it in 1945 when it was offered by King George VI. He said at that time that he did not think it appropriate to accept the Order of the Garter from his sovereign when he had just been given the Order of the Boot by the country (he had just lost the 1945 General Election).

R I Charles Earl of Ailesbury F4129

A mid-eighteenth century plate in the baroque style with an architectural compartment for Charles, 3rd Earl of Ailesbury (1682–1747) showing a full armorial. He succeeded to the earldom in 1741.

ARMS: Quarterly of nine, the pronomal quarter showing the arms of Bruce – or, a saltire and chief gules, on a canton argent a lion rampant azure.

CREST: A lion statant, tail extended, azure.

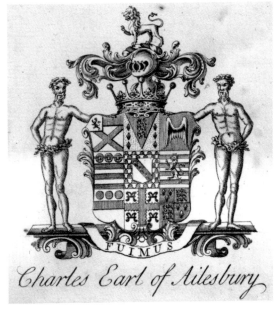

R I

Lansdowne.

R 3

R 2

R 4

SUPPORTERS: Two savages each wreathed about the temple and loins.

MOTTO: Fuimus – We have been.

R 2 **Anonymous** F27859

This is one of three similar plates from the second quarter of the eighteenth century all showing the Garter and motto. Philip, 4th Earl of Chesterfield was awarded the Garter in 1730. The arms are shown backed by a mantle surmounted by an earl's coronet.

ARMS: Quarterly, ermine and gules.

R 3 **Lansdowne** F10683

A mid-nineteenth century simple armorial with supporters showing the Garter and motto for Henry, 3rd Marquess of Lansdowne.

ARMS: Quarterly, 1 and 4, ermine, on a bend azure a magnetic needle pointing to the pole star or (Petty); 2 and 3, argent, a saltire gules and a chief ermine (Fitzmaurice).

SUPPORTERS: Two pegasi ermine, winged, bridled and unguled or, each charged on the breast with a fleur-de-lys or.

MOTTO: Virtute non verbis – By courage not words.

R 4 **The Marquis of Salisbury** NIF

A superb panel armorial for Robert Gasgoine – Cecil, 3rd Marquis of Salisbury.

ARMS: Barry of ten argent and azure overall six escutcheons sable, three two and one, each charged with lion rampant of the first.

CREST: Six arrows in saltire or barbed and flighted argent bound with a belt gules buckled and garnished gold, over the arrows a morion cap proper.

SUPPORTERS: Two lions rampant ermine.

MOTTO: Sero non Serio – Late but in earnest.

R 5 **ANDREW CARNEGIE** NIF

A panel pictorial plate showing a book pile with a torch of knowledge to the left and a ribbon inscribed 'Let there be light'. 'Andrew Carnegie' in base and a thistle at the top signifying his Scottish ancestry.

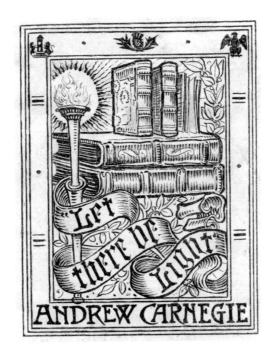

R 5

FIEL · PERO · DESDICHADO

R 6

R 6 **Anonymous** NIF

A panel armorial for Sir Winston Spencer Churchill K.G, signed Gayfield Shaw, Australia, Nov. 1955. This was probably a gift plate following his retirement from the Commons and the award of the Garter in April 1955. It is not known if it was used in Sir Winston's books.

ARMS: Quarterly, 1 and 4, sable, a lion rampant argent, on a canton of the last across of St George gules (Churchill); 2 and 3, quarterly, argent and gules, in the 2nd and 3rd quarters a fret or, overall on a bend sable three escallops of the first (Spencer); in centre chief an escutcheon argent charged with a cross of St George, thereon an escutcheon of France, azure three fleur de lys or as an augmentation of honour; all surrounded by the Garter and motto.

CRESTS:

1. a lion couchant guardant argent supporting in the dexter paw a banner gules charged with a dexter hand appaume of the first, staff or (Churchill);

2. out of a ducal coronet or a griffin's head, ducally gorged between two wings expanded argent (Spencer). The ducal coronet is actually shown as a duke's coronet, a mistake sometimes made by artists (see p 16).

Gayfield Shaw (1885–1961) was an Australian of Scottish extraction who lived in Sydney, New South Wales. He was a director of an art gallery, artist and printmaker.

Appendices

Appendix I

It has not been possible to cover all the dukedoms in detail in this volume so, for completeness, listed here, in alphabetical order, are the dukedoms granted in the British Isles since the first in 1337 (excluding the established royal dukedoms) with brief details of their creation and where appropriate their demise and recreation. Where available an illustrative bookplate has been placed at the end of the section (D1–D15) for those dukedoms not covered in the main text.

Dukedoms were created in the Peerage of England between 1337–1707 (E), in the Peerage of Scotland between 1398–1707 (S), in the Peerage of Ireland between 1661–1868 (I), in the Peerage of Great Britain between 1707–1801 (GB), and in the Peerage of the United Kingdom between 1801 and the present day (UK). The last dukedom to be created was Fife on 29th July 1889. Those titles currently extant are indicated in **CAPITAL BOLD TYPE**.

ABERCORN (I) James Hamilton, 2nd Marquess of Hamilton, was created Duke of Abercorn on 10th August 1868. The current holder of the title is James Hamilton, 5th Duke of Abercorn.

Albemarle (E) Sir George Monck K.G. was created Duke of Albemarle on 7th July 1660. The title became extinct on the death, without issue, of the second duke, his son Christopher, on 6th October 1688.

Ancaster and Kesteven (GB) Robert Bertie, Marquess of Lindsay, was created Duke of Ancaster and Kesteven on 26th July 1715 with special remainder, failing heirs male of his body, to the other heirs male of his parents. The title became extinct on the death of the fifth duke, Brownlow Bertie, on 8th February 1809.

ARGYLL (S) Archibald Campbell, 10th Earl of Argyll, was created Duke of Argyll on 23rd June 1701. The current holder of the title is Torquhil Campbell, 13th Duke of Argyll.

ARGYLL (UK) George Campbell, Duke of Argyll (S) was created Duke of Argyll (UK) on 7th April 1892. The current holder of the title is Torquhil Campbell, 13th Duke of Argyll.

ATHOLL (S) John Murray, 2nd Marquess of Atholl, was created Duke of Atholl on 30th June 1703. The current holder of the title is Bruce Murray, 12th Duke of Atholl.

BEAUFORT (E) Henry Somerset, 3rd Marquess of Worcester, was created Duke of Beaufort on 2nd December 1682. The current holder of the title is David Somerset, 11th Duke of Beaufort.

Bedford (E) (first creation) John Plantagenet, third son of Henry IV, was created Duke of Bedford on 16th May 1414. The title became extinct on his death on 15th September 1435.

Bedford (E) (second creation) George Nevill, son of John Nevill, Earl of Northumberland, was created Duke of Bedford on 5th January 1470 by Edward IV who intended him to marry his eldest daughter, Elizabeth. However the family were attainted, their estates forfeited and George was deprived of his peerages by Act of Parliament in 1478.

Bedford (E) (third creation) Jasper Tudor, second son of Sir Owen Tudor by Katherine, Queen Dowager of England and uterine brother to Henry VI, was created Duke of Bedford on 27th October 1485 by his nephew, Henry VII. The title became extinct on his death on 21st December 1495.

BEDFORD (E) (fourth creation) William Russell, 5th Earl of Bedford, was created Duke of Bedford on 11th May 1694. The current holder of the title is Andrew Russell, 15th Duke of Bedford.

Berwick (E) James Fitzjames (1670–1734) was the illegitimate son of James, Duke of York (later James II) by Arabella Churchill. He was created Duke of Berwick by James II on 19th March 1687. The title was forfeited, in England, in 1695 when the duke was attainted following the enforced abdication of his father. However, it continued to be recognised in France as one of the *de facto* Jacobite peerages.

Bolton (E) Charles Paulet, son of John, 5th Marquess of Worcester, was created Duke of Bolton on 9th April 1689. The title became extinct on the death of Harry, the sixth duke on 25th December 1794. (D1.)

BRANDON (GB) James Hamilton, 4th Duke of Hamilton a Scottish peer was created Duke of Brandon on 10th September 1711 with special remainder, failing heirs male of his body, to those of his parents. The title remains extant in the family and the current holder is Alexander Douglas-Hamilton, 16th Duke of Hamilton.

Bridgewater (GB) Scroop Egerton, 5th Earl of Bridgewater, was created Duke of Bridgewater on 18th June 1720. The title became extinct on the death of Francis, the third duke on 8th March 1803. (D2.)

BUCCLEUCH (S) Anne, suo jure Duchess of Buccleuch, married James Scott, Duke of Monmouth (E), acknowledged illegitimate son of Charles II. On his marriage on 20th April 1663, he was created Duke of Buccleuch with remainder to the heirs of his body by Anne. He was later executed for high treason when his English titles were forfeit but his Scottish titles passed to his grandson, his son having predeceased him. The current holder of the title is Richard Scott, 10th Duke of Buccleuch.

Buckingham (E) (first creation) Humphrey Stafford, 5th Earl of Stafford, was created Duke of Buckingham on 14th September 1444. The title became extinct on the death of Edward, the third duke who was executed for high treason on 17th May 1521 when all his honours were forfeit.

Buckingham (E) (second creation) George Villiers, Marquess of Buckingham, a favourite of James I, was created Duke of Buckingham on 18th May 1623. The title became extinct on the death of George the second duke, without male heir on 16th April 1687.

Buckingham (E) (third creation) John Sheffield, 7th Earl of Mulgrave, was created Duke of Buckingham on 23rd March 1703. The title became extinct on the death of his son Edward, the second duke who died unmarried on 30th November 1735.

Buckingham and Chandos (UK) Richard Temple-Nugent-Brydges-Chandos-Greville, 2nd Marquess of Buckingham, was created Duke of Buckingham and Chandos on 4th February 1822. The title became extinct on the death of Richard, 3rd Duke without male heirs on 26th March 1889. (D3.)

Buckingham and Normanby (E) John Sheffield, 3rd Earl of Mulgrave and Baron Sheffield, was created Duke of Buckingham and Normanby by Queen Anne in 1703. The dukedom became extinct on the death of his son, Edward, in 1735. (D4.)

Chandos (GB) James Brydges, Earl of Carnarvon was created Duke of Chandos on 29th March 1719. The title became extinct on the death of James the third duke on 29th September 1789. (D5.)

Cleveland (E) (first creation) Barbara Villiers, Countess of Castlemaine, mistress of Charles II, was created Duchess of Cleveland on 3rd May 1670 with remainder to her eldest son, Charles Palmer, acknowledged illegitimate son of Charles II. The title became extinct on the death of William the third duke on 18th May 1774. (see Southampton)

Cleveland (UK) (second creation) William Vane, 3rd Earl of Denbigh, whose grandfather had married Grace, eldest daughter of Charles, 2nd Duke of Cleveland, was created Duke of Cleveland on 29th January 1833. The title became extinct on the death of Harry George Vane the fourth duke on 21st August 1891.

DEVONSHIRE (E) William Cavendish, Earl of Devonshire, was created Duke of Devonshire on 12th May 1694. The title is still extant and the current holder is Peregrine Cavendish, 12th Duke of Devonshire.

Dorset (GB) Lionel Cranfield Sackville, Earl of Dorset, was created Duke of Dorset on 17th June 1720. The title became extinct on the death of Charles the fifth duke on 29th July 1843. (D6.)

Dover (GB) James Douglas, Duke of Queensberry (S), was created Duke of Dover on 26th May 1708 with special remainder to his second and younger sons successively. The title became extinct on the death of Charles, the second duke on 22nd October 1778.

Exeter (E) (first creation) John de Holland, younger son of Thomas, Earl of Kent, was created Duke of Exeter on 29th September 1397. He was deprived of his title on 3rd November 1399 for complicity in murdering the Duke of Gloucester and executed on 9th January 1399/1400.

Exeter (E) (second creation) Thomas Beaufort, youngest illegitimate son of John, Duke of Lancaster, was created Earl of Dorset on 5th July 1412 and Duke of Exeter on 18th November 1416. The title became extinct on his death on 31st December 1426.

Exeter (E) (third creation) John Holland, second son of John Holland, Duke of Exeter (first creation), was created Duke of Exeter on 6th January 1443/4. The title became extinct on the death of his son, Henry, the second duke in September 1475.

FIFE (UK) (first creation) Alexander Duff, 6th Earl of Fife, was created Duke of Fife on his marriage on 27th July 1889, to Princess Louise, Queen Victoria's granddaughter, the eldest daughter of Edward, Prince of Wales. There being no male issue of the marriage he was re-created Duke of Fife on 24th April 1900, with special remainder in favour of his first and other daughters and their male issue. The title is extant and the current holder is James Carnegie, 3rd Duke of Fife.

Gordon (S) (first creation) George Gordon, 4th Marquess of Huntley, was created Duke of Gordon on 1st November 1684. The title became extinct on the death of George the fifth duke on 28th May 1836.

GORDON (UK) (second creation) The title was re-created in 1876 on the insistence of Queen Victoria for the Duke of Richmond, a collateral descendant of the fifth duke. The current holder of the title is Charles Gordon-Lennox, 10th Duke of Richmond.

GRAFTON (E) Henry Fitzroy, second of three illegitimate sons of Charles II by Barbara Villiers, Countess of Castlemaine, was created Duke of Grafton on 11th September 1675. The title is still extant and the current holder is Henry Fitzroy, 12th Duke of Grafton.

Greenwich (GB) John Campbell, 2nd Duke of Argyll, was created Duke of Greenwich on 27th April 1719. This title became extinct on his death on 4th October 1743.

HAMILTON (S) James Hamilton, Marquess of Hamilton, was created Duke of Hamilton on 12th April 1643. The title is extant and the current holder is Alexander Douglas-Hamilton, 16th Duke of Hamilton.

Kent (GB) Henry Grey, 12th Earl of Kent, was created Duke of Kent on 28th April 1710. The title became extinct on his death on 5th June 1740.

Kingston upon Hull (GB) Evelyn Pierrepont, Marquess of Dorchester, was created Duke of Kingston upon Hull on 10th August 1715. William, his son and heir pre-deceased him and the title became extinct on the death of his grandson, Evelyn the second duke on 23rd September 1773.

Lauderdale (S) John Maitland, Earl of Lauderdale, was crated Duke of Lauderdale on 26th May 1672. The title became extinct on his death on 24th August 1682.

Leeds (E) Thomas Osborne, 1st Earl of Danby was created Marquess of Carmarthen on 20th April 1689 and Duke of Leeds on 4th May 1694. The title became extinct on the death of Francis D'Arcy Osborne, the twelfth duke on 20th March 1964.

Leinster (I) (1st creation) Lord Meinhardt Schomberg, third son of Frederic, Duke of Schomberg, was created Duke of Leinster on 3rd March 1691. The title became extinct on his death on 16th July 1719.

LEINSTER (I) (second creation) James Fitzgerald, Marquess of Kildare, was created Duke of Leinster on 26th November 1766. The title is still extant and the current holder is Maurice Fitzgerald, 9th Duke of Leinster. (D7 and 8.)

Lennox (S) (first creation) Esme Stuart, 6th Seigneur D'Aubigny, in France and cousin of James VI of Scotland was created Earl of Lennox on 5th March 1579 and became Duke of Lennox on 5th August 1581. The title became extinct on the death, without issue, of Charles, the sixth duke on 12th December 1672.

LENNOX (S) (second creation) Charles Lennox, Duke of Richmond, illegitimate son of Charles II by Louise De Keroualle, was also created Duke of Lennox on 9th September 1675 when only three years old. The title is still extant and the current holder is Charles Gordon-Lennox, 10th Duke of Richmond.

MANCHESTER (GB) Charles Montagu, 4th Earl of Manchester, was created Duke of Manchester on 28th April 1719. The title is still extant and the current holder is Alexander Montagu, 13th Duke of Manchester.

MARLBOROUGH (E) John Churchill was created Earl of Marlborough by William III on 9th April 1689 and Duke of Marlborough by Queen Anne on 14th December 1702. The title is still extant and the current holder is John Spenser-Churchill, 12th Duke of Marlborough.

Montagu (E) (first creation) Ralph Montagu, 3rd Baron Montagu of Boughton was created Earl of Montagu on 9th April 1689 and Duke of Montagu on 14th April 1705 The title became extinct on the death of John, the second duke on 16th July 1749. (D9.)

Montagu (GB) (second creation) George Brudenell (later Montagu), 4th Earl of Cardigan married Mary, younger daughter and co-heir of John, 2nd Duke of Montagu and assumed the name of Montagu on the death of his father-in-law. He was created Duke of Montagu on 5th November 1766. The title became extinct on his death without male heir, 23rd May 1790.

Montrose (S) (first creation) David Lindsay, Earl of Crawford was created Duke of Montrose on 18th May 1488. He was deprived of the title under the Rescissory Act of 18th May 1489 but restored to the title, for life only, on 18th September 1489. He died at Christmas 1495 when the title became extinct.

MONTROSE (S) (second creation) James Graham, Marquess of Montrose, was created Duke of Montrose on 24th April 1707 for supporting the protestant succession and Act of Union. The title is extant and the current holder is James Graham, 8th Duke of Montrose. (D10.)

Munster (I) Ehrengard Melsine von der Schulenburg was created Duke of Munster on 18th July 1716 by George I but only for life. He died on 10th May 1743.

Newcastle upon Tyne (E) (first creation) William Cavendish, nephew of William, 1st Earl of Devonshire, was created Duke of Newcastle upon Tyne on 16th March 1664/5. The title became extinct on the death of Henry, the second duke on 26th July 1691.

Newcastle upon Tyne (E) (second creation) John Holles, 4th Earl of Clare, married his cousin, Margaret daughter and co-heir of Henry, 2nd Duke of Newcastle upon Tyne, and as a consequence of that marriage was created Duke of Newcastle upon Tyne on 14th May 1694. The title again became extinct on his death on 15th July 1711.

Newcastle upon Tyne (GB) (third creation) Thomas Pelham Holles, 1st Earl of Clare, was created Duke of Newcastle upon Tyne on 11th August 1715. Because he had no one to succeed him he was further created Duke of Newcastle under Lyne on 17th November 1756 with special remainder, failing heirs male of his body, to Henry Clinton, 9th Earl of Lincoln, husband of his niece, Catherine, and their heirs male. He died on 17th November 1768 when all his honours became extinct except the dukedom of Newcastle under Lyne which passed to his nephew-in-law.

Newcastle under Lyne (GB) Henry Fiennes Clinton, 9th Earl of Lincoln, inherited the dukedom of Newcastle under Lyne from his uncle-in-law under a special remainder on 17th November 1768. The title became extinct on the death of Henry, the ninth duke, on 25th December 1988.

Norfolk (E) (first creation) Thomas Mowbray, Earl of Nottingham, was created Duke of Norfolk on 29th September 1397. He was arraigned for treason and his dukedom annulled but his other titles remained. He died on 22nd September 1399 and was succeeded by his brother, John, who had the dukedom restored to him on 30th April 1425. The title became extinct on the death of John the fourth duke on 16th January 1475.

Norfolk (E) (second creation) Richard Plantagenet, Duke of York and second son of Edward IV was married at the age of six to Anne (aged five) daughter of John, 4th Duke of Norfolk. On marriage Richard was created Duke of Norfolk on 7th February 1476/7 His young wife died as a minor in 1481 and Richard was murdered along with his brother Edward in the Tower of London in 1483 when the title became extinct.

NORFOLK (E) (third creation) John Howard, whose mother, Margaret, was daughter and co-heir of Thomas Mowbray, Duke of Norfolk (see above) was created Duke of Norfolk on 28th June 1483. The title, the senior dukedom, is still extant and the current holder is Edward Fitzalan Howard, 18th Duke of Norfolk.

Northumberland (E) (first creation) John Dudley, Viscount Lisle, was created Earl of Warwick on 16th February 1546/7 and Duke of Northumberland on 11th October 1551. However, for taking a leading part in appointing Lady Jane Grey queen after the death of Edward VI, to the exclusion of his sisters, he was found guilty of high treason and executed on 22nd August 1553 when all his honours were forfeited.

Northumberland (E) (second creation) George Fitzroy, third of the illegitimate sons of Charles II by Barbara Villiers, Countess of Castlemaine was created Duke of Northumberland on 6th April 1683 when aged seventeen. The title became extinct on his death without male heir on 3rd July 1716.

NORTHUMBERLAND (GB) (third creation) Sir Hugh Smithson (later Percy) Earl of Northumberland, by special remainder on the death of his father-in-law was created Duke of Northumberland and Earl Percy on 22nd October 1766. The title is still extant and the current holder is Ralph Percy, 12th Duke of Northumberland

Ormonde (I) James Butler, Earl of Ormonde, was created Marquess of Ormonde on 30th August 1642 and Duke of Ormonde on 30th March 1661. His son, James the second duke, a Jacobite supporter, was attainted on 20th August 1715 when his English and Scottish honours and estates were forfeited. His Irish dukedom passed to his brother Charles on his death in Avignon on 16th November 1745. Charles died on 17th December 1768 when the title became extinct. (D11.)

Portland (GB) William Henry Bentinck, Earl of Portland was created Duke of Portland and Marquess of Titchfield on 6th July 1716. The title became extinct on the death of William, 9th Duke of Portland, on 30th July 1990.

QUEENSBURY (S) William Douglas, Earl of Queensbury, was created Duke of Queensbury on 3rd November 1684. On the death of William the fourth duke on 23rd December 1810 the title descended under a special remainder to a cousin, Henry Scott, Duke of Buccleuch and is still extant in that family. The current holder is Richard Scott, 10th Duke of Buccleuch.

Richmond (E) (first creation) Henry Fitzroy, only illegitimate, son of Henry VIII was created Duke of Richmond and Somerset on 18th June 1525 aged six years. The title became extinct on his death on 22nd July 1536.

Richmond (E) (second creation) Ludovic Stuart, Duke and Earl of Lennox, was created Duke of Richmond on 6th October 1613. The title became extinct on his death without legitimate male heir on 16th February 1623/4.

Richmond (E) (third creation) James Stuart, Earl of Lennox, was created Duke of Richmond on 8th August 1641. The title became extinct on the death of Charles the third duke on 20th September 1673.

RICHMOND (E) (fourth creation) Charles Lennox, illegitimate son of Charles II by Louise DeKeroualle, was created Duke of Richmond on 9th August 1675 aged three years and a month later on 9th September Duke of Lennox. The titles are still extant and the current holder is Charles Gordon Lennox, 10th Duke of Richmond.

ROXBURGHE (S) John Ker, Earl of Roxburghe, was created Duke of Roxburghe on 25th April 1707. The title is still extant and the current holder is Guy Innes-Ker, 10th Duke of Roxburghe.

RUTLAND (E) John Manners, 11th Earl of Rutland, was created Duke of Rutland on 29th March 1703. The title is still extant and the current holder is David Manners, 11th Duke of Rutland.

St ALBANS (E) Charles Beauclerk, illegitimate son of Charles II by Nell Gwynne, was created Duke of St Albans on 10th January 1684 aged twelve years. The title is still extant and the current holder is Murray Beauclerk, 14th Duke of St Albans.

Schomberg (E) Fredrick Herman Schomberg was created Duke of Schomberg on 10th April 1689 by William III. The title became extinct on the death of Meinhard, the third duke on 5th July 1719

Shrewsbury (E) Charles Talbot, Earl of Shrewsbury and Earl of Waterford (I) was created Duke of Shrewsbury and Marquess of

Alton on 30th April 1694. He died on 1st February 1717/18 when the dukedom of Shrewsbury and the marquessate of Alton became extinct. His other titles passed to a first cousin. (D12.)

Somerset (E) (first creation) John Beaufort, 4th Earl of Somerset, was created Duke of Somerset and Earl of Kendal on 28th August 1443. He died on 27th May 1444 without male heir when the when the dukedom of Somerset and the Earldom of Kendal became extinct. His other titles passed to his brother Edward Beaufort (see below).

Somerset (E) (second creation) Edward Beaufort, Marquess of Dorset and Earl of Somerset, was created Duke of Somerset on 31st March 1448. He was slain at the Battle of St Albans on 22nd May 1455. He was succeeded by his son Henry who was attainted by Act of Parliament on 4th November 1461 when his honours were forfeit. They were reinstated by Parliament on 10th March 1462. However he deserted Edward IV and was captured at the Battle of Hexham and executed on 15th May 1464 when the reinstatement of his honours was declared null and void and they finally became extinct.

Somerset (E) (third creation) Henry Fitzroy, only acknowledged illegitimate son of Henry VIII, was created Duke of Richmond, Duke of Somerset and Earl of Nottingham on 18th June 1525 aged about six years. He died, unmarried, on 22nd July 1536 when his honours became extinct.

SOMERSET (E) (fourth creation) Edward Seymour, brother of Jane, queen consort of Henry VIII having already been made Earl of Hertford and Viscount Beauchamp was created Duke of Somerset on 16th February 1546/7. He was attainted and executed for treason on 27th January 1551/2 when his honours were forfeit. The titles were in abeyance for over one hundred years until they were restored to William Seymour, great grandson of the first duke, in 1660. The title is still extant and the current holder is John Seymour, 19th Duke of Somerset.

Southampton (E) Charles Fitzroy, illegitimate son of Charles II by Barbara Villiers, was created Duke of Southampton in 1675. He also inherited his mother's dukedom of Cleveland in 1709. His son, William, inherited both titles but had no offspring so the titles became extinct on his death in 1774. (D13 and 14.)

Suffolk (E) (first creation) William De la Pole, 4th Earl of Suffolk, was created Marquess of Suffolk on 14th September 1444 and Duke of Suffolk on 2nd July 1448. His grandson, the third duke, Edward, agreed with the king, Henry VII, to surrender his dukedom and marquessate voluntarily and be known only as the Earl of Suffolk on 25th February 1492/3. This was ratified by Act of Parliament in 1495.

Suffolk (E) (second creation) Charles Brandon having been created Viscount Lisle in 1513 was created Duke of Suffolk on 1st February 1513/14. His son Henry the second duke died of the 'sweating sickness' unmarried and aged fifteen. He was succeeded by his brother Charles who was duke for only half an hour dying from the same disease as his brother on 14th July 1551 when the titles became extinct.

Suffolk (E) (third creation) Henry Grey, Marquess of Dorset, was the husband of Frances, daughter of Charles Brandon, Duke of Suffolk (see above) and was created Duke of Suffolk on 11th October 1551. Having proclaimed his daughter, Lady Jane Grey, as queen after the death of Edward VI, with precedence before his sisters, he was attainted by Queen Mary and beheaded on 23rd February 1553/4 and his titles were forfeited.

SUTHERLAND (UK) Elizabeth Sutherland, suo jure 19th Countess of Sutherland, married, 4th September 1785, George Leveson-Gower who succeeded his father as Marquess of Stafford on 26th October 1803 and who was created Duke of Sutherland on 28th January 1833. The title is still extant and the current holder is Francis Egerton, 7th Duke of Sutherland. (D15.)

WELLINGTON (UK) Arthur Wellesley, the famous army general was in turn created Viscount, Earl, Marquess and finally Duke of Wellington on 11th May 1814. The title is still extant and the current holder is Charles Wellesley, 9th Duke of Wellington.

WESTMINSTER (UK) Hugh Lupus Grosvenor, 3rd Marquess of Westminster, was created Duke of Westminster on 27th February 1874. The title is still extant and the current holder is Hugh Grosvenor, 7th Duke of Westminster.

Wharton (GB) Philip Wharton, 2nd Marquess of Wharton, was created Duke of Wharton on 28th January 1718 in spite of being a staunch Jacobite supporter. He died without surviving male issue on 31st May 1731 when the titles became extinct.

D 1 The Right Noble Charles Duke of Bolton 1705 F*7

A fine early full armorial with inscription below, close cropped.

ARMS: Quarterly of four with pronomal arms in the first quarter, sable, three swords pilewise, points in base, proper, pommels and hilts or. (Paulet)

CREST: On a wreath of the colours, on a mount vert a falcon rising or, gorged with a ducal coronet gules.

SUPPORTERS: Two hinds purpure semi of estoiles and ducally gorged or.

MOTTO: Aymes Loyaulte – Love loyalty.

Charles Paulet was the second duke succeeding to his father's title in 1699. Born in 1661 and educated at Winchester he went to the Netherlands to assist William of Orange in his invasion of England. He served in many offices; Lord Chamberlain to Queen Mary, Lord Lieutenant of Hampshire. Lord Justice of Ireland, Governor of the Isle of Wight and he was a commissioner for the union of England and Scotland. He died in January 1721/2.

D 2 The Right Honble Scroop Egerton Earl of Bridgwater Viscount Brackley Baron of Elsmere 1703 F9642

A fine full early armorial design with inscription beneath but unfortunately closely cropped intruding on the design.

ARMS: Argent, a lion rampant gules between three pheons sable.

CREST: On a chapeau gules turned up ermine, a lion rampant gules holding in its forepaws an arrow, point downwards.

SUPPORTERS: Dexter, a horse rampant argent ducally collared; sinister, a griffin or ducally collared and chained.

D 1

D 2

MOTTO: Sic donec – Thus until.

Scroop Egerton (1681–1744) was styled Viscount Brackley from 1687 to 1701 when he inherited his father's earldom as 5th Earl of Bridgewater. He was created 1st Duke of Bridgewater in 1720. His maternal grandfather was Charles Paulet, 1st Duke of Bolton. His first wife was Lady Elizabeth Churchill daughter of John, 1st Duke of Marlborough whom he married in 1703. He married again in 1722, Lady Rachel Russell, daughter of Wriothesley, 2nd Duke of Bedford. He held various posts; Lord Lieutenant of Buckinghamshire, Lord of the Bedchamber and Master of the Horse to Prince George of Denmark, Prince Consort to Queen Anne, Lord Chamberlain to Princess Caroline, Princess of Wales and later Lord of the Bedchamber to her husband George II. He died in 1744 and was succeeded by the eldest surviving son of his second marriage, John, as second duke.

D 3 **B&C** F12795

This is a very dull inauspicious plate for a duke with five surnames. It comprises the initials 'B & C' within the Garter surmounted by a duke's coronet.

Richard Temple-Nugent-Brydges-Chandos-Greville, Duke of Buckingham and Chandos (1776–1839), had taken the surnames of Brydges and Chandos, by Royal Licence in 1799, because he had married the heiress of those families, Ann Elizabeth, daughter of James

D 3

John Sheffield,
Duke of
Buckingham & Normanby.

D 4

The Honourable James Brydges of Wilton Castle in Hereford Shere

D 5

Brydges, Duke of Chandos, in 1796 (see D5). He held various posts; Member of Parliament for Buckinghamshire, Vice-President of the Board of Trade, Joint Paymaster General and Lord Lieutenant of Buckinghamshire. He was given the Garter in 1820 and on 4th February 1822 was created Marquess of Chandos and Duke of Buckingham and Chandos by George IV. This was the only dukedom he created – it was said because of personal friendship but in fact it was a political appointment by which Lord Liverpool gained the support of the Grevilles for the Tory party. Sir Charles Bagot said at the time – '*I am glad that the Grevilles are taken into Government; and they come tolerably cheap. I see no objection to a dukedom at the head of the Greville family, but I see many to giving it to the actual blubber-head who now reigns over them.*' It seems that the new duke had a much exaggerated idea of his own ability and status. He was reputedly very greedy, never satisfied and always asking for more. He died, aged sixty-three, in 1839.

D4 John Sheffield, Duke of Buckingham & Normanby
F26643

An early full armorial, the shield surrounded by the Garter and motto and surmounted by a duke's coronet.

ARMS: Quarterly of fifteen with the Sheffield arms in the pronomal quarter.

CREST: On a wreath of the colours a boar's head erased.

SUPPORTERS: Two boars rampant.

MOTTO: Comiter sed fortiter – Politely but firmly.

John Sheffield (1647–1720) was the son and heir of Edmund, 2nd Earl of Mulgrave, who succeeded his father as third earl, aged only eleven, in 1658. He followed a naval and military career whilst at the same time serving as Governor of Hull 1679–82, Lord Lieutenant of the East Riding of Yorkshire 1679–82, Lord Chamberlain of the Household to James II 1685–8. He was created Marquess of Normanby by William III in 1694 and Duke of Buckingham and Normanby by Queen Anne in 1703. He married three times but only his third wife, Katherine, an illegitimate daughter of James II by Katherine Sedley, bore him any children, three sons of whom only the youngest survived to inherit the title when he died in 1720.

D5 The Honourable James Brydges of Wilton Castle in Hereford Shere F4191
(later Duke of Chandos)

An excellent, but incorrectly designed (see below), early armorial from the second decade of the eighteenth century showing the arms of Brydges with Lake in pretence and impaling Willoughby.

James Brydges, born on 6th January 1673 was the eldest of fourteen children of James, 8th Lord Chandos. His father died on 16th October 1714 when James became the 9th Lord Chandos and three days afterwards he was created Viscount Wilton and Earl of Carnarvon. Five years later, in October 1719, he was created Marquess of Carnarvon and Duke of Chandos. He was Member of Parliament

for Hereford 1698–1714, Member of Council to the Lord High Admiral (Prince George of Denmark, Prince Consort) 1703–5 and Paymaster General to the forces abroad 1705–13. Which 'lucrative post' it was said, enabled him to build a magnificent country house, Cannons, near Stanmore, Middlesex. All of which activities presumably justified his rapid rise through the peerage.

He married first, in 1696, Mary daughter of Sir Thomas Lake who bore him six sons, only one surviving to inherit the title. She died in 1712 and the following year he married Cassandra daughter of Francis Willoughby. The arms as shown are incorrect as on the death of his first wife her family arms would devolve on her children and her husband would no longer have guardianship of them so Lake in pretence should not be shown.

D6 Anonymous F25916

This plate is for Charles, 5th, and last, Duke of Dorset. It is a small early seal type armorial depicting the arms surrounded by the Garter and motto with supporters under a duke's coronet

ARMS: Quarterly or and gules, a bend vair.

CREST: Out of a duke's coronet an estoile argent (not shown).

SUPPORTERS: Two leopards argent collared azure.

MOTTO: Aut nunquam tentes aut Perfice – Either do not attempt or complete.

Thomas Sackville, son and heir of Sir Richard Sackville, was created Earl of Dorset by James I on 13th March 1603/4. Lionel Cranford Sackville (1687–1765), the seventh earl was Lord Warden of the Cinque Ports and envoy to Hanover to inform George I of the death of Queen Anne. Being a strong Whig supporter and in favour with the new king he was created Duke of Dorset on 17th June 1720. The title became extinct when Charles (1767–1843) the fifth duke died unmarried in 1843.

D6

D 7 **Anonymous** NIF

A fine twentieth century pictorial plate for Edward, 7th Duke of Leinster, by Henry James Haley (1874–1964) depicting a seascape with sailing vessel, observed by a figure probably St Christopher. The scene is topped and tailed by books and in centre chief crossed 'L's under a duke's coronet.

Edward Fitzgerald, known as Lord Edward until his succession in 1922, was the third and youngest son of Gerald, 5th Duke of Leinster. He succeeded his elder brother Maurice, 6th Duke (1887–1922) who died unmarried having lived in a psychiatric institution in Edinburgh for the last fifteen years of his life. The seventh duke was a spendthrift and a gambler. He married four times; first a chorus girl, second an American socialite, third an actress and music hall performer and fourth a waitress. He died, in debt, in a bedsit in Pimlico, in 1976 having committed suicide,

D 8 **HERMIONE**

An elegant panel pictorial plate by C.W. Sherborn featuring books, the lamp of knowledge, an inkwell, quill pen and profuse acanthus leaf scrolling, with a duchess's coronet in the centre. The motto above reads 'Non progredi est regredi' – To not go forward is to go back. In base is the name '*HERMIONE*'. It is signed and dated 'CWS – 1891' on the spine of the book on the far right.

Lady Hermione Wilhelmina Duncombe (1864–95) was the daughter of William Duncombe, 1st Earl of Feversham. She, and her younger sister Helen, were considered great beauties of their day. She married, in 1864, Gerald, 5th Duke of Leinster, and bore him two sons before becoming estranged from her husband due to her affair with Lord Elcho, son and heir of 6th Earl of March. In 1893 she had an illegitimate child by him and died two years later of tuberculosis aged only thirty-one.

D 8

D 7

D 9

D 10

D 9 The Most Noble John Duke of Montagu 1709 F20864

A full, dated early armorial plate with inscription below, produced in the year he succeeded to the dukedom as second duke.

ARMS: Quarterly, 1 and 4, argent, three lozenges conjoined in fess gules within a bordure sable (Montagu); 2 and 3, or, an eagle displayed vert beaked and membered gules (Monthermer).

CREST: A demi griffin or winged and beaked sable.

SUPPORTERS: Two griffins rampant or winged and beaked sable.

John Montagu was born in 1690 the son and heir of Ralph, 1st Duke of Montagu. He succeeded to his father's titles in 1709. He followed a military career rising to the rank of general. In 1717 he was granted a Doctorate of Medicine by Cambridge University and became a Fellow of the College of Physicians but there is no evidence he had any training or practised in that craft. He was however a founder member and supporter of the Foundling Hospital opened in London in 1739. He was a great practical joker, his mother-in-law wrote of him *'All his talents lie in things only natural in boys of fifteen years old and he is about two and fifty; to get people into his garden and wet them with squirts, and to invite people to his country houses and put things in beds to make them itch and twenty such pretty fancies as these.'* He died in 1749 when all his titles became extinct.

D 10 His Grace the Duke of Montrose F12445

An early armorial originally for James Graham (1682–1742) who was created Duke of Montrose, second creation, in 1707. It would appear to have been altered for William, the second duke. 'James' has been erased although the 's' can still be seen, and replaced by 'the'. Presumably 'William' would not fit the space.

ARMS: Quarterly, 1 and 4, or, on a chief sable three escallops of the field (Graham); 2 and 3, argent, three roses gules barbed and seeded proper (Montrose).

SUPPORTERS: Two storks argent beaked and membered gules.

MOTTO: Ne oublie (Ne oubliez) – Forget not.

D 11 The Most Noble James Duke of Ormond Lord Lieutenant of Ireland and Knight of the Most Noble Order of yᵉ Garter 1703 F*5

A fine early full armorial plate for James, the second duke dated 1703 with inscription below.

ARMS: Quarterly of four with the Butler arms in the pronomal quarter – or, a chief dancetty azure.

CREST: Out of a ducal coronet or a plume of five ostrich feathers argent, therefrom a falcon rising of the last.

SUPPORTERS: Dexter, an eagle or; sinister, a griffin argent.

MOTTO: Comme je trouve – As I find it.

James Butler, 12th Earl of Ormonde (1610–88), was an Irish career army officer becoming Lieutenant General of the army in Ireland in 1640. Following the English Civil War and throughout the Commonwealth he was in France supporting the young Charles II in exile. Following the restoration in 1660, he was created Duke of Ormonde (I) on 30th March 1661 and, some twenty years later in November 1682 he was created Duke of Ormonde (E). Of which honour he was said to have remarked that it was *'of no other advantage than precedency'*. Although he had eight sons and two daughters only his daughters survived him, consequently he was succeeded by his grandson James (1665–1746) as second duke in 1688. James was a staunch Jacobite supporter and after the 1715 Rising he was attainted and all his English honours forfeit but he retained his Irish dukedom.

D 11

D 12

D 12 The Most Noble Charles Duke of Shrewsbury Knight of the Most Noble Order of the Garter F*8

A small early eighteenth century shield armorial under a duke's crown, surrounded by the Garter and motto with inscription beneath.

ARMS: Gules, a lion rampant and bordure engrailed gules.

CREST: On a chapeau gules turned up ermine a lion statant or (not shown).

SUPPORTERS: Two talbots rampant argent (not shown).

MOTTO: Prest d'accomplir – Ready to accomplish (not shown).

Charles Talbot (1660–1717), 12th Earl of Shrewsbury, and godson of Charles II, was brought up a catholic but in 1679 he seceded from the Church of Rome and became an ardent supporter of the Church of England. He was instrumental in arranging the accession of William of Orange, taking money to the Netherlands and accompanying the Prince on his invasion of England. He was in high favour with the new king, becoming a Privy Counsellor in February 1688/9 and on 30th April 1694 was created Marquess of Alton and Duke of Shrewsbury. On his death on 1st February 1717/18 his dukedom and marquessate became extinct.

D 13 The Most Noble Charles Fitz Roy Duke of Southampton Knight of the Most Noble Order of yᵉ Garter 1704 F*22

A small full early armorial with impaled shield and inscription below, dated 1704.

ARMS: The royal arms debruised by a baton sinister ermine (Fitzroy); impaling, argent, a fess dancetty gules, in chief three leopards heads sable (Poulteney).

CREST: On a chapeau gules turned up ermine a lion statant guardant or, ducally crowned azure; collared compony counter compony ermine and azure.

SUPPORTERS: Dexter, a lion rampant or ducally crowned azure; collared as in the crest; sinister, a greyhound rampant similarly collared.

MOTTO: Secundus dubiisque rectus – Upright in prosperity and in perils (not shown).

Charles Palmer (1662–1730), later Fitzroy, was the illegitimate son of Charles II by Barbara Palmer, Countess of Castlemaine and later Countess of Southampton and Duchess of Cleveland. On 10th September 1675 he was created Earl of Chichester and Duke of Southampton. He married, in 1694, Ann Poulteney (see D14) daughter of Sir William Poulteney who bore him six children including an heir William who succeeded him. In 1709 he succeeded to his mother's title as 2nd Duke of Cleveland. He does not appear to have done anything outstanding in his life apart from a possible intrigue in the early 1690s for the return of James II. He died in 1730 and was succeeded by his son William, on whose death in 1774 without issue the titles became extinct.

D 14 The Most Noble Ann, Duchess of Southampton 1704 F*24

An identical plate to D10 but with the inscription changed for use by his duchess Ann (1663–1746).

D 13

D 14

Duke of Sutherland

D 15 **Anonymous**

A fine full panel armorial by Graham Johnston dated 1911 for Cromati Sutherland-Leveson-Gower, 4th Duke of Sutherland (1851–1913) who succeeded to the dukedom in 1892. It depicts a quartered shield with supporters beneath a duke's coronet and helm with five crests above and a profusion of mantling. The arms are not showing the correct tinctures.

ARMS: Quarterly, 1. barre of eight argent and gules, a cross flory sable (Gower); 2. azure, three laurel leaves or (Leveson); 3. three clarions, 2 and 1 with a canton showing two lions of England, (unidentified, possibly an augmentation of honour); 4. The basic arms are those of Egerton, argent, a lion rampant gules between three pheons sable. The design in chief has not been identified but may be an augmentation of honour. The shield in pretence is for Sutherland, gules, three mullets or, on a border of the second a tressure flory counter flory of the first as an augmentation of honour.

CRESTS:
1. A wolf passant argent collared and lined or (Gower);
2. A goat's head erased ermine attired or (Leveson);
3. A squirrel sejant, (unidentified);
4. A lion rampant proper (Egerton);
5. A Cat-a-Mountain sejant proper (Sutherland).

SUPPORTERS: Dexter and sinister, a wolf argent, plain collared and lined reflexed over the back or.

MOTTO: Frangas non flectes – Unbowed, unbroken.

Appendix II

List of courtesy titles used by the eldest son of current dukes, in their father's lifetime.

Duke of Abercorn – Marquess of Hamilton
Duke of Argyll – Marquess of Lorne
Duke of Atholl – Marquess of Tullibardine

Duke of Beaufort – Marquess of Worcester
Duke of Bedford – Marquess of Tavistock
Duke of Buccleuch and Queensbury – Earl of Dalkeith

Duke of Devonshire – Marquess of Hartington

Duke of Fife – Earl of Southesk

Duke of Grafton – Earl of Euston

Duke of Hamilton – Marquess of Douglas

Duke of Leinster – Marquess of Kildare

Duke of Manchester – Viscount Mandeville
Duke of Marlborough – Marquess of Blandford
Duke of Montrose – Marquess of Graham

Duke of Norfolk – Earl of Arundel
Duke of Northumberland – Earl Percy

Duke of Richmond Lennox and Gordon – Earl of March
Duke of Roxburghe – Marquess of Bowmont
Duke of Rutland – Marquess of Granby

Duke of St Albans – Earl of Burford
Duke of Somerset – Baron Seymour
Duke of Sutherland – Marquess of Stafford

Duke of Wellington – Marquess of Douro
Duke of Westminster – Earl Grosvenor

Appendix III

A list of Jacobite dukedoms created by the 'de jure' Stuart Kings in exile from 1689–1788. These titles were never recognised in Britain by any of the subsequent monarchs after the abdication of James II and mainly died out in the eighteenth century through failure of male heirs or lack of recognition and usage.

James II died in exile at St Germain on 16th September 1701. His son the Old Pretender and 'de jure' James III died in Rome on 1st January 1766 and his son Charles, the Young Pretender, 'Bonnie Prince Charlie' and 'de jure' Charles III died in Rome on 31st January 1788. All three issued titles in great profusion including dukedoms, each duke was also given a number of subsidiary titles ranging down all five ranks of the peerage.

Albany (S) Charlotte Stuart, illegitimate daughter of James III was born in 1753 and in March 1783 was created Duchess of Albany by her father. She died, unmarried on 14th November 1789 when the title became extinct.

Albemarle (E) (first Jacobite creation) Henry FitzJames, second son and youngest of the five children of James II by Arabella Churchill, spinster sister of John Churchill, 1st Duke of Marlborough was created Duke of Albemarle and Earl of Rochford by his father in exile on 13th January 1695/6. The honours became extinct on his death in December 1702.

Albemarle (E) (second Jacobite creation) George Granville second son of Bernard Granville, Groom of the Bedchamber was created Baron Lansdown by Queen Anne on 1st January 1711/12. His sympathies however were with the Jacobites and he was created Duke of Albemarle, Marquess Monk, Earl of Bath, Viscount Bevel and Baron Lansdown by James, the Old Pretender, on 3rd November 1721 with remainder failing heirs male of his body to his younger brother Bernard Granville and his heirs male. He died, without male issue, on 31st January 1734/5 and was succeeded by his younger brother who died, unmarried, on 2nd July 1776 when all his Jacobite peerages became extinct.

Arran (E) Charles Butler, second and youngest surviving son of Thomas Butler, Earl of Ossory, was created Earl of Arran, Viscount Tulloch and Baron Cloughgrenan by William III on 8th March 1693. Having played an active part in the Jacobite Rising of 1715 he was, on 2nd January 1722 created Duke of Arran by James the Old Pretender with remainder to the heirs male of his body. He died without male issue on 17th December 1758 when his Jacobite titles became extinct.

Fraser (S) Simon Fraser, 1st Lord Lovat, a strong supporter of the Jacobite cause was, on 14th March 1740, created Duke of Fraser, Marquess of Beaufort and Earl of Strathterrick by James, the Old Pretender. He supported the 1745 Jacobite Rising and was later tried for high treason and executed on Tower Hill, 9th April 1747. His Barony of Lovat was forfeit but his Jacobite titles devolved on his son, Simon, and then his grandson Archibald who died on 8th December 1815 when the Jacobite honours became extinct.

Inverness (S) Colonel the Honourable John Hay, third son of Thomas Hay, 6th Earl of Kinnoul, and a Jacobite supporter in the 1715 Rising was attainted for his part and retired to the Jacobite Court at St Germain where he was, on 4th April 1727 created Duke of Inverness by James the Old Pretender. He died without issue in 1740 when the honour became extinct.

Mar (S) John Erskine, 23rd Earl of Mar and 11th Baron Erskine, a strong Jacobite supporter was, on 22nd October 1715, created Duke of Mar, Marquess of Erskine, Earl of Kildrummie and Viscount Garish by James III with remainder to his heirs general. He was attainted by Act of Parliament on 17th February 1715/6 when his Scottish titles and estates were forfeit. He was later created Duke of Mar in the peerage of Ireland by James on 13th December 1722. He died at Aix-la-Chapelle in May 1732. The Jacobite peerage passed through seven generations of the family either in direct line or via cousins but these unrecognised titles were little used by the family. On 17th June 1824 the then head of the family John Francis Fraser had the Earldom of Mar restored to him, by George IV, he was in his eighty-third year at the time.

Melfort (S) The Honourable John Drummond, second son of James, 3rd Earl of Perth, was born c.1650. He was Secretary of State for Scotland 1684–8 and in 1685 was created, by James II, Viscount Melfort (S) and Baron Drummond (S) being further raised to the earldom of Melfort in 1686. At the Revolution he escaped to France and later went with James II to Ireland. On 17th April 1692 James created him Duke of Melfort, Marquess of Forth, Earl of Isla, Viscount Richerton and Baron Castlemains. He was outlawed and attainted by Act of Parliament 2nd July 1694 when all his honours were regarded as forfeit. He died on 25th January 1714/15 but his Jacobite titles continued to be used by his descendants. His great grandson, James, 4th Duke of Melfort, succeeded in 1766 and in 1781 succeeded a cousin to another Jacobite peerage, the dukedom of Perth (S). He did not use either titles. He was, however, created Baron Perth (GB) and Baron Drummond (GB) by George III in 1797. He died, without issue, 2nd July 1800 when his baronies became extinct. His Jacobite titles passed to a cousin, James Lewis Drummond (see Duke of Perth) The dukedoms of Melfort and Perth fell into disuse on the death of George Drummond, 11th Duke of Perth and 6th Duke of Melfort on 28th February 1902. Neither titles were used by subsequent descendants

Northumberland (E) Philip Wharton, 2nd Marquess Wharton, was born in 1698 and succeeded his father in 1715. He visited the exiled James II in France a year later when he was created by him Duke of Northumberland, Marquess of Woburn, Earl of Malmsbury and Viscount Winchendon. However, so anxious were the English Government to retain his support he was allowed to take his seat in the Irish House of Lords in 1717 and in 1718 George I created him Duke of Wharton (E). In 1726 he left England and openly declared his support for the exiled James II. He died in 1731 when all his honours became extinct.

Perth (S) James Drummond, 4th Earl of Perth was born in 1648 and succeeded his father in 1675. He was a Privy Counsellor and one of the original Knights of the Thistle. In 1686, during the Revolution, he was imprisoned for four years and then exiled. He joined James II's court in exile at St Germain. Sometime before 1701 he was created by James, Duke of Perth, Marquess of Drummond, Earl of Stobhall, Viscount Cargill and Baron Concraig all in the peerage of Scotland. He married three times and died on 11th May 1716. His Jacobite titles passed through twelve generations being finally discarded by the 12th Duke, William, on his succession in 1902.

Powis (E) William Herbert, 3rd Lord Powis, was born in 1617 and succeeded to the barony in 1667. He rose through the legitimate ranks being created Earl of Powis by Charles II in 1674 and Marquess of Powis by James II in 1686. At the Revolution he remained loyal to James II and as a result was created Duke of Powis and Marquess Montgomery by James in January 1689, after his abdication. He died at St Germain in June 1696.He was succeeded by his son William and then by his grandson, William, who died, unmarried, in 1748 when his Jacobite honours became extinct.

Rannoch (S) William Murray, 3rd Marquess of Atholl, was born in 1688 and had a naval career before joining the 1715 Jacobite uprising. He was attainted but managed to escape to France where he joined James III. On 1st February 1717 James created him Duke of Rannoch, Marquess of Blair, Earl of Glen Tilt, Viscount Glenshie and Baron Strathbran. He accompanied the young Prince Charles to Scotland in 1745 but surrendered after the Battle of Culloden in 1746. He was committed to the Tower in June 1746 and died there, unmarried, a month later. His honours devolved on his younger brother, James. The Jacobite titles died out when they were inherited, but not used, by John James, 7th Duke of Atholl, in 1864.

St Andrews (S) and Castelblanco Don Joseph de Bozes, Count of Castelblanco (Spain) was an active Jacobite involved with the attempted Restoration of 1715. He was created, by James III, on 4th February 1717, Duke of St. Andrews and Duke of Castelblanco, Marquess of Boreland, Earl of Fordan, Viscount of the Bass and Baron Divron. He was succeeded by his son, a Spanish national who married a Spanish heiress. His Jacobite titles fell into disuse.

Strafford (E) Thomas Wentworth, 3rd Lord Raby, was born in 1672 and succeeded his cousin as 2nd Earl of Strafford (E) in 1695. In 1711 Queen Anne created him Earl of Strafford (GB) and Viscount Wentworth with remainder to his heirs male and failing that to his younger brother. Following the accession of George I in 1714 he took no further part in public affairs but entered into private negotiations with the Jacobite party. Subsequently the Old Pretender (James III) appointed him Commander-in-Chief of all his forces north of the Humber on 4th January 1722 and the following day created him Duke of Strafford. He died at Wentworth Castle 15th November 1739 and was succeeded by his son, William as second duke etc. William died, without issue, in 1791 when his Jacobite dukedom became extinct and his other honours devolved to his cousin and heir male.

Tyrconnel (I) Richard Talbot who was born in 1625 was, in 1685, created Earl of Tyrconnel, Viscount Baltinglass and Baron Talbotowne by James II. He became Captain General of the Irish army and Viceroy of Ireland in 1686 until the arrival of James in Dublin 24th March 1689. Six days later, whilst still 'de facto' as well as 'de jure' King of Ireland James created Richard Talbot Duke of Tyrconnell (I) and Marquess of Tyrconnell. The new duke was present at the Battle of the Boyne on 1st July 1690. He died in Limerick on 14th August 1691 when the dukedom and marquessate of Tyrconnell became extinct.

York (E) Henry Benedict, younger son of James III was born 6th March 1725 and shortly thereafter was created Duke of York by his father. On the death of his elder brother Charles III (bonny Prince Charlie) he became, 'de jure' King of England, Scotland and Ireland as Henry IX. He died, unmarried, in Rome 13th July 1807 when the male line of the House of Stuart and the whole issue of James II became extinct.

Bibliography

Burke's Peerage, Baronetage and Knightage, 101st edition, 1956

G.E. Cokayne, *The Complete Peerage*. Revised editor, E.V. Gibbs, 1910

Debrett's Peerage, Baronetage and Knightage, London, 1926

Arthur Foss, *The Dukes of Britain*, Herbert Press, 1986

Joseph Foster, *The Peerage of the British Empire*, 1883

A.C. Fox-Davies, *Armorial Families*, 1st edition, 1895, E.C. Jack, Edinburgh

Stephen Friar, *A New Dictionary of Heraldry*, Alpha Books, 1987

Adeline Hartcup, *Below Stairs in the Great Country* Houses, 1980

John, Duke of Bedford, *A Silver-Plated Spoon*, 5th edition, Cassell, London 1961

Kelly's Handbook to the Titled, Landed and Official Classes, London, 1935

Edmund Lodge, *Portraits of Illustrious Personages*, 1834

E.S. Turner, *Amazing Grace*, Michael Joseph, 1975

Peter Youatt, *Bookplates in Arundel Castle*, Bookplate Society Journal, NS 8:2, 2010